FROM HEAVEN TO THE PRAIRIE

—When you know, you know!—

The Story of the 972nd Living ECK Master

Sri Darwin Gross

FROM HEAVEN TO THE PRAIRIE
—When you know, you know!—
The Story of the
972nd Living ECK Master

Copyright © 1980 by Darwin Gross
ISBN: 0-914766-30-9

Library of Congress Catalog Card Number: 80-69589

Printed in U.S.A.

With the assistance of:
Bernadine Burlin
Joan Jenkins
Steve Dewitt

Cover Photo by Patricia Duncan

Additional Books by Sri Darwin Gross:

ECKANKAR, A WAY OF LIFE
YOUR RIGHT TO KNOW
GEMS OF SOUL

Dedicated to my sister Adeline Froeber and to all fellow travelers of God's many levels of Heaven who understand ECK and ECKANKAR.

May you enjoy reading this as I have lived it.

Affectionately,

Darwin Gross

TABLE OF CONTENTS

Prologue: The Chosen One

The departing Master always leaves on our calendar date of October 22nd, and in turn his successor always accepts the Rod of ECK Power on the same day, at midnight, in the full of the moon in the Valley of Shangta, in northern Tibet, near the Katsupari Monastery. The ritual takes place at the site of the ancient Oracle of Tirmer under the direction of the ancient sage Yaubl Sacabi, whose age is beyond the imagination of the normal senses.

The Adepts of the ancient Order of the Vairagi meet at the time of the handing of the mantle of spiritual power from the departing Master to his successor.

— *The Spiritual Notebook*

It is the evening of October 22, 1971. An audience of 3,500 people sit in expectant anticipation, backs rigid, hearts pounding. Before them on the stage, Gail Twitchell, young, petite and pretty in a blue jumpsuit, reads "The Golden Hour," an unpublished poem written by her late husband, Paul Twitchell.

"We are very fortunate in being present when a Living ECK Master is introduced to the world. Bringing forth the works of ECKANKAR should be utmost in our hearts, in our lives and in our Souls. Paul laid many cornerstones and he placed many building blocks and it's up to us, individually and collectively to continue spreading this

vii

message to the waiting world. To guide us and show us the way, we have a Living ECK Master in our presence. Our Living ECK Master—Darwin Gross!"

Breathlessly they watch as she moves down into the audience and hands a single blue carnation to a tall, slim, young man, his face aglow, his smile warm and shy. Together they return to the stage.

Flashbulbs explode, movie cameras whir and official audio equipment spins into action to register a momentous spiritual occasion. The applause is deafening as exuberant hearts display their joyful acceptance of the choice presented them in the form of a new living Master. But the historical accounting will go unrecorded for every camera and recorder refuses to register this moment in time.

The newcomer or the curious can only speculate in wonder at the furor they witness as this young man ascends the stage. But the ECKists have come from all over the world to be a part of this moment, their first look in the physical realm at the man who has succeeded Paul Twitchell as their teacher, spiritual guide and companion.

Darwin Gross moves toward the microphone, the blue carnation in hand. The houselights dim in the large ballroom of the Flamingo Hotel in Las Vegas, Nevada, and a hush instantly sweeps the room.

"The surprises on this path of ECK and its teachings of ECK within ECKANKAR are many. There are many things to talk about within ECK and I don't know why precisely I have been chosen, yet I do. Fubbi Quantz, when he first experienced ECKANKAR, went into a contemplation for eight years before he started giving out the message of ECK to the world. There are those on some of the planets within this galaxy in the universe that are Masters, present here this evening, that work in this field of ECKANKAR.

"The majority of the people outside of the teachings of ECK and ECKANKAR are seeking phenomena, but this is just mere child's play, just an everyday occurrence with an

ECKist, because you really become a co-worker with the Sugmad (God) and are responsible for every action.

"To reach the ECKshar Consciousness takes a little doing. It can be done very easily. It cannot be heard, though, from another person. You cannot expect that person to do it for you, be it a Master or your neighbor, your friend, husband or wife, because each and every individual is responsible for their own vibrations that they set forth and these manifest, be it in the thought form, in the form of an uttered word, a feeling, or even an action or emotion."

Hours earlier at midnight in the Valley of Shangta at the Oracle of Tirmer in Tibet, Darwin Gross, known spiritually as Dap Ren, accepted the Rod of ECK Power. He became the 972nd Living ECK Master in an unbroken line of ECK Masters that date back to the beginning of time as we know it. His predecessor, Sri Paul Twitchell, known spiritually as Peddar Zaskq, had translated (died) from the physical on September 17, 1971.

But earlier this night, in his light body, Darwin stood beside Paul, his teacher, master and friend, receiving homage from the great ECK Masters Fubbi Quantz, Rebazar Tarzs, Yaubl Sacabi, the many rulers of the worlds of God, and the Nine Silent Ones who had selected Darwin after Paul had submitted his name for consideration as the next Living ECK Master.

Sri Paul Twitchell, modern-day founder of ECKANKAR, served as the Living ECK Master from 1965 to 1971. He traveled extensively giving lectures, and authored many books, discourses and articles on the ancient spiritual teaching of ECK.

Now Darwin faces the vast audience of Paul's chelas (students) and those who want to know more about ECKANKAR, a direct path to God: "Every teacher that has taught the true teachings of ECK and ECKANKAR that have been on this planet, have taught the Light and Sound. Some of the offshoots have taught it but they can only go so far ... there is nothing held back, nothing other than your own state of consciousness, you are given help ... Getting beyond these lower worlds is not easy. This is where the Living ECK Master of the time can help guide and show and assist those individuals, those chelas of the past Masters, as well as those that are initiated during the span of a present Living ECK Master, the way through these lower worlds into the pure positive God Worlds. Many times the curtain is pulled on many of us and there is a reason because of some of the fear that has been built up in past lives and lives not only here on this planet, but perhaps elsewhere. But the majority of you have been on this planet many hundreds of thousands of years."

As Darwin finishes speaking and steps off the stage, a line forms as he shakes hands with all who come forward. One young man recognizes Darwin as the man he had seen in a vision after an initiation earlier that very afternoon. As he approaches, the Master extends his hand and says, "Hello, Mark."

"Wow!" Mark thought, "How could he know my name? I'm not even wearing a name tag!"

A feeling of festivity, joy and awesomeness pervades the room. The historic impact of the passing of the Rod of ECK Power is felt by all.

CHAPTER 1

From Heaven to the Prairie

It was not unusual for the prairie lands of Denhoff, North Dakota, to be blanketed with snow or aswirl with howling blizzards such as the one that heralded the arrival of Darwin Gross on January 3rd at nine o'clock this particular morning. The clapboard house moaned under the wind's fury while inside Adina Schmidt Gross delivered the third of five children she and her husband, Paul Patrick Gross, were to have. The blizzard negated the possibility of a doctor or midwife to assist Adina, but under the skilled and soothing hand of a neighbor lady, the baby's body entered the physical world, the body that was to be the vehicle for the Supreme Being to use as ITS contact in the lower realms.

Dad Gross was away on a business trip, but Adeline, eight, and Harry James (Jim), six, welcomed their new brother, Darwin. Within the next five years, Ruby and Donald were to join the family.

Darwin's paternal grandparents were about nine or ten years old when they migrated with their families from Russia to America. Maria Kleinsasser and Paul F. Gross were married January 6, 1889, lived for a while in a Hutterite settlement in South Dakota, then homesteaded in North Dakota, throughout their 43 years of married life. During this time Grampa Gross became a member and minister of the Kimmer Mennonite Brethren, creating a marital wound that never healed.* They had thirteen children, one of them Darwin's father.

*Joe D.M. Gross, *The Rev. Paul F. Gross Family Record* (Nov. 1972).

11

The Hutterites (named after one of their leaders, Jacob Hutter) lived communally, "a unique survival of the Anabaptist movement, that important but little understood middle religion between Catholicism and Protestantism. Originating in the Austrian province of Tyrol in 1528, they have since lived in many countries and under many governments without ever compromising their allegiance to God.... Over 70,000 strong in the Austrian empire, persecution reduced them to a hundred haggard souls who fled to Russia in 1773. In America, they now number 15,000."* Many also reside in Canada.

"The language of the Hutterites is a distinctive dialect of High German known as Tyrolese.... In the old Chronicle the names of Gross, Hofer, Mendel, Mueller, Walter, Wollman and Wurtz are found. These seven family names can be traced back to the origins of the sect in Slovakia or Velky Levary."**

Darwin indicates that he "wasn't born" but "stepped into the family from elsewhere." There is some mystery about his birth, a birth certificate not being available, and he was born beside a small lake, "a factor that just about all Masters in the past have been born on or near a body of water." He remembers "falling through the universe" about the time his Grandfather Gross, a Baptist Mennonite preacher, was leaving the family home following a visit.

Darwin did not care for his Grampa Gross. During this visit, when the tyke was three or four years old, Grampa Gross wanted to hold him for a photograph but Darwin rebelled. He kicked, cried and wiggled, throwing his little cap to the ground, wanting to get away from the man. "I didn't like his appearance, the black suit, hat, coat and tie,

*Paul S. Gross, *The Hutterite Way* (Saskatoon, Canada: Freeman Pub. Co. Ltd., 1965)
**Paul S. Gross, *The Hutterite Way* (Saskatoon, Canada: Freeman Pub. Co. Ltd., 1965)

the garb of the Mennonite. It was the combination of the dress and the little goatee beard, a vibration you'd call it, that I felt even at that age a difference between our ways of thought."

It was during this period in Darwin's young life where he would awaken from dreams screaming and crying, unable to tell his concerned parents about the experiences he had had in the dream state. Dreams became the true reality to the boy and he could not explain the beauty and bliss he found in these inner worlds. He did not wish to return to the physical existence. Thus the child resisted and came back to the physical realm in a state reminiscent of a nightmare. It distressed his parents who seemed unable to fathom the boy's problem. "If the child screams and hollers during sleep," Darwin explained, "It isn't a nightmare; the Soul doesn't want to come back to the human state of consciousness: I fought it until my spiritual guide assisted me. I was only three or so at the time and after about three months of this, my parents were about to give up on me."

These unexplainable occurrences made the child restless; he daydreamed much of the time and suffered severe headaches. Darwin was inwardly going beyond the universe, the stars and planets in the galaxies. He could travel from planet to planet as though he were going from one house to another, preferring the heavenly worlds because of the total freedom he experienced there with his spiritual guide.

"One morning about three o'clock," Darwin recalled, "I sat right up in bed for I could see this gentleman from the waist up, clad in very light blue. I sat there and stared at him. No communication took place verbally, only silently and subtly within myself and between the two of us. I lay back down in my feather bed after a time and pulled the covers over my head and went to sleep. From that moment on, all fear of going beyond myself and the universe passed by the wayside."

He was not to know who this being was until his adult

years, when he shared a book given him by his cousin, Edith. It was *In My Soul I Am Free,* the biography of Paul Twitchell by Brad Steiger. Darwin immediately recognized the picture of Paul. "I first met Paul Twitchell in the physical body in October of 1968, at the Third World Wide Seminar of ECKANKAR. I found that when I met him in the physical, it was like renewing an old acquaintance. I knew that he'd been in my dreams for a number of years. He worked with me from there on in a very subtle basis."

As a toddler, Darwin earned himself the unauthorized title of "streaker" when neighborhood boys found him coming into town "to help Papa," undisturbed by the fact he was stark naked. Some years later, he went swimming in the lake with his buddies in typical Huck Finn style, ignoring the trivialities like time and dinner calls. Sister Adeline, sent as usual by Mom to locate him, decided this was the last straw, spotted the nude swimmers and ran off with their clothes. While the other boys didn't live far from the water, Darwin had to take a long and circuitous route down the back roads and alleys to stay hidden from the eyes of the townspeople.

Darwin was close to his brother Jim and his sister Adeline. Adeline came down with polio when she was seven, leaving her with a limp, but she always had time to listen to Darwin and take care of him. In time, her husband-to-be, Walt Froeber, became one of Darwin's trusted friends. Adeline understood her brother's inner experiences because she too was a spiritual traveler. She knew how to go beyond this world and go into the heavenly worlds. In many instances, Darwin's life experiences paralleled those of his spiritual guide and teacher, Sri Paul Twitchell.

Darwin's mother, Adina, was a staunch Nazarene and her religion was as important to her as her family. When she was eleven years old, living in a sod hut on the prairie of North Dakota, she felt the presence of someone in the room while she was sleeping on the floor. She gazed upon a figure she thought to be Jesus. She looked to Jesus and devoted her life to him. It was not until as a widow she lived with her son, Darwin, at the end of her life, that she recognized a picture of the ECK Master Fubbi Quantz as the figure she had seen those many years before. Fubbi Quantz and Jesus resembled each other.

"I was placed in this family environment for my spiritual education," Darwin commented. "I didn't look like my mother, father or sisters or brothers, and that's not unique, but the vibratory rate may be closer. The vibrations are partially right and the essence of experience is gained through that time when one is given birth and by their parents. I had a happy time with my parents. Billions lack spiritual guides and their families are chosen for them. Some Initiates of ECK* choose their families; occasionally the Lords of Karma** will place individuals in a karmic situation."

Darwin remembers as a youngster lying in his little wagon, looking up at the clouds and wondering what lay beyond that blue, blue sky. Sometimes he was shown, but he didn't know who was showing him these wonders until he was older. "I would talk to the wind, to the stars, and to the moon." And they would respond. "The wind spoke back to me, it was very subtle and interesting. Sometimes the stars would dip a little bit, wave or oscillate back and forth. I communicated with birds. I enjoy all life and always have. I've never had any trouble with animals."

Darwin's first dog was a little white dog given to his father. They called the dog Topper since Darwin's father was known as "Big Topper" and his middle son, "Little Topper." When Topper was hit and killed by a motorcyclist, the youngster experienced his first pangs of death. Dad Gross soothed the saddened boy with some ice cream.

Years later when the family moved to the West Coast,

*ECK: Holy Spirit, the source of all, the audible life current.
**Lords of Karma: The distributors of karma to Souls in the lower worlds.

Darwin was forced to give up another dog, Jacky, a Belgian Shepherd who was an outstanding sheepdog. Unable to find room for Jacky in their crammed car, the family left Jacky with a sheepherder eight miles outside of town who bought him for six dollars. But a divine love existed between Jacky and Darwin and neither wanted to be separated from the other. They had spent hours together daily, roaming the prairies, going to school together, sleeping together. Heartbroken, Darwin had to leave Jacky in Denhoff but the dog refused to stay with its new owners. He broke loose and returned to the Gross home, but everyone had gone. Neighbors tried to feed and care for him, but Jacky had lost his heart and finally starved to death. Jacky's spirit still lives, and many were to tell of seeing Darwin, after he became the Living ECK Master, take their pets across the boundaries of heaven or heal them. Darwin's affinity with animals began at a very early age, and he always had a dog around him "for protection" throughout his life.

Two buddies and Darwin became known in the town as the Three Musketeers. Adventures were presented with every get-together. What one didn't think of, the others did. One warm summer afternoon they decided to learn to swim, so they began pestering the bigger boys to take them swimming with them in the dam about three miles out of town. Even though there were some small lakes on the edge of town, one even in Darwin's backyard, they felt they weren't deep enough. The older boys winked at each other, amused with the Musketeers and their enthusiasm, "Sure, kids, we'll teach you how to swim!"

Once out there, everyone stripped down to their birthday suits. No one else was around. The older boys rowed the threesome on a raft out to the middle of the lake. One Musketeer began to have second thoughts. Afraid, he cried, but Darwin sensed some mischief afoot and whispered to his buddies, "Don't be afraid. If you're afraid, it can be worse. Just know that even if we're thrown in, we'll swim to shore."

Darwin's premonition proved to be true. They were thrown into the lake. The water was deep, thirty feet, and they were quite a distance from shore. Darwin dog-paddled furiously for shore with one of the Musketeers, but the third member had trouble staying up and began to go under. The older boys stayed on the raft, laughing, but when Darwin yelled that the boy was drowning, the older boys pulled him onto the raft and headed for shore.

While telling this story, Darwin added, "I don't know what spiritual significance that might have had, but to me, even at that age, every moment of my life was of spiritual significance. I looked at each moment as such and lived it to the hilt."

When five or six, the Three Musketeers decided to try their hand at smoking. One of the three went up to the barber of the hotel and "snuck a pack of cigarettes, I think they were Lucky Strikes," sharing them with the other two. They leaned back against the old outhouse and lit up. Smoke billowed around them and curled its way around the small building, catching the eye of Paul P. Gross who was on his way home from work. He peered curiously down the alley on his way home for lunch, walked up on them and grabbed his son by the shirt collar, and headed him for home. Once home, Dad Gross sat Darwin down, lit up a large cigar and made him smoke it, much to Mom's chagrin. While it didn't make Darwin ill, he didn't feel like eating for a while and his smoking desire came to a halt.

When Darwin's father offered him a beautiful, gold railroad watch, the youngster, about seven years old, turned it down. He would have to be careful of such a fine and expensive instrument and it would get in the way of climbing trees and digging caves. Darwin recalls, "My little brother, Ron, playing the big shot, took the watch and wore it. He was out on the edge of town in a pasture and lost the watch, came home crying to me and told me about it. At that moment of time, I got out of the body, raised above the area and saw the watch, where it was.

"I told him not to worry about it, that we'd find it. I went out there with him, walked up to this gopher hole which was close to a rock that I'd seen from overhead, reached down in there and pulled out the watch. Otherwise Ron, then only around three or four, would have gotten a severe spanking from our father. Dad used what was called the razor strap in those days. It had a straight edge to sharpen the shaving instruments so it could sting!"

While Ron was relieved that his big brother Darwin had saved his hide, he was not overly impressed with Darwin's unusual abilities. Darwin had learned at an early age not to speak about his inner experiences. "This out-of-the-body ability wasn't uncommon," he continued. "I would use it only for myself or the good of others, without sometimes even knowing it."

Darwin's father was a jovial, happy-go-lucky person, but stern and stubborn when the situation merited it. He would listen to others and allow the children to be adventuresome in life, and Darwin developed a special rapport with his father. But dissension grew between the parents when Dad Gross drank and socialized and Adina pressed too hard with her religious views.

Dad Gross wanted to invest in some far land and buy a piece of property. It had rained heavily and automobiles often got stuck in the dirt and mud. "You're going to get stuck!" Mom exclaimed. She repeated this remark several times. Darwin was in the car with them, and recalled saying, "Oh, let him drive, Mom, he knows how to drive."

But she insisted and he did get stuck. He couldn't move the car, in mud clear up to the axle. "My father deliberately got stuck, just to anger her more, and it did. She was also trying to set up the condition and I was trying to stop it. She'd use the Bible, the church and the scriptures against him, and this, of course, got under Dad's skin. We finally got a farmer to pull us out."

Darwin learned early to give individuals their psychic space. He didn't like to hear his parents arguing and bickering, feeling that it had a detrimental effect on the children, and he would walk away or ignore one who wished to argue with him. He felt that arguments caused inner frustrations.

The rapport between father and son increased as Darwin grew from child into boy. Paul Gross was a self-educated man in the mechanical field. He took an industrial school course in Fargo, North Dakota, and began repairing engines in the early steam tractors and other farm equipment. He was an inventive man, vital and enthusiastic, and he loved his children. He contributed to the town's assets by building the first sidewalk. He owned the first telephone, automobile, camera and motorcycle in town. He ran one of the earliest automobile agencies, then a confectionary/beer parlor and hotel/cafe business in their turn, had a hand in bootlegging, farming, and politics, losing the election for County Sheriff by only a handful of votes.

When his father would go on business trips, Darwin often went along. Although an apparently normal human being, Paul P. Gross had certain abilities that are considered abnormal and psychic. Between Darwin and his Dad existed a silent communication called mental telepathy. "And I learned later," Darwin added, "that there is an even greater communication that can be had with a loved one or especially with the Living ECK Master* and with the ECK Masters** in the Golden Wisdom Temples."

One time when Darwin was nine or ten years old, he was driving down a dusty, muddy, unpaved road with his father. As they approached a certain corner, the lad turned right because he understood that his father wanted him to, yet no words passed between them. Darwin did not question the incident, just glanced knowingly at his dad who smiled in

---

*Living ECK Master: The messenger of the Supreme Being, the Sugmad, in all the worlds of God, physical, psychic and spiritual.
**ECK Masters: Work on every plane and planet in the universes of God to help forward the evolution of humanity, to find and train disciples who are brought to the Living ECK Master for their return to the Godhead.

return.

Paul Gross's drinking proved to be a jarring factor to his wife, but the bootlegging escapades were high adventure for the youngster Darwin. When revenue agents raided the Gross household periodically, Darwin would hide under the front steps with the dog, hugging the grain alcohol cans close to his body. Or he'd pretend he was sleeping with the liquor snuggled in bed with him. No one thought to search his bed or disturb him.

As Darwin remembered, "Dad did drink and liked to socialize. Everybody loved him; he was a man who had no enemies." But Dad Gross's reveling came to a halt one night when he came home inebriated following a winter evening at the confectionary and beer hall he had opened after the car agency had closed. On his way down cellar to stoke the furnace for the sleeping household, he forgot the missing step he had been meaning to repair. He fell and broke his arm, admitted that he had "learned his lesson with liquor," and never drank again.

The German language was used almost exclusively in the Gross home until just before Darwin went to school. To some extent, it made school difficult for Darwin since English was used at school. The curricula and routine of school were dull, but Darwin particularly enjoyed geography, English, arts, crafts and music. Spelling and grammar were his least favorite subjects. He would daydream much of the school day away amazing the teacher by answering correctly when she sought to trap his apparent inattentiveness by tossing a question his way. Darwin had the ability to rally instantly as though he had been listening to every word, despite the fact he was journeying into the inner realms of God with Peddar Zaskq.

Summers were full of opportunities to enjoy the wildflowers, lilacs, and chokecherries that could be gathered on picnics. Blackberries and raspberries grew wild along the roads but chokecherries made the finest jam. Darwin would pick them as fast as possible and go "over the hill," his mother amused by his "eating three and putting one in the bucket." Being adventuresome, the children dug out caves in the hills. Leisurely swimming, games, and good times with friends, summer jobs and relating to life and living filled Darwin's days to overflowing.

Darwin used to go walking out in the prairie, among the birds, animals and wildflowers, tall grasses and openness as far as the eye could see. "In the springtime," he reminisced, "the prairies have such a beautiful fragrance with the new grass coming up, the crocuses, all kinds of beautiful flowers, fields of flowers and tall grasses. There are white owls, ground owls, tree owls and birds that migrate from south to north, geese and swans."

Darwin learned to shoot inanimate objects with a bow and arrow. With a buddy, it was a pioneering experience for the young trail-blazers to live off the land in an area that contained only rocks and a few trees. But there were always water, lakes, wild onions that tasted like garlic, and Indian potatoes that used to grow wild in North Dakota. Darwin and his friend enjoyed the Tom Sawyer spirit of adventure in their bones, with their only "weapon" a slingshot that each carried.

When a robin was slain by the buddy's slingshot, it upset Darwin who did not care to destroy life unnecessarily. His buddy prepared and roasted the robin, eating it alone, while Darwin enjoyed the potatoes and onions and watched his buddy grow sicker and sicker.

In explanation, Darwin stated: "I always have had a love for birds and all animals. I didn't think anything of eating chicken at home, but this robin wasn't necessary. There's quite a difference between the two birds that I was to learn about later in life. I didn't know it at the time, but chicken, turkey and some of the fowl such as ducks and geese are very edible and it's good meat, if it's cooked well, for the food you eat has nothing to do with one's spiritual growth. It's far better for you than beef, venison or other meats, but

21

the songbirds have a particular function in this world, and very few people know of it. They are not here to be eaten. They are to be enjoyed and watched and observed. Man actually can learn things from them, from the animals, as well as the birds and learn some spiritual lessons. The use of sex is only for reproduction, not for just the pleasure of their mate; it's just cut and dried in that kingdom. Man doesn't know that. Man has evolved, in a sense, but in the states of consciousness, some people are lower than an animal or a bird, because of their actions, their words, their thoughts."

From a previous time, an individual will have certain characteristics that they have developed within themselves, whether it's from another dimension of time or a past life. It drew out the inventiveness within Darwin. He could build his own radio, take clocks apart and put them together again, rebuild a Model-T or -A car. One afternoon he ascended a thirty-five-foot water tower with a set of wings he had fashioned. Usually Darwin's "flights" were relegated to the chicken coop roof, but the water tower presented an exceptional challenge. However, the venture failed for he froze on the spot and had to be carried down by a couple of the men from town, the incident horrifying his mother.

Darwin invented a special gopher trap but it was the invention itself that interested him, not its ability to harm the animal, so the trap was set aside once it was built. He considered every incident in his life a spiritual experience, and still does. His struggle for the Mastership began early in his life and presented test after test that he was to look upon as a learning experience.

He tackled his daily duties quickly so he could be free to work or play with his friends in the afternoons. He took odd jobs to be independent financially. He and his Dad cut ice from the lakes in the winter to store the ice blocks for summer use; he weeded his mother's large garden in the summers from which the family received most of their food throughout the year, and Adina canned much of it. The kitchen always smelled warm and fragrant from Adina's baking and canning. Darwin carried his own weight by following through on tasks he was given to do.

He was mischievous and innovative and the family enjoyed him. He was often in the limelight and warmed to it. In his imagination, he envisioned himself a movie star or musical performer, but his daily existence was punctuated with adventures and fun, accompanied by the constant and growing awareness of his spiritual guide and friend. He was shy and bashful and still is.

Music was an important part of Darwin's life. "I enjoyed music. It is an excellent vehicle for that which man calls 'Spirit' to work through, that which supports all life. I used to whistle as a kid all the time, and sing. I composed my first song on horseback. It lifted me over hurdles, whether I sang or went out in the country to play my trumpet. I even took my father's violin out one day. I believe it was a copy of a Strad, and it had a beautiful tone; it was built for a left-handed player. I always wanted to learn to play it. Dad gave it to me one day and told me if I could learn to play it, I could have it. But something else came along and I went off in another direction."

The family had many instruments and each member played at least one of them. Darwin's father played by ear, and Darwin did also. He played the trumpet before he was school age and was taught to read music, but singing and composing songs were his first-loves, a cowboy song being his first attempt. While he appreciated all types of music, negative harsh tones did not appeal to him. Music was to be an important vehicle for Darwin, the boy and the man, to express his feelings and experiences within the universes of God.

When his brother Jim was given piano lessons, Darwin wanted to learn piano also, but family finances did not allow it. Darwin took out his anger and frustration by carving numbers in the piano one afternoon following a stint of

23

cutting the firewood. He never quite knew how his father learned he had been the culprit, but Darwin received a sound spanking for his efforts. Since Paul Gross was also spiritually aware, he may well have had an inner knowingness that his middle son's anger had evidenced an outlet at the piano's expense.

Later when the family moved from Denhoff to Kensel, Darwin was to experience seeing his first black man: "I was about eleven years old. I heard about this band coming into town and I was interested because I played trumpet. I went to the school house that night because they were playing in the gym. I sat outside and watched through the windows for a full four hours. I was fascinated, not by their color, but by the music they were playing. It was the kind of music I enjoyed and listened to occasionally on the radio. I believe it was King Oliver's band with Louis Armstrong!"

Darwin's inner spiritual guidance and protection came to his assistance many times in his youthful escapades. A blizzard came up one time when he was on his way home from school, obliterating the view completely and disorienting direction. Instinctively, he dug a little hole or cave in a snowbank, keeping calm until the wind stopped blowing and everything settled down. Most of the day passed, a long period for a youngster, but when the storm was over, he emerged warm and protected from the cold wind and harsh snow. He knew that to remain calm in the time of stress, to relax the best way he could and not worry about it—like the swimmer who relaxes and stays buoyant, not fighting the tide of events—all should go well, as indeed it did, and he continued on his way home.

The boys would ice skate on the ponds near the house and Darwin would ski out alone on the prairie hills on skis he had made from barrel staves.

When Darwin's Grandfather Schmidt translated (died), his parents offered to help run the farm. Dad Gross kept his business in town and the house in Denhoff, but the family moved in with Grandmother Schmidt, a warm and loving woman who baked kuchen, cheesecake and cookies for her grandchildren. The farm was less than three miles from town and the family stayed there for a couple of years until Darwin's uncle was able to oversee the farm's care.

Blizzards were a way of life in the Dakota winters but this one particular day it caught them unprepared. Although the cattle were already in the barn, the horses were still out in the pastures and could freeze to death. The only adults at the farm were Darwin's mother and grandmother, so Darwin, about nine years old at the time, slipped out of the house and bridled up his favorite white horse. He went out in the blinding snowstorm to locate the missing horses. No one knew he had gone. He painstakingly gathered together twenty to thirty of them, up to their bellies in snow, and brought them into the barn without mishap. Although he was scolded, his father was justifiably proud of Darwin. It was this inborn ability to communicate with animals that has served him well throughout his life. "Kids and animals are closer to Soul and to Spirit," Darwin stated. "A child is very open to IT. You will find that in life adventures and living life that certain things take place with animals and human beings that are not understood by mankind as a whole.

"Children and animals like and want strict discipline. They know just what they can get away with. I have no fear of snakes or animals of the jungle. I could go out into the jungle and not be eaten by the wild beasts, because of my spiritual knowledge of how to send forth love that they understand and react to. This is inborn in each of us, yet there are spiritual lessons one must learn before trying this out."

One lazy summer afternoon, Darwin eyed Grandma Schmidt's tractor. He had been told to stay off the vehicle but the temptation beckoned. Suddenly he foresaw himself falling off. He was being warned by his spiritual guide not to pursue this, that there would be an accident. He even saw himself lying on the ground, knocked out completely. But he chose to disregard the warning. He got on the tractor and cranked it up. It lurched forward. The narrow front wheels hit a boulder. Darwin was knocked off and hit his head on a rock. "I learned from that to adhere to instructions given me by my elders in the future," Darwin remembered.

"While we were out on my grandmother's farm, I'd always wanted to fly in airplanes, getting up in high places. This one nice day I climbed the windmill, which was higher than the barn and any of the trees. I was enjoying myself up there, without hanging on to anything particularly, and my mother came out of the house and saw me. She almost had a heart attack, nearly fainted, tried to holler to me but couldn't get a word out.

"When I saw that, I knew what was happening so I immediately got down and hid in the hayloft and proceeded to get beyond myself and go to the top of the barn and observe and watch that my physical body was safe. When my father came home that evening, she wanted him to give me a spanking because I had climbed the windmill and almost frightened the life out of her. I thought better of out-of-the-body experiences and in the future used more of those to get the experience of heights in this physical world than attempting to use the physical body. And the experience is the same."

One day the pharmacist in town, who also doubled as a dentist of sorts, pulled one of Darwin's teeth with a pliers, creating a sea of blood. Darwin assured the dubious "dentist" that he felt no pain, for he had traveled beyond the physical realms, moving his attention away from the pharmacist's tools. "Effortlessly I found myself outside my physical body, watching the whole event from a separate vantage point, a point I know as my Soul body."

The townspeople leaned on Darwin, sometimes for guidance physically, sometimes for their spiritual needs. He was a good sounding board. He became known as "Little Doc" when people talked to him about their health, but when a healing would take place, he'd answer them with

"Well, Spirit knows best." Darwin knew that when an individual is a vehicle for healing, the individual who realizes and accepts the responsibility doesn't really care to be praised. They are just grateful to be of assistance for the good of all.

According to Darwin: "When I was a youngster, I was able to get up into those areas of heaven—back and forth—and wanted to go further and I couldn't. I got into what the Eastern man called the Void, also spoken of as Bliss or Nirvana. It is a dark tunnel, black, coal-black and dark." But Darwin no longer feared the worlds of duality, for he longed to move into the levels of heaven that knew of no negativity, those known as the pure positive God Worlds of ECK. And this he did under the guidance of his spiritual guardian.

CHAPTER 2

Music from Beyond

In these early years, music and what others called daydreams played a central part in Darwin's life. Ever since he could remember, he had experienced sound and light in his dreams, night and day, in heavenly tones. It was the force of these experiences that urged him to take up his father's trumpet and teach himself to play by ear. This was the underlying reason for the burning anger at being denied piano lessons in favor of his older brother Jim, which had prompted the young boy to cut numbers into the piano with his pocket knife. How could he express the beauty and harmony found within, but by his music?

Once, on the vast North Dakota prairie as Darwin rambled alone in a field of wheat, he suddenly heard beautiful music, seemingly coming from nowhere. It rippled in waves like the wind rippling the golden grain of the fields. He found himself being drawn into the sound as he looked around for its source. It seemed to be coming from a rock, but when he lifted it he found nothing. The music continued to flow through his being and in the next instant he found himself riding on the sound into worlds of exquisite beauty that he would someday know as the Ocean of Love and Mercy, Source of all, which flows from the SUGMAD.

Outwardly, the youngster had no words for the awe-inspiring levels of consciousness that came to him from beyond the physical perception, but when he played his music, sang or whistled to himself, he felt a happiness and closer to God than at any other time.

*   *   *

When Darwin was thirteen, he had grown into a tall, but thin teenager, with thick wavy hair combed straight back, and deep serious blue eyes. He was friendly to all, yet kept a distance to most people. The few to whom he was close knew him to be generous, a friend to be trusted and full of laughter. But like the rose encased in the bud, his real self emerged only in his travels within his own consciousness and beyond this physical world.

One day, his father assembled the family together and told them he was thinking of going to Oregon. Since the outbreak of the war in Europe and the Pacific, the shipyards in Portland were booming, and a man could earn more in a month in the shipyards than in a year of hard work in North Dakota.

Before moving out to the West Coast, the family spent the year in Carrington. Darwin commented, "The snow was so deep that you could barely get into town for shopping, and tunnels from building to building had to be made in the snow. That spring in school I was out for the track meet. I was going to get into a pole vaulting team and somehow, I don't know how it happened, but I missed the hole and broke my arm. And I didn't feel any pain. It could have been the pretty girl I was looking at; however, I learned a lesson. I knew it was broken because of it hanging. I didn't cry or that sort of thing. It hurt, yet it didn't bother me, I guess is the expression." This was a recurrence in Darwin's life—the ability to rise above pain—from the time he was four years old and broke his arm falling from the piano bench "with a cuff on the side of the head for marking the piano with my knife."

Preparing with his family for the move, Darwin heard many of the rumors and stories about Oregon circulating in Carrington, North Dakota. They would talk of the fresh fruit to eat all year round! The nice houses, and every one of them with indoor plumbing! And the weather, mild and so much better, especially the summers and winters!

Darwin's anticipation heightened. Finally, the family set

out, cramped in the overloaded car, boxes and suitcases on top, ready for a two-thousand-mile-long trek through the flat plains of the American Midwest, over the passes of the Rocky Mountains, across the thinly populated stretches of Western Montana and Idaho, climbing the winding roads of the Blue Mountains, suffering the heat and dust of Oregon's eastern desert. Slowly, the hills grew greener, the Juniper and Ponderosa Pines being replaced by the great Douglas Firs, rivers appeared, orchards lined the road—they were nearing the coast!

Their car caked in dirt, the Gross family arrived in Portland with thousands of others, worried about their future, tempers strained from the long journey. But Darwin was excited.

"There are people everywhere!" he exclaimed. "And it looks like there's a store on every block. No wonder, with people living in houses so many floors high."

After being turned down at two motels, they at last found a small motel with two rooms left. Thunderclouds were piling up in the sky, as dad and mom and the children hastily unloaded the car to get their few belongings inside. Soon the forces of nature were released in a furious rainstorm that swept the entire state. Day after day the torrents continued, rivers rose, and roads were closed. People began to worry.

Standing by the window, Darwin was amazed at the amount of rain. Vaguely, he wondered to himself why there was always such heavy weather whenever a great change occurred in his life? But he felt no fear—the natural forces of the Earth would never harm him personally.

A few days later, Dad Gross announced to the family that he had found a place in a temporary housing project for shipyard workers where they could stay until they found a suitable home to buy. It was called Van Port City.

Van Port City was a small district of wooden, two-story houses, where many families like the Gross family were crowded. Daily, Paul Gross would go out after work to look at houses up for sale. It took him about a month, but the result was pleasing to all. Located in St. Johns, an unpretentious, older suburban area of Portland, it was a two-story asbestos shingled home well maintained and surrounded by a huge garden.

Immediately after moving in, Darwin, accompanied by his youngest brother Ron, explored the garden.

"It's full of fruit trees!" he delighted. "Cherry trees, apple trees, pear trees ... and these must be yellow and purple plum trees, filberts, quince, and, oh look, even a grape arbor and a fig tree!"

Both were impressed. Fruit to them had been an orange or two a year, maybe an occasional banana—and in the fall some crab apples and wild chokecherries, so this seemed like a garden of Eden offering its delicious goods for free. The two boys frolicked around the yard like excited puppies, while mom and dad stood in the back door, smiling. The house had indoor toilets, running water, and plenty of room for everyone. It would make a good home.

The day after they moved in, the rains started again. This time the waters rose so strongly that the residents of Van Port City had to be evacuated—the shipyard housing project was completely destroyed.

Since Jim and Adeline had moved out and started families of their own, Darwin, as the third child, was now the oldest of the children still at home. Having a reputation as the family tease and always making jokes in all kinds of situations, Darwin still took his role seriously, especially with Ron.

Portland at first was an overwhelming experience for Darwin, who had lived all his life in a small country town where everybody knew everybody else. Life was much more anonymous here, and a single person seemed lost in the multitude of the city people. The high school he was attending, the Sabin school for boys, was miles away from where he lived in St. Johns, and the bus ride took nearly two hours each way. This prevented him from making many friends in the immediate neighborhood and added to his feeling of loneliness created by the very fact that he could not talk about what influenced him most — his spiritual experiences and music.

Later Darwin recalled, "I couldn't talk to anyone about what was really important, other than to my father and Adeline, whom I felt always had time to listen to me, for she was a fellow spiritual traveler, and being so, when you know, you know."

Darwin resented school and was frustrated by it. Where his younger sister and brother found school in Oregon easier than the strict education of Dakota, he was behind his classmates. He knew the educational system was trying to fit him into a very limited pattern, and his way to get beyond that was to increase his ability to explore the worlds within as well as the outer universes, to contact knowledge and wisdom no ordinary school taught.

He became adept at bringing into his own consciousness the lessons of his dreams and of his travels from beyond this world, and his self-explorations, and to consciously appreciate the subtler feelings of others. At the same time, he was well aware of what went on around him. He would surprise his teachers when called upon by repeating their questions word for word, although obviously his real attention had been focused elsewhere.

Amid his loneliness and isolation, music provided the outlet he needed. The blues on his trumpet flowed like the rivers — smooth and haunting. Whenever Darwin's problems would press too hard in these early Portland years, he would find solace in Pier Park, a short distance away from his house down North Pier Park Avenue.

The rolling hills of the park were forested with huge cedar and pine trees, which emitted natural fragrances, and the entry paths were lined with azaleas and rhododendrons splashing the green of the forest with bright colors. The voices of children playing ball carried far through the clear air, mixing with the shouts of youngsters at the pool and the conversation of the lovers strolling under the trees. Birds chirped and squirrels chattered overhead in the tree-tops where the gentle breezes rustled the leaves. At Pier Park, Darwin could merge his worlds in harmony. Under the distant gaze of the majestic peaks of Mount Hood and Mount Adams, when the huge fir trees glowed in the red light of sunset or sunrise, Darwin enjoyed communicating with the small animals and birds. Here he maintained his perspective.Many of his own love songs and blues were born in this place, where contact with inspiration and divinity came more easily.

In company with people outside the persons he was close to, Darwin was quiet and spoke very little. But he observed people closely—from their auras he would discern their negative or positive feelings. Being sensitive, he empathized with others, their pain, their anger, the limitations of their self-imposed imprisonments. He was saddened by the wrongs and deceptions they practiced on one another. His urge was to shout of the serenity, wisdom and beauty of the heavenly existence so far beyond the misery and dangers of the lower worlds, but life had taught him to stay silent. No one would listen, or if they did, they would not take him seriously. The frustrations built up in the youngster, and his severe headaches began to recur.

In reflecting on this point, Sri Darwin, the Living ECK Master, said: "Children are more receptive and accept more readily than most older people, yet there is the individual who is sort of receptive, as man thinks of sensitivity. This can be dangerous if one develops sensitivity without developing spiritually to retain that balance. One can misunderstand the signals given from a very low nature such as astral or causal or mental."

Much of the balance that Darwin gained for himself in the difficult years of his adolescence resulted from his music. He rarely indulged in self-pity, regrets or complaints. He looked forward to every day being a new day, welcoming the things it brought him. There was the high school band he played in, baseball which he played as shortstop and outfielder, and various activities, including basketball which appealed to him, although his participation did not earn him a spot on the school team. Hating conflicts, he never got into fights and never made enemies. On the other hand, he was not one of those kids that always got bullied by the aggressive ones. He had a physical and inner strength which others were wary of testing.

"I don't look for fights, but nobody had better push me around," he told one of his friends. "I can run faster than they can."

In being above the usual little aggressions, bickerings and defeats that occur between teenagers, Darwin was truly a rare individual. He had a knowledge of rhythms, harmonies and principles given to him via his spiritual guidance that few others had.

"There were times in my youth when I would rather express myself musically than verbally," Sri Darwin explains, looking back. "Music is a creative form of expression; each note, or the accumulation of notes or what we call a chord or set of chords, can be uplifting and positive, or negative. The negative aspect of that is detrimental to the various sheaths or auras of the bodies of man. This is not common knowledge throughout the outer world. Most of the music you hear on the airwaves today on radio and television is very detrimental. I'm talking about the rock music and some of the jazz music.

"You can heal people with music. Plato taught it to some of his students whether it was on the lute or some of the instruments of those days. You could present a chord on a three-stringed instrument and there are records of people being healed. There is certain symphonic music that is uplifting and healing to Soul, soothing to the Soul, some that is not. In all types of music, there is some positive and some negative, or some good and some bad, whatever terminology you choose to use there. There were certain types of music I didn't care for as a child, and it wasn't all jazz. I wasn't that narrow in my scope of appreciation and I appreciated all types of music and learned from all types of music. I still enjoy it."

From music Darwin derived much pleasure and sense of achievement, since it did communicate in its own way some of his experience with the "heavenly" worlds to those who listened to him play but would not listen to his words. Or even when he sat alone and played his trumpet to himself at Pier Park, it gave him release from the frustration of seeing things he could do nothing about. He composed songs and tunes with his family, his teachers and friends in mind, hoping to uplift them with his music so they, too, would have a touch of those exalted states.

He often received encouragement from his teachers. One told him: "You really have talent, Darwin. I like your songs and melodies. You should keep it up."

"Thank you," Darwin answered, thinking of the future, "maybe it wouldn't be such a bad idea to make a career out of it."

Years later, his dream would fulfill itself when he enrolled in a Portland music school after leaving the army. Only then did he learn to write the music he now composed intuitively, playing by ear and using his talent for picking up tunes from the radio or themes from sounds in his environment—birds, people, machines, the wind and rain, and melodies from within.

As a teenager, Darwin loved playing in the high school band. At the dances he was more up on the stage playing the music than on the dance floor. He did have a few girlfriends, but never went steady or spent much time with them. But during his sophomore year in high school, he began dating one girl regularly. She was a nice-looking, pleasant girl with a slight, well-built figure and dark, short hair. She went to a different school than Darwin and they saw each other only on the weekends, but they got along so well that their relationship did not suffer.

On one particular occasion, this girl was to learn that she

was dating a young man who did not as readily accept the conditions and limitations of the world of physical reality as others did.

Since her parents liked Darwin and because she lived across town from his house, after a date he sometimes slept on the couch in their living room instead of going home. Early one morning, she came down from her bedroom to get his shirt to wash it while he was still asleep in the living room. He awoke by the slight sound of her footsteps and, still groggy, said:

"What are you doing to my shirt?"

She said, "I was going to wash it, but it's clean, even around the neck!"

"Dirt won't cling to a shirt if you think and act right," Darwin answered.

She smiled and said, "You're not serious." But when she looked in his eyes, she knew he was serious, as he said, "A person can raise his vibrations so that a shirt never gets dirty, you know." Today Sri Darwin Gross works beyond that area of spiritual development.

Throughout the years of his youth, Darwin's ability to anticipate danger through contact with his spiritual guardian, Peddar Zaskq, never left him. Where Pier Park ended, a steep downward sloping bank stopped abruptly at the railroad tracks. The neighborhood boys often made a game out of sliding down the bank. Though usually a great organizer of games and in the forefront of anything that took boldness and courage, Darwin stayed away from that bank. They taunted him, but he had been warned by his inner guide and didn't join them; in fact he warned them of the danger that existed. Shortly thereafter, a train rolled over one boy who had been unable to stop his slide in time, and crushed him to death.

On the other hand, Darwin didn't always listen to the premonitions coming from within. He was a normal and lively youngster and couldn't always resist a challenge.

At fifteen, he owned his own car and was always generous about giving someone a ride. On one such occasion, the neighborhood boy riding with Darwin talked him into stopping at a department store. His friend needed an automobile part and said it wouldn't take long. While Darwin was waiting in the car, he felt the nudge of that silent voice to drive away. But he had no other plans, and so he decided to go inside.

In the store the other boy pulled him close and said, "Dare you to steal that part for me."

It was a part worth forty-nine cents. Darwin had eight or nine dollars in his pocket from working after school and could have bought the part without feeling the loss, but thinking he would gain more in the eyes of his friend, he stole the trinket when he felt no one was looking. The theft did not go unseen, however, and the two lads were met at the door by a store detective. The other boy was let go, but Darwin was taken to the police. His parents had to come and get him out. The embarrassment he felt burned in his face and heart.

Through the lessons he learned, his upbringing, and the understanding flowing in from his contact with higher levels of consciousness, Darwin developed an unusually strong sense of what was right. And his conscience kept that feeling foremost in his mind. In fact, one day his way to school led him past a garden with an apple tree heavily laden with large, ripe apples. The apples seemed to beckon with their rounded, shining cheeks, and unable to resist, Darwin quickly looked right and left, swung over the fence and plucked one. No sooner had the apple parted with the branch than the owner rushed out, waving a shotgun. Darwin felt no need to hang around for exchanging pleasantries, and so he ran as fast as he could, vaulting over the fence in one leap and expecting buckshot from behind at any moment. Yet, despite the trouble he had gone through, he found he couldn't eat that apple.

"I can't get away with anything," he thought sourly to himself. Later in life he realized, "This has been true throughout my life, for I have to be truthful even though it hurts at times. Even in my youth I knew I had to be true to myself, truthful to God."

Foremost as one of Darwin's motivations was independence, not having to rely on someone else for the things he wanted in his life. He earned his own money, bought his own clothes, and even the school lunches and expenses were paid from his own wages. The shipyards had accepted him as a welder at age fifteen, because he knew how to weld from helping in his father's garage back in Dakota. He also worked odd jobs, picked fruit and used every opportunity to maintain his independence. If other children borrowed money from their fathers, Darwin never did. Even when Papa Gross, knowing at times that Darwin needed some money, would give him ten or twenty dollars, his son would later always pay him back.

In the wartime years to follow, family life changed for Darwin. Although the family often had happy picnics in Pier Park or drove the eighty-five miles to the ocean beaches — where the pounding surf, the sand, the caves and rocks, winds and cool water were exciting to Darwin and gave him many opportunities for good-natured pranks shared with his brothers and sisters and their families — he yearned to be on his own. No longer was life a struggle for survival, with shipyard work paying well, but the family was not as close as they had been in Denhoff. The anonymity of life in Portland had changed his father. He became more subdued, where before in Dakota he had been exceedingly vivacious, knowing everyone and always being out somewhere to make money with some scheme or another. The older children were raising their own families, and the younger ones were being drawn to separate activities in the diversity of the large city.

Darwin was growing toward young adulthood himself, and at this stage, he began looking at his parents with different eyes. There was very little physical affection between them, he noticed. They hardly ever embraced or

39

touched, yet there was a reliability in their relationship. All the Gross children knew that whatever happened, they would never be neglected or pushed away. Mom and Dad would always be there and stand behind them if needed. It was not a clinging relationship the family had, for although they liked to be around each other, the need for being on one's own was also recognized.

Darwin later recalled: "The love between parents and children in my family, though admittedly not physical, was more detached. That sort of love is more like divine love."

The independence of knowledge gained from his inner travels, and the strength that was imparted through his contact with the force of Spirit increased in their effect on the shaping of Darwin's life. The limited religious beliefs of his mother more and more felt like a vise grip on his expanding spiritual vision. Finally, through quiet but determined opposition, Darwin won his mother's reluctant agreement that he no longer attend church with her. His feelings about church he later related: "I met Peddar Zaskq many times in the dream state and also had seen some of the ECK Masters, such as Rebazar Tarzs, and was introduced to some of the others as I grew older and progressed spiritually. I had various insights when taken to my mother's church. They said one thing on Sunday and lived differently the rest of the week.

"My mother did have some degree of influence in shaping my life, but I dropped out of her church at an early age. The negative atmosphere, the songs depressed me. The atmosphere became emotional because of it. It bothered me internally."

As happens with many father-son relationships, there comes a time when both realize that the son is growing up and is put on equal footing with the father. For Darwin this came at age sixteen through a confrontation that was both intense and brief. The incident was triggered by Mom Gross and Ron, the youngest of the children. Ron was supposed to accompany his mother by bus to a field to pick berries. At the bus station Ron saw there were no free seats left on the bus, and not wanting to stand all the way, stubbornly refused to go.

Adina Gross didn't discipline her youngest son, but waited, as usual, for Dad to come home to report Ron's misbehavior to him. The small boy knew he was in for some punishment, but not the incredible thing that happened then. Dad got out the razor strap and then suddenly erupted into a red rage, throwing Ron to the floor, beating him with the length of heavy leather and yelling at him all the while. The child writhed helplessly on the floor. Red welts appeared all over his arms and back as he rolled on the ground trying to escape the mighty blows from the heavy man whose temper was running wild. Darwin's sister Ruby screamed, but neither she nor her mother were in any way capable to interfere. Darwin, hearing the racket in the living room, rushed down the stairs and stopped short at the shocking scene.

Immediately, Darwin grabbed his father's arm in midswing and told him, "If you strike him once more, you'll have to take me on!"

The determination in Darwin's voice penetrated his father's rage. Still shaking with anger, Paul Gross turned and looked at the young man whose hand gripped his arm. The confrontation lasted only a second, yet the elder Gross recognized the stronger. He dropped the razor strap and walked away.

Darwin and his father had always been close, often sharing instant communication through mental telepathy, and so the inevitable conflict between father and son was resolved without a fatal break in the relationship. They continued on the good terms they had always had.

"My father had a heart of gold and he loved all the children, but his anger was aroused by my mother who often waited until he came home to tell him about our childish misdeeds. She didn't discipline the children; she wanted him to discipline them, and he didn't like it. He'd rather give the children love, and it hurt and angered him to the point that he sometimes over-disciplined us."

Despite his greater knowledge on what was good for him on the spiritual as well as physical level, Darwin was by no means immune to the temptations of consumption habits offered by the society of the time. Although he had tried drinking and disliked it, he had picked up the habit of smoking somewhere along the line in the struggle of his adolescent years. He knew it was bad for him and disliked it because of the messiness with the ashes, the smell that clung to his clothes and the smoke that got into his eyes. But, once the habit was formed, it wasn't easy to get rid of. Darwin talked to Spirit about it, to his Inner Master and spiritual guide. He hadn't been left alone, but he didn't get any answers, either. "I'll be darned!" thought Darwin in frustration. He wanted to get rid of the smoking habit so badly, he even cried once and pleaded to Jesus, but no answer came from Jesus. This was the point in Darwin's life when he realized that past teachers, saints and saviors are unable to help us here on Earth. His parents were sympathetic, his father had given up smoking himself, but there wasn't much they could do. Finally, Darwin gave up his struggle. "Okay, God, I need your help." He had to learn the lesson not to lean on other beings and people, that it had to come from within himself and no one else: "My parents left it up to me, just as the Masters in ECK did, and once I realized that I was fighting with myself and with nothing else, I was able to get above it and control it."

At sixteen, the wish to be on his own and his yearning for adventure motivated Darwin to apply for enlistment in the U.S. Army. He wanted to leave school and be away from home, not because he was unhappy with his family and didn't want to be around them, but because he wanted independence and to see the world and meet people of different countries and races. The Merchant Marine seemed best for this purpose, but because of his flat feet, the lad was turned away.

Seeing how great Darwin's disappointment was, one of the doctors told him, "You can strengthen your feet and build up the arches by picking up marbles with your toes." So, with his customary dedication, Darwin picked up marbles with his toes every day. After two years, his feet passed the army requirements, and at age eighteen he won his enlistment.

But, by that time, World War II was over; he understood, then, his spiritual guardian had kept him from actual combat, which the sixteen-year-old would have experienced had he been admitted earlier to the armed forces.

During all these two years, Darwin's desire to get away grew within his heart. Once out on his own, he felt he would be free to work more directly towards what from his inner experiences he made out to be his destiny. These unusual experiences, his contact with his inter guide,* his ability to go beyond himself, all this made it clear that he was different from most people. Different not in the sense of being superior to them in human standing, only that he had work to do that was somehow vastly important. Once on his own, his road would lead to success—success in living the life of Spirit, working with his unique talents that often surpassed the skills learned under the forming hands of society's school and university system.

Darwin relied on Spirit and his inter guide, whom he would later call Peddar Zaskq, known to this world as Paul Twitchell. He had contact with other ECK Masters, such as Rebazar Tarzs and Fubbi Quantz, Adepts of great wisdom who taught him in the dream state, and he was confident the future would bring even greater understanding of the worlds of God. One way this understanding would come during his assignment with the army was through a meeting with Sato Kuraji, an ancient Japanese ECK Master,

*Darwin distinguishes *inter* guide from *inner* guide. An inner guide is limited to the lower worlds, while inter guide has ability to lead Soul through the lower worlds into the pure positive God worlds.

43

who led young Darwin to greater knowledge of the intricate world of the mind.

CHAPTER 3

The Angels—Hell From Above

The 492nd Screaming Eagles Division of the United States 11th Airborne Army known as "The Angels, Hell From Above"—by reputation the toughest division in the airborne—was Darwin's assignment. He worked for it and well earned that division's choice tour of duty in Japan. A land of mystery, intrigue and antiquity. An opportunity for adventure in a far country that would have spiritual significance to the young man, culminating in an unsuspected meeting with an ancient Japanese Master of the Vairagi.

Adventuresome but practical, Darwin signed right up when told at Fort Lewis in Tacoma, Washington, that he would earn fifty dollars more a month if he joined the airborne troops. After basic training in Fort Knox, Kentucky, he met with three months of rigorous paratroop training at Fort Benning, Georgia. Here his determination and self-discipline were a help in meeting his immediate goal.

During the early part of paratroop training a test came that temporarily froze him. The trainees had to climb to the top of a tall tower and jump off. Wearing only a trim harness attached to a lead cable, that first step was a big one. To simulate the shock of a real jump, there was fifteen feet of free fall. Then the cable tightened to bounce the trainee like a ball on the end of a string, before he could slide down the lead wire and into the dirt and sawdust pile for his landing. Although Darwin had been watching those before him meet the challenge, some shaking and pale in face, when his turn came he could not move. Even the sergeant's helpful "boot" could not budge him. He was told he had "washed out" and to report to the C.O. A big lesson was learned for he and some others, while waiting for the instructor, had made fun of those below.

Determined to return to face and lick the fear that had gripped him, Darwin asked the officer in charge to give him another chance. Though somewhat irregular, he returned to jump that afternoon. His jump and landing were in order. But just to make sure, he climbed the tower a second time and repeated the jump with the same success. During the course of his military career he made more than 23 jumps without mishap. He was among the honored.

Even here his intuitive powers he had learned to recognize and listen to as he was growing up came forth. On one jump in Japan, a sudden wind caught his canopy, pulling him off target and over some jagged, hazardous rocks. Recognizing the danger, he pulled down on the parachute straps. Then a split second before impact, released these risers, which gave him an accurate soft landing that amazed his companions.

Typical of all significant moves in Darwin's life, the forces of nature would mark his voyage to Japan with unusual intensity. Before the troop ship that left San Francisco reached Yokohama harbor, it encountered a violent and intense storm. The merciless rocking jolted and sickened the men. Yet Darwin remained calm. His innate ability to go beyond himself through use of the creative imagination enabled him to ride out the storm on the ship's bow with the fresh air in his face.

Although stationed in Jamachi in Central Honshu, Japan's main island, at one point Darwin was sent to the west coast town of Moto for glider training along the China Sea. An ideal setting for long daily swims beyond the breakers in the warm sea. One day the forces of nature again assailed him. Huge tidal waves began to crest far from shore. As they swept by, they raised Darwin high into the air before they crashed on the distant shore. The strong undertow created by their return drew Darwin far out to

46

sea. At first he struggled to keep his position, but was quick to recognize the futility of such exhaustion. He turned over on his back and surrendered to that spiritual source within that he called Spirit, which is known in ECKANKAR as the Inner Master, and that later he would come to know as the ECK. "It's up to the Divine Spirit," he thought. "Whatever I am to do, I will do." Instantly a force surged through his body. He swam all the way to shore and collapsed on the warm, welcome sand.

Another experience Darwin encountered on the Japanese coast was not soon forgotten. Years later in speaking to a seminar audience as the Living ECK Master, he referred to it as an illustration of how creativity and flexibility can get you through almost any situation:

"I had a unique experience in my Army career, which took some swift creativity on my part. On this particular evening, I sort of broke the rule at the camp and went into this little neighboring town that was close to the camp that we were bed-rocking in, to become more acquainted with the people in that community and to see how they lived. There were three of us that had gone into this little community. Upon returning to camp that evening, it was dark, and we were going through this field of rice, walking on a narrow dirt path; it was a dike to separate the fields. And if you know how the Japanese fertilize their fields, you know what a little honey-bucket is, that's buried in the ground. It was level with the ground that opened, and it had been filled with human waste. We were sort of running because coming up the beach was a jeep with some M.P.'s. Well, the two fellows that were running in front of me later said, 'What happened to you?'

"I had disappeared in this honey-bucket, and I crawled out of there faster than lightning and headed for the beach and ocean, which was about 500 yards from this little field, and dodging the M.P.'s. I spent all that evening and most of the morning swimming in the ocean trying to cleanse the physical body from the delightful unpleasant odors. Spirit works very swiftly sometimes. It was interesting. The salt water itself did not take away all of the stench. It was through the ECK and Spirit that showed me—at the time I was not aware that this was Peddar Zaskq working with me—to take the seaweed, and using the juices that I could squeeze out, rub through my hair and on my body to cleanse it. Staying loose or flexible sometimes can be very exciting and yet rewarding in what one gains in wisdom." Darwin many times has said that all through his life he never really could get away with anything. "You see, this little village was off-limits to us!"

The Screaming Eagles Division of the 11th Airborne was in Japan on a peace time occupation mission, their main duty "to put their best foot forward." Darwin had received a good conduct medal and was considered a good jumper in the division, as well as an expert rifleman. He was never required to fire at anyone, but he knew he could to defend himself or his unit. Although he avoided fights and would walk away from emotional arguments over religion or politics—he could see no sense in arguing about something he already knew within himself—he was respected as a tough soldier. He had a few buddies and especially enjoyed the company of some of the older men who had more experience in life. Easy to be with, Darwin's courage and honesty was sensed by the officers in charge. They more than once came to him for help in resolving what seemed to be an impossible situation.

One incident in particular led to a rather miraculous experience that Darwin came to understand from a spiritual point of view. A well-liked top sergeant, veteran of many battles, had gotten drunk and gone berserk more than once. This time, however, he had stolen a truck to get to town to drink, and then had wreaked violent havoc on everything and everyone within reach, even holding some of his own men hostage in back of the stolen vehicle. Darwin was sent to bring him back, being told he was the only one who could do it.

Darwin found the drunken top sergeant and talked him into letting the hostages go. The two agreed to return to camp together, but the sergeant insisted upon driving. It was a wild ride over a steep and narrow mountain road, but before reaching camp the sergeant took a detour, jumped truck and began to attack a farmer's wife. By the time Darwin got him into the truck and back to camp, the charges against the sergeant had accumulated. He was put under guard and scheduled for a court martial.

One by one, several of the sergeant's close friends came to Darwin and threatened him not to testify against the sergeant. Yet Darwin had learned long before that he had to be true to himself, to that part of God within. His inner guidance saw him through. When the trial came, he told it like it happened. There were many other witnesses, including some Japanese. There was no question of the sergeant's guilt and misconduct. He was sentenced to six months.

True to their word, more than a half dozen of the sergeant's friends soon after surrounded Darwin's bunk. At first they only attacked him verbally, shouting insult after insult. Then they began to kick at him and to beat him with belts and fists. He could not fight them all at once. Within him his inner guide repeated, "Have no fear." He protected himself as best he could, using his arms in an attempt to ward off any blows to his body or head. He completely relaxed and went beyond himself, becoming an observer of the scene, knowing he would not be harmed. They got their revenge, but after the severe beating there was not a mark on him. No bruises, not even any soreness. Darwin later came to understand this miracle from his meetings with an ECK Master of the Vairagi from the mental worlds. He recalled: "I learned from Sato Kuraji that the use of the aura can be pulled in so tightly surrounding one's being that no injury could befall him or no fire burn him." Darwin advises not to try this unless you know you can do this.

Darwin's main army duty at Jamachi was to divide up

49

the whisky rations, an assignment envied by many a man. But there was no temptation here for Darwin. He had no interest in that area. He finished his duties quickly and used his free time to visit the Japanese inns and city temples. The people were polite and good natured. Japanese ladies often sang and danced with the troops. It would have been easy to get involved, but Darwin never did. He enjoyed the good natured camaraderie, but needed and looked forward to time by himself. He took many solitary walks through the pine covered hillsides, the lush green valleys with their lakes and streams, snowcapped mountains on the horizon.

It was on one of these walks that his inner spiritual guide, whom Darwin thought of as a guardian angel, set up conditions for him to meet Sato Kuraji, a great Japanese spiritual traveler and ECK Master of the Vairagi.* Darwin reflected on the importance of this meeting:

"I had passed this place numerous times. Our camp was in a valley surrounded by the magnificent and beautiful mountains, with lots of pine trees. Regardless of what direction I would go in, I'd come across a little shrine along the pathway.

"A meeting at this particular place had been prearranged to meet Sato Kuraji. He appeared to me, not in the sense of a vision, but in the form as we know of it as form, yet it could be thought of as a vision. The embrace as we parted was as solid as a rock.

"Sato Kuraji is the guardian of the Shariyat-Ki-Sugmad who watches over this section of the sacred book of the ECK Masters. It is also known as The Way of The Eternal. This ECK Master teaches those who are fortunate to be able to reach these spiritual heights via the Atma Sarup (Soul body) to study under him. He is a no-nonsense

*An ECK Master at the Golden Wisdom Temple, sometimes known as the Hall of Brahmanda, in the city of Mer Kailash on the mental plane. He is slight of build, wears a maroon robe wrapped kimono-style, and has close cropped black hair and dark penetrating bright eyes.

teacher. One learns as he unfolds spiritually that in the levels of heaven one must earn and work for what he wants in heaven just as here on Earth. This is not understood nor taught by the major religions.

"I grew spiritually and learned an enormous amount about the works and teachings of Spirit (in ECKANKAR, it's called ECK) through Sato Kuraji, since he works from the Golden Wisdom Temple. On prearranged meetings that took place after this first meeting, an enormous amount of spiritual insight and guidance was imparted to me on all levels of consciousness."

Through all these years Darwin was being protected and tested and watched. He became more aware of how it all inter-related and gained spiritual insight into the mental realms through his studies with Sato Kuraji of the Golden Wisdom Temple where years later Darwin himself would guide ECK chelas to study in the dream state with this amazing Japanese ECK adept.

*   *   *

Upon his return to Portland Darwin's family welcomed him with eager interest to hear about his adventures. Many tales he could share, but those that were really important to him, his meetings with Sato Kuraji, his inner experiences and growth in awareness and understanding, could not be expressed. Darwin recalls: "After getting out of the service, my father wanted me to work right away, but I wanted to lay back and rest, to collect the money I was entitled to from the 52-20 Club. The 52-20 Club was for ex-servicemen who could collect twenty dollars a week for fifty-two weeks."

Nevertheless, being strongly independent, Darwin did work several odd jobs for brief periods, including a stint on an assembly line where hot water heaters were made. It was on this job he learned an interesting lesson in cause and effect, as well as responsibility.

"I had caught up with my work this particular day, having been there for two or three weeks. There was a window

51

near the assembly line where I worked. I looked out and breathed the fresh air, waiting for the line to move, and as I leaned out a pretty little lady walked by and I whistled at her. The boss heard that and fired me. I learned at that time when you are working for someone else, you do what you are supposed to do or there are repercussions if you go beyond a certain thing, in other words, in conduct only. It's like an airplane pilot, he's flying with all these pretty stewardesses and he's married. He can't really play around with those stewardesses. He's going to get in trouble. This boils down to individual conduct, regardless of where one is at."

Post-war jobs were scarce and hard to come by. For a while Darwin moved from job to job among the logging mills. When his friend Wayne, a fellow veteran working the mills, suggested they hop in his car and head south where jobs were reportedly more plentiful, Darwin grabbed his bag and trumpet and they were gone.

They traveled south in Wayne's car, only to find that available jobs had already been taken and what few odd jobs there were, were short lived. By now two other men had joined them and Wayne was thinking of trying his luck on the coast. Darwin was getting ready for bed and heard a knock on his door.

"Darwin, you better start packing. We're leaving in about half an hour."

Darwin responded: "OK, I'm always ready to go and flexible." He packed and loaded his suitcase and trumpet in the car. They pulled off into a side street.

"Hey, that's not the way to the coast!" Darwin remarked.

"We got one stop here to make," said Wayne as he pulled into an alley. They parked the car facing outward toward the street away from a tavern. Wayne and the other two got out.

"We're just going behind here to pick something up. You watch the car. If anyone comes, let us know."

They disappeared behind a nearby building next door to the closed tavern. Darwin later recalled, "I was sitting in the car and got very nervous. In case somebody came, I was going to get out of there. I got out of the car, and here come these guys carrying beer and cigarettes that they had stolen from the tavern. They filled up the car floor and back seat and the trunk. We drove most of the night and got into this coast town, and through Spirit the Inner Master was nudging me, telling me to get away from these people. So when they stopped for breakfast or lunch, I asked for the keys for the trunk, got my suitcase and checked into a motel across the street. I had told them I would be either in for lunch or walking down the highway to be picked up. Later I could see from my motel that they came running out of the restaurant, didn't pay for their meal, jumped in the car and raced off towards the coast. I listened to Spirit and to the Inner Master at that point in time, got a good night's sleep, hitchhiked back to Portland with a clean conscience and glad I got out of that. They got thrown in jail, got caught at Seaside, but I had kept out of trouble."

Darwin had to walk a good many of the 85 miles back to Portland, but he was grateful for his freedom. He says: "I was happy about it, because I knew what was going to happen. I had taken nothing of the beer and cigarettes and was not karmically involved with the theft." He didn't like being implicated in something that was not of his own choosing. His inner warning had been well heeded. Knowing what was going to happen, he wanted no part of it, though it was being forced upon him. So he simply removed himself from the scene, thankful for the inner guidance and awareness.

Back in Portland Darwin worked at various small jobs here and there, and began giving attention to what he would like to make his career. His attention was more and more on music. He had always enjoyed it as a growing boy. It was always an inspiration, creative, spontaneous. A means of communication as well as source of sharing joy. Yet he realized if he was going to make his living with it, he needed to know more about it from a technical point of view.

An ad in the paper caught his eye: "Careers in music are a thing of the future." The Portland School of Music, run by Aeriol Rubinstein, was seeking new students. Darwin enrolled. He didn't have much money, but was eager at this new adventure and opportunity to realize a goal he had had within him since he was a boy. He got a part-time job in a furniture store, lived in a modest attic room and ate sparingly, at times half-starved, but it was worth it. This was the first time in his life he had the opportunity for formal training in trumpet and piano, in composition, in music history. He was delighted with the school, whose atmosphere was serious and career-oriented. Finally he could write down the music he heard within, that he was constantly composing through improvisation.

Darwin gave up the trumpet as "his" instrument and instead focused on the vibraharp. Although he had overcome the mouth injury he sustained in Japan—when he had lost footing stepping off a slow-moving train, tripped and landed full square onto an iron pipe across a ditch—and could play the trumpet quite well, it was not the same. Besides, the "vibes" offered more variety in sound, greater range and more subtlety of tone. He enjoyed all kinds of music, and composed pieces from old as well as new sources, combining different sounds and types of music to yield his own unique style.

He organized a combo that played in local clubs. They called themselves "The Subtle Tones." Lee, a talented young man about Darwin's age, played the piano and trumpet. Bonnie, an older woman with a heart of gold, played the bass. If you closed your eyes you thought it was Ray Brown playing. Darwin played the vibraharp. They became well enough known to require a manager. Darwin served this function himself, booking them up and down the West Coast between Portland and Seattle. They had what Darwin later described as an "M.J.Q. sound," long before the advent of the Modern Jazz Quartet. He knew that to be successful, music needed the proper combination of elements: the intention of the composer, the technique and feeling of the artist, and the attitude of the listener. To him, music was much more than an emotional release; it was a way to reach the heights of experience "within the worlds from the physical plane of existence to the mental worlds of heaven" and beyond. The tone of a sound can lift one to greater inner spiritual heights than mere words.

In this regard Darwin reflected: "I've played some jazz, contemporary music and many of the old standards, but I played a different sort of sound, it's soft, it's gentle, it's uplifting. I've had people say that the soft sounds were so easy to listen to that they were going to sleep, but I, as well as the group, was enjoying what I was doing, even though it may have been putting some people to sleep. That's quite a good character of the sound that's being produced. They didn't realize what was actually taking place. They were used to the harshness of certain sounds. Music can be very healing. There's an old statement, 'Music is the meat of Soul.' There have been many connotations put on Soul, like soul music or soul food. That's really misusing the word Soul. It's not true. However, it was a way that I was able to express myself.

"At an early age, I learned that certain music punctures the astral aura, or the astral body, and lets other negative currents flow through. On the other hand, if his attitude is right, a person can have a physical healing from some music. You won't close up the aura, completely, unless a certain chord is struck. There may be one or two musicians in this whole world who may know how to do that. There might be more—I could be surprised, but I hardly doubt it. The training in music and the way it has been for the past ten years or more has gotten very bad, very negative. I would like to see it change, but I'm not here for that, to change the trend of music. It's not my purpose or goal.

There are certain individuals who don't want it to change because of the control they have over certain groups of young people and some adults, and the greed factor of how many millions of dollars they can make. Some of this in the record industry, and other individuals who get involved."

Darwin enjoyed playing music with the combo, yet there were drawbacks. The clubs were smoke filled and noisy. The clientele were more interested in what drink could do for them than in the music. The club managers were only interested in making money. The joy of playing music was lessened in this atmosphere. Darwin soon realized he did not want to make this his life's work.

Partly from this realization and partly due to added responsibilities he had taken on in his personal life, Darwin determined to seek employment in other areas. He began working in a plywood mill. Since much of the operation was indoors with loud machinery humming and whirring, Darwin would whistle and sing, composing songs to the rhythm of the machines. His supervisor nicknamed him "Hambone." A steady and conscientious worker, Darwin soon earned a promotion, but a mishap one day took him out of work and gave him the opportunity to re-evaluate his position.

A few strips of flooring had been removed in a part of the plant to get at and repair some equipment beneath. As Darwin came around a stack of materials, he stepped into the pit with his right leg. He was able to keep his balance on his left leg and avoided falling into the hole, but the force of the downthrust had wrenched and cracked his left kneecap. He asked that his brother Ron be called, and in the ambulance on the way to the hospital he refused an injection to ease the pain of the smashed kneecap, saying he didn't feel any pain.

At the hospital, x-rays revealed that Darwin had two kneecaps. Darwin explains: "The ECK set up the condition for leaving the plywood mill. The top kneecap was shattered, the bottom one was cracked. The other two in the other leg are still intact. They're superimposed on each other. That's very uncommon. I came into this world whole, directly from the God Worlds as a specific function to assist in bringing out this message of ECK."

Ultimately, both of Darwin's kneecaps on his left leg were to be removed. He got about with the use of a cane while on the mend. When just about healed, his love of the outdoors resulted in a slip on the ice. This tore the cartilage of his injured knee anew, and required more surgery. The surgeon was not optimistic. He told Darwin that he doubted he would regain much use of his left leg. "No way, Doc," Darwin replied, and asked what he could do to get it back into use. The doctor told him exercise was the only possibility, but that at best he should expect to regain only 20-40% use of it.

Darwin was not about to accept the limited conceptions of another, even if he were a doctor and surgeon. The great inner awareness Darwin had throughout his life came to the fore again. He *knew* he could regain full use of his leg. For nearly eighteen months he worked diligently, repeating the exercises over and over. First, he repaired the muscles. Then with assistance of a cane, he learned to walk on the leg. In time he could do without the cane, and ultimately without even a limp. His determination and inner resources saw him through. He returned to skiing and ice skating for recreation, and turned his attention to pursuing a new career.

* * *

Electronics came to Darwin as naturally as music had. He was quite aware of the corresponding relationship between the musical scale with its frequencies and wavelengths, and the different components of electronics with their frequencies and wavelengths. The scientific study of sound went hand in hand with his own inner experiences, from the piano and vibraharp to electronics to the light and sound of the spiritual worlds.

Although he already knew how to repair television sets

—which he learned on his own from taking apart his own set to find out how it operated and what could malfunction —he went to the Portland School of Radio and Television to get his diploma in electronics.

In Portland Darwin went to work soldering components in electronic units for an electronics company. He was a meticulous employee and often came up with beneficial ideas to streamline and improve operations in production. His supervisors noticed him and offered him a promotion. To their surprise he turned it down, instead requesting a chance to work in the test lab in engineering. He got his opportunity.

He worked a year in the test lab, went to night school, and for the next three years had the good fortune to work with a professional engineer as his project design engineer. He learned all he could from him and kept amazing the man with his innate abilities and knowledge. With relatively little technical background, Darwin could get results on problems that baffled the "experts." He thrived on such challenges, and with his ability to go beyond himself could often bring back solutions from the inner worlds that others wouldn't even begin to think of. This happened with a Sperry-Rand project for an output transformer for an automatic testing system for the B-58 Hustler airplane. Sperry-Rand had tried all over the country to get results on that project and in a last-ditch effort offered the job to the company Darwin worked for. As design engineer he worked with the project engineer. In a few weeks they succeeded, using completely unorthodox techniques. But it worked! The unit met and exceeded the design specs.

Opportunities for talented men in engineering were tremendous at that time. As Darwin and his work became known, he received many job offers. He finally accepted one in the San Francisco Bay area and shortly became the chief engineer. The man he was replacing had a Master's degree in mathematics, but Darwin's reputation was all the credentials he needed. His responsibility was to oversee construction of electronic filters and the manufacture of magnetic components such as transformers for guidance control computers of spacecraft.

It was here that he sustained a back injury that would flare up later in his life. Of a very generous and giving nature, Darwin was always ready to help others on their projects. So it was natural for him to volunteer to help his boss, Loren Schoof, move a heavy piece of equipment from the factory loft one Saturday afternoon. In doing so a sharp pang shot through his upper back. In pain that evening, he called his boss who took him to Stanford Hospital the next day. He was in traction for two weeks, but it didn't help. His muscles were in spasm from badly torn muscles and pinched nerves. It took nearly eight months of treatment with a Palo Alto physical therapist to work out the knots below his left shoulder blade. Once again, his determination and inner strength saw him through the ordeal. The insurance company refused to compensate him because the accident occurred outside of the normal work week.

Many times he used his ability to go beyond himself and look at things from a 360 degree viewpoint to resolve a given problem. In one case in particular this ability and Darwin's innate capacity to draw on information beyond himself not only was a boon to his career, but saved his company a great deal of embarrassment as well as expense. The firm had hired a Stanford physics Ph.D. to build an electronic unit to be part of a device whose function was top secret, and thus not revealed. The Ph.D. had followed the specifications and design requirements but the unit would not work. Darwin was called in to review the situation, and in two days he had built a prototype that did work. His boss was thrilled and shipped the device off to the subcontractor. But when they inserted it in their prototype, it wouldn't work. Again Darwin was called in by the general manager, Loren Schoof. They looked at the physical unit, then at the schematic design. In an instant Darwin was above himself viewing the situation from a

360 degree viewpoint. He knew what to do. He suggested they put a resistor in front of the unit as a source resistance. They balked at the suggestion, but finally tried it, to discover it worked beautifully.

After two years Darwin accepted a job as a magnetic design engineer with a Seattle firm. He moved north again, into a small apartment on a hillside overlooking a park as well as a small houseboat marina on Puget Sound above Lake Union. It was here that Darwin would have a near meeting with his inner spiritual guide, Peddar Zaskq, a man who would later be known to him as Paul Twitchell, whose mission was to bring forth the modern-day ECKANKAR teachings that were very ancient.

At this time Paul lived in one of the houseboats in the marina. He was totally immersed in writing, reading and his spiritual experiences, as well as studying every teaching known to man. Often in the hours before dawn he would walk in the park below Darwin's apartment. Set on an incline on the hillside, the park had many pathways winding through it. One morning, which was not unusual, for reasons he didn't understand at the time, Darwin couldn't sleep. He decided to walk through the park, an activity he enjoyed and often pursued at any hour of the day or night. A light, misty fog had settled in the predawn hours. As he hummed a new tune, he became aware of another man coming toward him down the path. He had a hat pulled down over his eyes and Darwin couldn't make out his features in the misty light, yet a feeling of love flowed from this stranger. As they were about to meet, the other man turned off on a side path, so they did not pass one another. Darwin felt a pang of disappointment on this lonely night as he watched the other figure disappear in the mist. Years later, looking back on the incident, Darwin commented: "He didn't want to meet me yet. He was just looking me over for he was an Eagle-Eye Adept!"

Less than a year after moving to Seattle, Darwin was offered another job back in the San Francisco Bay area that was too good to resist. As he drove towards Portland, out of Seattle, that area experienced one of its worst storms with sheets of rain and 100-mile-an-hour winds. Darwin almost expected it, for as so many times in the past, the forces of nature marked major moves in his life with extreme activity.

Darwin's electronics specialty had become the reduction of costs and size of complexity of electronic components. He could do things others could not and earned quite a reputation for himself. After two years with a company in San Mateo, he was transferred to their new plant in Grand Junction, Colorado, to become a staff engineer working in areas of administration, production and engineering. On a weekend skiing trip to Aspen with the president of the company, chief chemist, and personnel director, Darwin's spiritual capabilities to go beyond himself saved their lives.

As he was driving his car, Darwin took a curve too fast to see the boulder in time. It was in the middle of the road in his lane. There was a car approaching rapidly in the other lane. The shoulder to the right edged a steep river bank. Suddenly Darwin found himself above the scene looking down at it. He could see that his car was about to hit the boulder and immediately knew there was only one way to avoid disaster. Back at the wheel in the next instant he swerved to the right slightly. The boulder passed just inside the left front tire and raised the left side of the car into the air. With only the right wheels on the ground, the car balanced precariously at it passed the boulder. When it returned to all four tires, Darwin stopped the car. The only damage was to the floor on the driver's side. One of the men in the back seat was visibly quite shaken. The other two men were a bit unnerved themselves. The president of the company said, "It must have been the hand of God." Darwin just looked at him and said, "Yeap!"

Although he enjoyed the job in Colorado, the company was running into some financial difficulties, so Darwin decided to leave before conditions worsened. He returned to the San Francisco Bay area, and true to form, his departure was marked by a violent, immense rain storm that blocked out the daylight and streaked the sky with bolts of lightning.

When Darwin returned to the San Francisco Bay area, he took a job with an electronics firm in Sunnyvale. He also undertook an interesting side project of his own. Roughly 100 miles southeast, in the small town of Los Banos, California, he considered opening a coffee house with sandwiches and light music, a place to talk for young teenagers who had nowhere else to go. As New Year's Eve approached, he realized that most of the young people in town, especially those who were in the lower income brackets, had nothing in particular to do. Darwin talked with the local radio stations and the police. All agreed it would help to have some activity going as an alternative to roaming the streets, drugs and drinking. However, the radio manager's son had a dance band and they didn't want to accept the competition of Darwin's advertising, so he went to another town to do the advertising.

Darwin set up a New Year's Eve party at the Portuguese Community Hall which was advertised with flyers and on the radio. He hired a young rock group from San Jose to provide entertainment. He provided music and soft drinks at very reasonable prices. The party was open to any young people who wanted to come. Over 250 showed up. Darwin opened the evening with his "vibes," talked to the young people for a short time, then turned the program over to the band. It was quite a success. Everyone enjoyed themselves, especially Darwin.

On the job, Darwin was often called upon to be intermediary in handling conflicts between antagonistic parties. Where others couldn't, he would often work out satisfactory compromises. He would often support the underdog. In one case, he was protective of a deaf worker who suffered harassment from the other men. The others respected Darwin and his admonition that they stop teasing the fellow. He and the deaf worker would often pass notes to each other and they became good friends. Later they discovered they didn't need the notes for they could communicate very effectively without them.

Darwin's unusual abilities often came to the forefront. During his years in the electronics industry he had become an inventor, often working on projects for his employers, and sometimes for himself. He was able to tap the secrets of the universe with ease and apply them to practical objectives. Key elements in this were his ability to simplify even the most complicated matters, to listen and to use common sense. His musical background was an asset. And, more important, as he told anyone who asked, it was his attitude and his visualization of a successful result, his positive approach to every situation as an opportunity where others saw only a problem.

With a physicist co-worker, George Neilands from Edinburg, Scotland, Darwin worked on a project that applied space technology to the germination of lettuce seeds by radiation and electron bombardment. This procedure enabled them to germinate within twenty-four hours without fungus and produce a constant yield of 96%. He set the experiment up with parts from an old Model-T and an antique refrigerator converted to a vacuum pump at a cost of $12. This technique, properly applied, could raise food production throughout the world by a minimum of 40%.

Some of the other inventions Darwin developed during his time as an engineer include special electronic filters, a practical way of creating an electronic automobile using components off the shelf, an automatic explosion-release mechanism for parachutes for use with return space vehicles, and a way to make heaters out of glass mirrors.

In a little less than a decade and a half Darwin had worked his way up from a manual laborer to being a dynamic and respected engineer. He had proven himself to be hard working, capable and creative. "In fourteen years,

I've missed two days of work," he once said to a co-worker. "Once I goofed off and once I had a cold."

In Portland he had worked with light phenomena, including lasers and research in the field of photography and optics. Without the background of a formal education, he demonstrated his abilities as an inspired inventor, respected in the industry and capable of achieving results that even those with extensive formal training and experience could not bring forth.

His managers and supervisors always gave Darwin high recommendations as he moved from company to company in the electronics industry. This often occurred in two-year cycles, usually in October. His co-workers remembered him fondly.

More than 18 years later, one co-worker was traveling on the highway listening to a call-in radio talk show on ECKANKAR from KXRX Radio in San Jose, California. He heard references to "Sri Darwin Gross" and stopped his car at a roadside phone booth to call in. "I'm not exactly sure why I'm calling," he said. "I was driving down the street listening to your program. Years ago I guess maybe 17 or 18 years ago, I knew Sri Darwin Gross before he became the Living ECK Master. He was a very kind and sensitive person. I had the feeling when I worked with him, those many years ago, that he was undergoing a great change in his life. We were both engineers together at a company and I think that environment wasn't very sensitive to the change he was undergoing.

"I would like to say that he's a very real person and I'm very pleased that his personal transition has happened for him. I only knew this five or six years ago when I happened to pass an ECKANKAR booth at a fair and I saw his photograph there and kind of had a little personal tickle and a little personal thrill to see that. At that time I dropped him a line and I received a very gracious, highly spiritual answer. I still have that letter; I feel very pleased to have that."

In addition to being a designer, Darwin occasionally sculpted, wrote poems and composed music. He was never bored but always into some new project. Although not much for reading books in his youth, from the time of his near meeting with Peddar Zaskq in Portland, Darwin became an avid reader in areas beyond the immediate business and technical requirements. He read books on the world's religions, metaphysics, psychic phenomena, biographies of seers and mystics and related subjects. He was not too interested in novels or fiction. His own inner life made such literature seem dull. "Because of my travels in the various worlds of the physical, astral and mental, flying saucers and space people were everyday common experiences," he recalled. "I didn't read science fiction—I lived it!"

He got to the point where he could pick up a book and instantly know if it was worth his reading. It wouldn't be long now before he would be handed a book he couldn't put down. It would be the link for him between his inner experiences and his outer life, and eventually lead to his meeting with the Living ECK Master.

CHAPTER 4

The Return to the Heavenly Worlds

With many individuals the finding of their true spiritual path is preceded by a period of apparent failure, bewilderment, loneliness, the fleeing of one's material possessions, or ill health. In ECKANKAR, this period is known as The Dark Night of Soul. It is shortly before that individual is to come into the knowledge of his divine origin, and his inherent potential of realizing God, that he suddenly feels the world turning against him. Everything he does seems to end in frustration, many of his friends turn their backs, and it is as if the guiding spirit had forsaken him and dropped him into some dark pit. This is the cleansing of Soul from many impurities—attitudes that might hinder Its progress towards Its heavenly home—which is the preparation for the opening of the individual's eyes for the wonders of the worlds of Divine Spirit.

Though to the individual who is experiencing his dark night of Soul it seems that the world around him is in upheaval, for most people the drama is acted out on the stage of the personal universe. However, when Darwin's inner preparation drew to the point where he was to meet his master and teacher in the physical, the implications of what was to be his period of intense struggle and nightmare, affected the course of the entire Earth planet.

At the time, Darwin was living near Concord, California, working as a staff engineer for a small computer firm in digital circuitry. His line of work involved marketing, design, procurement and production engineering. Company security had become a major issue, for technological espionage in highly sophisticated ways had resulted from the strong competition in the electronics field. Some of this technological espionage involved wire-tapping, deception, illegal break-ins, use of drugs, and even injuries or death of some of the scientists and agents who were the targets of various operations. The San Francisco Bay area, being one of the most concentrated centers of technological research in the world, was the scene of much company intrigue and activity by foreign intelligence agencies as well as the CIA.

As an inventor and innovator, Darwin had already been a victim of having his ideas stolen. So he resolved to get a patent on any new project that promised to be successful. He always brought many ideas for inventions from his inner travels, and often he would set up experiments in his apartment in the Walnut Creek area, which he had turned into a small but efficient laboratory.

His experience in a large variety of engineering fields helped him a great deal with the experiments he was conducting in some of the most advanced areas of technological progress. He had held a government clearance for top secret information in his engineering positions. From his studies in the spiritual worlds under the ECK Masters, he possessed a wealth of knowledge in areas of particular significance to his special interests: frequencies of sound and light and magnetic effects.

Working in his free time — employing not only his knowledge gained from his career experience, but also his inner ability to move into higher areas of awareness and contact the knowledge he needed directly—he developed a simple electro-magnetic device that he knew would revolutionize the transportation industry. It would change everything: the engines that used fuel, the air pollution choking the cities, the dependence of many countries on imported energy. The way he put it was, "The device, built into a car, could make it go from New York to San Francisco without being charged."

He took the design and idea to a patent attorney and showed it to him. The more Darwin explained it to the attorney, the less he seemed to understand what was put before him. A physicist was called in from another office in the same building and although the design was sound, and it was plain to see that it would work, neither of the two experts could understand how it functioned.

Finally, Darwin left, with a promise from the patent attorney to further look into the matter. But whenever Darwin would phone back in the next few days, the attorney was never available and continued to delay his reply. Many days passed, and there was no action from the attorney's office. Darwin began to wonder if there was a reason behind all this.

During this time, he came home twice to find his apartment had been broken into. The place was in shambles, but nothing seemed to be missing. He began noticing men standing outside the building or sitting in a car across the street, watching the house. One night, when lying in bed and all was quiet, he heard humming sounds coming from some kind of electronic equipment installed in the apartment next to his. Suspicious that he might be the target of surveillance, he got up without turning on the lights, and carefully went over his own rooms with a flashlight, searching for hidden wires, bugs, and other devices. It didn't take long to find the wire coming in from the adjoining apartment. Darwin produced a short with a pocket knife and immediately reaped a surprised voice saying on the other side of the wall, "He must have found out! The boss will be mad."

Darwin needed no more confirmation that he was being watched. His sense of personal freedom and integrity was deeply violated. He yelled back through the wall, "They'll be even more unhappy when they're sued for five million dollars!"

The humming of the surveillance devices stopped, but there was no reply — only silence.

Shortly thereafter, Darwin's sense of physical well-being dropped sharply. The daytime was filled with strange things happening, and at night he was tense and slept poorly. He began seeing bright visions of colors and changing pictures and images, which had nothing to do with his spiritual experiences and the ECK Masters working with him on the invisible side. He felt light-headed and at times wondered if he was hallucinating. In his work, he wasn't going at his usual full capacity, and he was having trouble with keeping his wits when he was always very calm.

Maybe I'm working too hard, both at the company and at home, he thought to himself. Perhaps I should speak to the manager about it.

The manager advised him to take some vacation time, so Darwin left his apartment and drove to the Northeastern Californian mountain resort of Lake Tahoe. He arrived there worn out and weary from the lack of rest at night, the feeling of giddiness during the day, and the constant harassment from the surveillance he was subjected to. At Tahoe, at last, he got some respite and rest. He awoke at 3:00 a.m. on Monday morning, had some breakfast and hopped in his car for the four and a half hour drive back to the San Francisco Bay area. He felt good—this had been the rest he needed. Now he would be going at his full capacity again.

After driving about 30 miles on the mountainous road of the Sierras, he noticed the presence of someone making itself felt to his consciousness. First, he saw an unusual ultraviolet light on the reflectors along the highway. It changed from purple to blue; then he noticed that he seemed suspended in time—the whole car, inside and out, was engulfed in this blue light. He stopped the car at a turnout, and as the sound of the engine died down in the early morning stillness, a voice spoke to him out of the blue light. It said, "I will only tell you once, so listen closely, Darwin."

The voice had a southern accent. "Gee, that's strange," Darwin thought, "that God should have a southern speaking voice!"

The words spoken were imprinted deeply on Darwin's consciousness. After the message was imparted, he started up the engine and drove the rest of the way to his apartment.

The rooms seemed untouched and unchanged. Darwin returned to work, but in a few days he was having the same bizarre feelings which he could not understand. There seemed to be no escape from them, no matter what he tried. Darwin had always been a very healthy person, having grown up in the rugged farm country of North Dakota, and had always lived healthily, never taking drugs or drinking much alcohol. He couldn't understand what was happening. He clung to his contact with his Inner Master, held to his knowledge of Spirit, but it seemed to him that they were watching him benignly, yet letting him work it out for himself.

Soon after his return to the apartment, however, the nightmarish feelings and horrible illusions started again. He couldn't continue his work and had trouble thinking straight. Finally, there seemed no other avenue to take but to pick up the phone, call a friend and ask for help.

"Wes, you won't believe this story, but there are strange things happening to me." He poured out the entire story of mysterious troubles.

"Is there anyone you can absolutely trust, Darwin?"

"Well, there's my sister Adeline and her husband Walt, in Medford."

"Then let's get you on a plane."

Wes got Darwin on a plane to Medford, and there, in the restful two weeks that he spent with his sister's family, the world seemed to come back into balance. The San Francisco Bay area remained very unfavorable in Darwin's mind at that time, and he resolved not to pursue matters with his invention, leave his work there and never return.

"I'm not going back there," he told Adeline. "I don't want to see that apartment anymore, and I'll leave everything— the books, clothes, my vibes—I don't care."

However, Adeline and her oldest son, Mark, drove to Darwin's apartment and picked up his belongings. Having gotten a grip on his own life and his usual cheerful self again, Darwin went on to visit his family in Portland. While there, he was traced down and an attempt was made by persons to have Darwin committed to a state hospital, because of the strange experiences he had been having. Adeline and her husband Walt got him released with the aid of the Veterans Hospital, after a thorough physical and mental examination proved him healthy.

To Darwin, like many other people in a similar situation, it seemed that God had forsaken him. "I'm going through all these tests," he said to himself, "but what's it for?" He couldn't get any answers. One day in particular, he seemed to have reached the bottom line. He bought a bottle of wine and took himself down to a park to drink away his troubles. He drained the whole bottle. Not being a heavy drinker, he usually could take only a glass or two, no more. But now, even the entire bottle didn't have the desired effect of peaceful oblivion—he didn't get drunk, at all. He only felt ill, miserable, and it gave him a violent headache.

Only when he left his apartment for a while did the up-ended situation of his life seem to level out a little bit. On one of his rides out into the countryside, he crossed the Columbia River into the State of Washington and drove up on top of the plateau area, away and above the river. He parked the car and just relaxed, looking out into the sky, daydreaming, when something happened that was to remain vividly in Darwin's memory ever since: "...I was daydreaming, letting go of questions, and thought to myself, 'If I am supposed to know, if I have enough faith in God, then I'll be shown.' The moment I let go of all the internal turmoil and questions, there were only two fluffy white clouds in the sky, against a pretty blue sky, nice bright wintry afternoon; there was snow on the ground. All of a sudden these two clouds came closer together and closer and started forming like two separate crab claws, and they grabbed each other. And you can make many things out of that, but I had a hold of something and didn't want to let go of it, and God had a hold of something and didn't want to let go of it.

"So I said, 'OK, I give up, I'm in your hands,' and from that moment on things changed drastically. I always went back to that moment when I found that in thought or verbally I was committing myself to something to hang onto, a way of committment that I should live this moment and let the past months that are gone go, past years, past centuries, whatever it happened to be in time."

From Portland, Darwin stayed in touch with his former chief engineer to find out what had happened in Walnut Creek. After an investigation, it was found that someone had been putting LSD in Darwin's can of coffee. He was actually being drugged every time he made a cup of coffee, while at home working on his experiments! Darwin was more puzzled than angry. The only explanation he could find, why someone would do this, was that they were involved in some kind of industrial espionage.

He decided to remain in Portland, however, and went back to work with an electronics firm that he had worked with before. He often met with his cousin Edith, who worked in Rose's Bakery and Restaurant in downtown Portland. Edith and Darwin had talked about some of the experiences and ideas about religion and philosophy in the past, and liked to exchange books and viewpoints on the subject. The books ranged from metaphysical and occult topics to stories about ghosts and mysterious appearances. One day Darwin strolled in for a roll and a cup of coffee, and Edith came over and handed him a book. "I thought you might be interested in this one," she said.

Darwin took the book. Its title was *In My Soul I Am*

Free, a biography of a man named Paul Twitchell, by Brad Steiger. A sudden tingling ran through Darwin as he held the book in his hand.

"Have you read it?" he asked his cousin.

"No, I didn't get a chance yet. I have to get back to work, but you can give it back to me when you're through."

"Okay. Thanks!" Darwin said, as she left his table.

The book seemed to tingle in his hand. He turned it over. On the back cover was a black and white photograph of the subject of the biography, Paul Twitchell, a man that seemed to be in his early forties, with a full, squarish face and startling, wide-set eyes that seemed to penetrate to the very core of things, yet held humor and warmth. Darwin looked at the photo and a tremendous feeling of love, a burst of light and sound flooded through him. He knew that man! This was the one he knew as Peddar Zaskq, his spiritual guide whom he had thought of as his guardian angel. The one who had appeared in his bedroom and taken away his fear of dreams, who had warned and protected him time and again all through his life! He who had led him to other Masters such as Rebazar Tarzs and Lai Tsi, and showed him the worlds beyond the veil of the senses!

Darwin was surprised and yet not surprised to find that his teacher was a man of flesh and blood, that he actually existed physically and could be met and talked to in this world. But—here he was, and someone had written a book about him! And the caption under the photo read: "The Living ECK Master."

Darwin hurried home, hardly able to wait, and read the book without once putting it down. It seemed to open new doors for understanding, while confirming everything he had experienced and already knew about ECKANKAR. It was like coming home after a storm. More than that—it was gaining a harmony and upliftment that came from finally reading an all-encompassing, authoritative statement on all those things he had been unable to communicate to others.

His enthusiasm was so great he immediately searched through the book stores for more books on ECKANKAR. He found one called *The Tiger's Fang*, written by Paul Twitchell himself about his own journey through each of the planes of existence. "Why, it's almost as if he had written about me!" Darwin thought. For here were the descriptions of the worlds he had been visiting, meetings with the Spiritual Travelers and Masters of whom he had been aware, and all the principles of spiritual life spelled out. He had known about the word ECKANKAR and its meaning (all-inclusiveness in God), but not that it existed in the physical and that many others were also involved in its study.

Darwin had previously given talks about the heavenly regions and his experiences in them, one as early as 1963 in Grand Junction, Colorado, but found that people would always try to argue, or ask for the written material that he based his theories on. Many would only accept the Bible as the last word on heaven, but Darwin always knew there was more to it than knowledge from books. "There is no last word on heaven or God," he said. "It has no beginning or ending."

But here was a path that accepted his experiences for real. Here was a Master who could lead him even past the astral, causal and mental worlds into the positive God worlds of pure being. He had come home. This was his destiny. His long search was over.

Darwin was eager to advance in his studies, and wrote to the ECKANKAR Office, which at that time was located in Las Vegas, Nevada, for a list of their publications. Some ten or fifteen books had been published by Paul Twitchell on ECKANKAR at that time, some of the titles being *ECKANKAR, The Key to Secret Worlds, The Flute of God, Stranger by the River,* and *The Key to ECKANKAR*. There were also monthly study discourses available for a yearly membership fee.

Immediately Darwin wanted to enroll in the discourses,

but found after having purchased some of the books that his money had run out. He had just started working as a project engineer at Tetronix, Portland, and the little money he had went to support his two children from his first marriage. It was hard for him to be patient, when here was the learning material he had looked for all his life, but as always with Darwin, his responsibility came first.

A little earlier, his father had left this world. He had been seventy-seven years old. Darwin wasn't sorrow-struck, but the death of the one person in his life who had been understanding about his unusual experiences did cause a feeling of loss within him. He felt honored to be there at the time of his father's translation and help him across the borders to his place in afterlife. On the material side, however, he hadn't left Darwin's mother much, and since the payments from Social Security didn't suffice to provide for her, Darwin invited her to live with him in his apartment on North Central street in Portland.

While waiting till he had saved enough money for the discourses, Darwin read and reread *The Tiger's Fang*, *The Flute of God*, and all the other books, underlining passages of special interest for him and possibly for others. He listened to taped lectures Paul had given to various audiences. In these few short weeks, Darwin's spiritual and intellectual development focused into a harmony of awareness—the inner and the outer worlds merging together in the understanding of their continuous interaction.

Living in one apartment with his mother opened an avenue of understanding between them that hadn't been there previously. They spent many hours of the evenings talking about the days in North Dakota and the family years in Portland. Now that Darwin had the invaluable knowledge from Paul Twitchell's books to back up his own experiences, he could talk about his attitude towards his mother's church with much more confidence. One evening his mother said, "You really resisted church from a very early age. Is the church and the Christian faith in Jesus as the

76

Lord really that wrong?"

"It isn't wrong, Mom," Darwin answered. "Only my own experiences in traveling the regions of heaven showed me that there is more to God than the Bible and church. Jesus was a past teacher and way-shower, but I have my own guide within who is here now and capable of leading me into the God-realm."

"And this guide appears to you and protects you like a guardian angel?"

"Yes, he has done so countless times."

Adina Gross looked thoughtful. She hesitated with her next words. "You know, Darwin, I have my own inner spiritual guide, too."

Her son was surprised. "Really? Tell me about it."

"When I was eleven years old, our family lived in North Dakota in a two-room sod hut on the prairie. I was sleeping on the floor, and one night I woke up feeling that someone was there. I looked up and there stood the figure of this man. He was tall and solidly built, with a long, grey beard and brown eyes. He was dressed in a glowing white robe. Why, of course I thought he was Jesus. Ever since, he has been with me, and I devoted my life to Jesus and his faith."

Shortly after that conversation, Darwin met a man in one of his dream travels whom he knew as Fubbi Quantz. Fubbi Quantz had been the Living ECK Master in the time of Buddha, and was now the Guardian of one of the Golden Temples of Wisdom that Darwin had often visited. He usually wore a maroon colored robe, but in this meeting, this vision, he appeared in a glowing, white robe. This was about six months before Darwin's mother died. He wondered at that time why Fubbi Quantz would appear to him like that. But a few days later he had a chance to talk to his mother again.

"Remember when you told me of the man that visited you that night? I had a vision of him a few days ago, and he appeared to me just like you described him. I've known him for a long time. He is Fubbi Quantz."

He showed his mother a picture of a drawing of Fubbi Quantz that was available from the ECKANKAR Office. She exclaimed, "That's him! That man, that vision, has helped me all my life, in all my troubles. Why didn't he say he wasn't Jesus? He didn't say a word."

Darwin explained, "When a Master appears that way, without words, he has a greater communication. It is not right to tear someone out of his life's background where one is rooted, and change that person's state of consciousness. He would appear to you, help you in the times of crisis in your life, but never upset your belief in the Christ, upon which you depended for spiritual survival in your time and with the people around you. The ECK Masters aren't here to change the world."

In these last two years of her life, Adina Gross began to understand more of the ways of Spirit and heaven through conversations with her second son than in all her previous religious activities. She learned about the realm of the beyond from one who could actually go there at will, and when she died, she was at peace, knowing she would be met by Darwin on the other side and taken care of.

* * * * * *

It took Darwin three months to save the little money needed for the membership fee in order to get the discourses. He could have borrowed the money, but that was not his way. Many times it is necessary to let go of something, to learn patience, before it can come to one. In his own words, "This is letting go with the mind, and turning loose of this material world. We can have the things, but being attached causes problems. Well, I let go of it and said, okay, I'll study through the books, and then the right job opened up, a sufficient amount of money was earned, and I was able to start the discourses."

Darwin progressed by leaps and bounds. He had learned well from the spiritual forces within himself and his inner guides. He was adept at experiencing his dream states as real and controlled events, and he could venture without

78

fear from one plane to another. He had been with the ECK Masters to the astral, causal, mental and etheric planes and had proven their existence to himself. The Masters became as familiar to him as his own image in the mirror—Rebazar Tarzs, a swarthy man with short, black hair and black beard cropped closely, looked like a Tibetan lama except that at six feet he was much taller than most. His most outstanding features were his black eyes, piercing and humorous, deep pools of loving fire and shining spirit. Rebazar Tarzs liked to laugh, and many times in their travels to the various temples of Golden Wisdom they shared the humor of their experiences.

Lai Tsi, the guardian of the Golden Wisdom Temple on the etheric plane in the city of Arhirit, was small and slender, with hands that tapered to straight, polished nails. His hair was worn straight back, leaving his dark eyes to shine prominently, and his Chinese face adorned with a constant smile. He dressed in a heavy maroon robe and high Chinese hat and was surrounded by a silvery light and a humming sound that seemed to come through him from some other source. From Lai Tsi, Darwin learned many things about the subconscious forces that affected him and others, and how to control them in his everyday life, such as turning off pain, avoiding accidents and implanted subconscious wishes, and helping others.

In the course of his studies, Darwin had numerous occasions to prove to himself that the techniques and methods of contact with Spirit and the Inner Master really worked. One such experience involved a problem that was bothering Darwin, stemming from an old injury that pained him now and again. Darwin wrote a letter to Paul about some spiritual difficulties he was having, sealed it and took it to a mailbox. Just as he shoved the letter in, he felt a warm vibration and received a physical healing of that old injury. Paul Twitchell, the Inner Master, had already read the letter and acted to remove whatever was causing the difficulties to his student. Others would have called it a miracle or dismissed it as coincidence, but Darwin knew that the all-pervading, divine Spirit that was the body and instrument of the Master had helped him.

In turn, his desire to help the Master with his work of spreading the message of ECK grew ever stronger within him. "There must be some way I can help Paul and ECKANKAR to show others this joy I feel, know and have experienced," he thought. Though never a man to push himself on anyone, his eagerness to be of service finally prompted him to write a letter to Paul in September of 1969. He was willing to get some sort of discussion class going or perhaps even a group studying the Satsang discourses.

But before he received an answer from Paul, he received an announcement of great importance in his monthly mailings from the ECKANKAR Office: the Third World Wide Seminar of ECKANKAR was going to be held at the International Hotel in Los Angeles on the weekend of October 30 through November 3. Paul Twitchell, the Living ECK Master, was to be the main speaker.

Darwin could hardly wait to go. Finally, he was going to meet the man in the physical whom he had known all his life as his inner guide, who had helped and protected him countless times, the man with the southern accent who had spoken to him out of the blue light on the road from Lake Tahoe. What would the meeting be like? Would Paul recognize him?

At the seminar Darwin was delighted to see that there were over five hundred people, from all over the United States, Canada and some other countries, including Sweden, Switzerland and Australia. They were of all ages, backgrounds and races. Many had been invited to receive an initiation from Paul, while for others this was their first contact with the ancient teachings of ECKANKAR brought out by this Master for the spiritual growth and benefit of modern man.

Before Paul came on stage, there were various talks by

ECKists who had already been studying with Paul a little longer, some poetry was read and music performed. Darwin had come early to get a good seat so he would be close to Paul in person for the first time—Peddar Zaskq who had been his Inter Guide since the earliest years of his life. He felt the growing excitement of the audience, ECKists and newcomers alike, to each of whom Paul meant more than just a man with something interesting to say, but a possible bridge to the heavenly regions in this lifetime.

Just before Paul's talk, the emcee led the seminar participants through what he explained as a "rolling HU Chant." The audience sat with their backs erect, their feet flat on the ground; they closed their eyes and chanted or sang a long drawn out "H-U-U-U-"—the word HU being a very ancient name for God and a means of contacting Spirit or ECK force. Darwin knew about the word HU and used it in his contemplations, and in the two or three minutes of the rolling chant his consciousness was lifted into an awareness of brilliant light and heavenly sound. He opened his eyes.

Up on the low stage, not fifty feet away, sat Sri Paul Twitchell. He was a slight man, not very tall, dressed plainly in a light blue shirt and trousers that were loose, if not a little baggy, his suit jacket draped over the back of the stool he was sitting on. He spoke slowly and in a soft voice, his speech pattern a curious combination of the accents spoken in England and the Southern United States. Emphasizing his points with precise gestures, Paul talked clearly and authoritatively on the ancient science of ECKANKAR, but interspersed his lecture with many humorous stories from his own life or funny observations that drew warm laughs from the listeners.

Darwin listened and soaked in every word Paul said. The words seemed to be flowing into him on a different plane of being than on the usual level of mental reception —it was as if the Master was only using words and speech to carry his communication directly to the Soul of every listener. Thus, when Paul finished, the strongest impression that remained with Darwin was the feeling of joy and love that emanated from this man, his genuine laughter making it plain to see that Paul was truly enjoying his work.

After the talk was over, there was a chance for people to walk up to the Master, exchange a few words with him, shake his hand, see him and be seen by him. This gaze of recognition given by the ECK Master to his chela (student) is known as the Darshan. There are three parts to the Darshan, meeting with the Master outwardly and being recognized by him; meeting with him inwardly and traveling with him, seeing, and being seen by him; and the enlightenment which comes with this act. There does not necessarily have to be physical contact for the Darshan. It can happen in the dream state or while the Master is speaking from the stage. You don't have to shake his hand or touch him.

As the audience got up and crowded towards where Paul had stepped down from the platform, Darwin got up with them and moved forward. Paul greeted many people by name, bantering with them, shaking hands, smiling warmly at all. He moved through the crowd, briefly giving his full attention to the person he was shaking hands with. As Paul came nearer, Darwin wondered what to say to him. He wanted to thank him for all he had done, but how can you thank a person for a lifetime of guidance, love and protection in a few words?

Before Paul came close enough for Darwin to meet him, however, he looked up and beyond Darwin for a moment, then turned the other way. He seemed not to have noticed Darwin, at all. He went on, shaking other people's hands and talking to other people. But, somehow, Darwin wasn't disappointed. He had no questions to ask the Master, for these had been answered long ago on the inner. There was no real need to talk to Paul in the physical. In fact, Darwin felt very grateful that he had heard a lecture given by the Living ECK Master of his time. He felt so happy that he chuckled to himself, thinking how fortunate he was. "In fact, I didn't stay in the hotel where this seminar was taking place. I stayed in a motel a mile down the road."

Darwin flew back to Portland infused with a tremendous amount of enthusiasm and energy for helping with Paul's work. He understood now that an organization in the field under the Living ECK Master's direction was needed to make the teaching of ECKANKAR available to anyone who, like himself, had been prepared by spiritual experiences for the outward acceptance of this ancient path to God. "Truth is in every man and woman," he thought. "But every person needs a living Spiritual Guide who is both the Inner and Outer Master to lead him through the lower worlds and the traps of the negative force."

Paul's work was to establish the ancient teaching of ECKANKAR in the written form and as a path open to all who were interested. The ECK Vairagi Masters had decided that the message of ECKANKAR could, in these times, be made public. Man was ready for a huge step forward in spiritual understanding, which was to bring him spiritual results greater than the material results gained from the technological progress of the industrial revolution. Paul Twitchell had, in scores of manuscripts, described the entire system of age-old truths of ECKANKAR in modern language that anyone could understand, internally consistent, yet allowing for the extreme breadth in levels of experience and knowledge. Paul was the first to say, "They were translations from the Shariyat-Ki-Sugmad, the sacred scriptures kept in the seven Golden Wisdom Temples in the various levels of heaven."

Darwin sensed it was his duty to advance the teachings in Oregon to his greatest ability. On November 16, he received an answer to his letter to Paul in September:

Dear Mr. Gross:
Thank you for your letter of September 12,

asking about a Satsang group in Portland.

If you are at all interested, I would be most happy to see that you take a Satsang discussion group and run it for us in your area.

A discussion group is different from the regular classes because the individual who is taking the leadership of it does not teach but holds discussion classes. This means that he must arrange for a group to meet once every two weeks to discuss the books, tapes or anything else used in the class, along with the ECK Satsang discourses.

If you would be interested in taking over this discussion class in Portland, I will be glad to publish your name in the next issue of *The Mystic World*.

Please let me know right away if you can do this.

I am always with you.

> Affectionately,
> Paul

Darwin answered in a handwritten note by return mail:

In reply to your letter of November 14, 1969, about the Satsang discussion group in this area. Yes, Paulji, I am your servant and would be greatly honored to lead the discussion group in the Portland area.

Please forward any information and literature, if needed.

> Spiritually yours to mold,
> Darwin Gross

Darwin started by contacting two ECKists in the Portland area who had joined ECKANKAR a little earlier than he had and were willing to become active. Both were women, Polly Dornberger, a retired business executive, and Jean Quigley, a business woman, who had traveled to the Los Angeles seminar and met Darwin by sitting in the seat next to him in the audience. When the three of them got together for a meeting at a restaurant, Darwin outlined his goals for the beginning of the class for which Paul had given him permission, and possibly opening a place where the local ECKists could meet and information material and books could be distributed.

"We need an open place where the public can come, like a Reading Room or an ECK Center," he said. "Also, where the ECKists can gather for their meetings and work from."

Polly nodded. "Jean and I have already thought of that. We looked through the papers and at many locations up for rent, but it's hard to find something that we can afford right now."

"Well, I see. How about some place just to meet occasionally?"

Jean and Polly both offered their own homes.

But Darwin shook his head. "Many new people are hesitant to come to someone's private house when they don't know the owner. It embarrasses them, or they are too skeptical. Besides, I feel we should pay for what we get, not impose on any one person's private space."

"Libraries and banks often have public rooms for free. Why don't we check those?" Polly suggested.

"I already checked into that," Darwin replied. "The Community House has agreed to let us use a room now and then, so let's set a date there."

Soon, the discussion group started and gave the local ECKists and all interested newcomers a bi-monthly chance to get together and exchange viewpoints on the spiritual teachings. In addition, Darwin went out into the communities to give introductory lectures, hand out books or supply the bookstores with them, advertising the lectures and the discussion groups through small personal ads in the papers and posters. He kept up his correspondence with

Paul, sending him regular reports on his activities.

Sri Paul:
I wish to thank you for your guidance and help with my request on establishing an ECK-Satsang class here in the Portland and surrounding area. I am looking forward to learning much from this experience.

As stated to you in our discussion on February 22, 1970 in Sacramento, California, I am able to take leave from my work whenever needed. I would be HONORED to help you build up the northwest in ECKANKAR.

I will be at the Seminar in Vancouver, B.C.
SPIRITUALLY YOURS TO MOLD,
Darwin Gross

Dear Darwin:
Thank you for your letter of February 23, referring to an ECK-Satsang class in Portland and surrounding area.

I would appreciate it if you would go ahead with my suggestion of forming a class and trying to develop it into a sizeable number of chelas. If you can do this, I will be most happy to find a spot sometime next year to visit Portland to make a talk and to give you a hand in arousing more interest. Further still, if time ever permits it this year, it can be possible that I will run into Portland and give you a helping hand by talks with our own people and friends. Meanwhile, I would be very happy if you would go ahead and start building up a group which will give you an opportunity to either teach a class or have a discussion group which is the getting together with a group of people to listen to tapes and discuss the subject of ECKANKAR.

86

I am very happy to hear that you will be at the Vancouver Seminar and hope that you will participate in the music program with Irwin Webb who is coming all the way across the country from Ft. Lauderdale, Florida, to be the music director and organizer of this program.

I do want to give you the initiation while you are in Vancouver at this time and hope that you will be ready for your third or fourth initiation by the next time we get together.

I wish to thank you for your interest and enthusiasm for the cause of ECK.

May the Blessings be!

Affectionately,
Paul Twitchell

On the short trip to Vancouver, B.C., Darwin shared a ride with some ECKist friends. Polly Dornberger seemed upset about something, and, feeling concern for her, Darwin asked her when they were alone for a moment:

"What's the matter, Polly? Anything bothering you?"

"Oh, not really, but I got a letter from Paul saying I could have my Second Initiation at the seminar. It somehow doesn't feel right."

"How come?"

"It's the smoking business. You know what Paul says about smoking. That as you become aware it will drop away, but it doesn't seem to happen with me. I've smoked for fifty years, usually two packs a day, and that's a hard habit to break."

"You don't have to force it. Just don't worry about it, it will happen when the time is right."

Polly took her initiation at the seminar. Two months later, without forcing herself or suffering any strain, she laid a half-empty pack of cigarettes aside and never smoked again.

For Darwin, the seminar was to hold a series of important events. He knew he was going to meet with Paul, receive the Second Initiation, and also he would participate in the musical part of the program. He had been asked to perform on the final day. He sang a new song he had composed: "Oh, How I Love Thee, Blessed SUGMAD" — written in admiration for Sri Paul Twitchell. Everyone enjoyed it, and many hummed the tune to themselves as they left the session.

Darwin felt a sudden thrill when someone sent by Paul told him to go to Paul's room in the hotel. He knocked, and Paul called for him to come in. They shook hands and sat down. Darwin felt immediately comfortable and at ease in Paul's presence. They sat facing each other, and during the initiation the Master gave him his own secret word to use in his spiritual exercises. Then they contemplated for a short period with their eyes closed, Darwin being aware of the presence of his old friend Rebazar Tarzs, even hearing his footsteps in the room as well as smelling the sweet aroma which surrounds him.

Afterward, Paul invited Darwin to join him for lunch with another ECKist. They talked about organizing new areas and ideas for spreading the message of ECK. As a Second Initiate, Darwin was now an Arahata, a teacher in ECK, and could hold a Satsang class, which is a monthly or bi-monthly meeting of members of ECKANKAR on the Satsang discourses for the purpose of studying this material. It was not long after the Vancouver seminar, that Darwin began conducting his first Satsang class. In the first of his monthly reports to the Master which every Second Initiate or higher is requested to do, Darwin wrote:

> I am unable to truly put on paper with man's numerous words just how I feel about the darshan and the initiation that you gave me up in Vancouver, B.C. The wisdom and knowledge you passed on to me far exceeds the small self. "Thank you" just does not seem to fit. The

words to the song which the ECK spirit helped me write start to say it. It is called, "Oh, How I Love Thee, Blessed SUGMAD..."

Sri Paul, being invited to lunch with you and the young ECKist was a blessed thrill.

The first ECKANKAR discussion was held on the seventh of April. This went very well for the first session. I did appreciate your warm thank you as I put the physical body to rest that night.

The first Satsang class consisted of the following...

To evaluate each person that attended the Satsang class at this time is beyond my present ability. From what I heard as questions, I'm only able to repeat your statement you have made quite often: "We, as individuals, are at different levels of understanding."

Your servant here and above.

From then on, Darwin was always full of ideas and plans for ECKANKAR in his area. Once the class and various activities were established in Portland, he began looking outward to other areas to open up. Even in the dream state he worked for ECK, as he wrote Paul in his report on May 22, 1970:

Sri Paul:

....I played your tape called "The Rudiments of ECK-Satsang Teachings." It was well received by the class.

The morning of the 18th in the dream state, I found myself talking to a group in the Palo Alto or Sunnyvale area. Then on the morning of the 19th, no the 20th, for this was after the ECK-Satsang class, you asked me to go easy. Should I be correct you were talking about the teachings?

I am trying to get out as often as possible to our own people and other groups to talk on ECKANKAR. On the 29th of April I talked to Fern Hall's Meditation group. I left there with the feeling that some of the folk would read a little of the works of ECKANKAR; I turned it over to Spirit. I will try to get back up there in the Tacoma area again.

On the 10th I spent a couple of hours with Mr. Mosely. He will help me set up a talk in the Dalles or Hood River area. Then on the 16th I talked with Mrs. Hershberger's group, a very happy one. On June 10th I will be starting a discussion group in the home of Marsha Miller down in Eugene, Oregon. I hope to turn it over to one in that area soon.

I found something I enjoy doing and have you to thank for both the inter joy and the outer. I found that going out and talking to your Chelas is a step beyond.

WITH THE MAHANTA

He received many invitations to give introductory talks in various communities and more often set up presentations himself. Some of the towns he went to in early 1970 were Seattle and Tacoma, Washington, and Hood River, Salem, Seaside, and Sutherlin, Oregon. His usual approach was to contact a member of ECKANKAR in that particular town and suggest a lecture. When there was no one to arrange the hall or meeting place and take care of the advertising, Darwin would often do a special trip there four to six weeks in advance of his lecture. And, most frequently, the money for these expenses came out of his own pocket.

His lectures and meetings, including a question and answer period, seldom lasted over an hour. Always there was a table with the ECK books and tapes available for sale at the back of the room, a "No Smoking" sign posted on the wall, and a chart of the God Worlds of ECK and a picture of the Living ECK Master set up. Sometimes, in the discussions, he would play parts of tapes or records of Paul's lectures, and often he would refer a questioner to a chapter in a specific book to find his answer there.

The impression chelas gained from witnessing his style of presentation was described by some as "painfully honest and ethical," by others as "impersonal" or "low key." He seldom talked about himself or went into Paul's personal life, since it had always been his strong belief that an individual's personal life was his or her private matter. On the other hand, he did not approach the teachings of ECKANKAR with too much emphasis on the philosophical, metaphysical or intellectual side—his remarks were simple and based on common sense; and always the joy of dwelling in Spirit shone through, accounting for the humor and laughter shared in his classes and meetings.

Darwin was soft-spoken and never tried to push ECKANKAR onto people. He actually felt relieved after having given his talk, for now it was up to the individual and the divine Spirit, whether they accepted ECK or not. But this was not weakness. He seldom tolerated undue interference with getting the message out. He would not hesitate to point out to one of the chelas that copying the discourses without permission from the author was being dishonest. When one lady insistently interrupted his talk, he told her to stop and act like an adult or he would have to close the meeting. She stopped.

One young man once asked the question, "I don't want to kill anything..., but I have a cockroach in my kitchen that really bothers me. What can I do?"

Darwin answered, "Ask it to leave. If it doesn't, help it out the door or step on it in the name of the SUGMAD."

Aware of the discipline in the guidelines that issued from the ECKANKAR Office, Darwin continued to send Paul monthly reports on his area activities, excerpts of which follow:

...Mrs. M. is going through a little negativeness that some go through when starting out on the path of ECK.

...Some of the chelas are starting to experience some changes within their lives, as they are starting to go within to the temple. It is true that the most difficult task is to get across the point that the inter life is to be realized and only the chelas can do this. However, in the short time with this class I have seen a change in some and it is the one that believes and practices the daily spiritual exercises. I thank thee for the opportunity to study with and work for Thee. If I can be of assistance to Thee full time in ECK for ECKANKAR, I am yours to guide.

...The students are just starting to ask questions and opening up. Each meeting has been a new experience for me. Not just knowing but feeling and seeing the SPIRIT of ECK now and then (the Blue HU). Your Presence during the class hour and at each talk that I have given on ECKANKAR as well as each Moment of Man's time is ... On the morning of July 31, 1970, I was asked if I wanted to come to Las Vegas? My reply was positive. The question I had, was this for the physical body or the higher self? I am free to go anywhere, my LORD. The talk I gave here in Portland, Oregon on Aug. 20, 1970 was fruitful. However, I did open myself up and will take it as it comes. The one thing I am not sure of is just where I went negative. On the morning of the 22nd of August there was something said to me but all I retained was suffer.

...In observation of the students there is a noticeable change in the one who practices the

ZIKAR daily. Due to the forces beyond the small self, the Discussion Group is held on the third Monday of each month and the ECK-Satsang class is held on the first Monday of each month. I thank Thee for WISDOM, FREEDOM and CHARITY Thou hast given me.

...The class collectively is improving in the outer sense. One question I have had, is it required to call by phone, those who are not attending the class regularly? I do have much to learn and know there is a never-ending work.

...The interest of the class has grown in the study of this great teaching of ECK. There is a vast spread of understanding within the class. However, I feel that the class is just starting to get a toe hold on some of the fundamentals.

...In the class this month and the class last month we have been reviewing. This has been from the first through the sixth ECK-Satsang Discourse. A review once in awhile sure helps to freshen one's thoughts as well as brings out some new questions. My activity this past month has been: a talk in the Sutherlin and Roseberg area, a talk and the playing of a record of Sri Paul on Sunday in the home of Jean Quinn. This was for those who work nights or unable to get to the classes.

Enclosed you will find several clippings. I ran an ad for three days in both of the Salem papers. The evening before the talk I received a call from a newsman wanting to know about ECKANKAR. As you can see some things are not in order, however, some would not have come out had it not been for the free lines. They had missed the ad that ran for the three days.

...The attendance has dropped on some of the early ECKists. I have not called to see if they have dropped the class completely. I will do this before the next Satsang class. I have been able to see a change in some of your chelas, from a sad and lonely look, to a happy and peaceful look of love. It is with Joy, to be a channel for Thee to flow through. For without Thy WORD this Microcosm would be blue.

...In the dream state I seem to be a bit slow grasping, such as reading, like a note or hearing. I'll bring just a part of it back and then tend to become frustrated not knowing all I read or what the Dream Master has said to me. I know this will improve, for this SOUL to become a better channel.

...I enjoyed being with you and Gail at the Second International Youth Conference. At times I feel I know nothing, for there is much to bring through to the physical part of myself to be a wider channel and go beyond it. Till the screen is pulled aside, the ECK is my eyes...

Your servant in ECK
Darwin Gross

In 1970, the October World Wide Seminar was to be in Las Vegas, Nevada. A month before the event, Darwin got another letter from Paul:

September 19, 1970

Dear Darwin,

I'm late as usual with mail—for your letter August 22/70, giving report, etc.

I see you're on the program for the World Wide Seminar in Las Vegas this year. If you feel capable, I would like to see you get the next initiation — I want you pulled up to the Fifth quickly as possible, so you can officially be the

ECK representative for Oregon. Glad to hear you're doing well with classes and lectures.

Affectionately,
Paul

At the seminar Darwin gave a talk on Satsang classes and received much applause for speaking with authority and sincerity. To his own surprise, he was also given the initiation into the Fifth Circle. The Fifth Initiate is the Mahdis, working directly as the representative of the Master to spread the message of ECK imparted to him by the MAHANTA. Darwin had expected his Third or Fourth, but the Master had known his inner spiritual unfoldment had been prepared for a long time and that he was ready for the Fifth. It did not mean that he was above his fellow ECK students who generally took much longer to reach this stage, but only that he was ready to accept more of the burden and responsibility.

Darwin returned to Portland with his thoughts focused entirely on his new responsibility. He was now the area representative of Oregon, appointed by the Living ECK Master. He would receive a letter from Paul a month later asking him to attend the Pacific Coast Seminar in Los Angeles the following January, and adding "I have some projects which would like to discuss with you in detail about helping with ECK!"

At this time, Darwin reached an important decision at his job. His ECKANKAR activity had used up his whole vacation time, and he had taken so much unpaid leave that complaints about his continued absence had reached the ears of his superiors. Still there wasn't enough time for his work in ECKANKAR. But this was his true calling, so the only alternative was to find a more flexible job. He thought nothing of giving up what he had struggled and toiled for so hard, a career that had been suited to his creative technical abilities and paid a good salary besides, if this stood in the way of spreading the message of ECK. He asked for a transfer to a job in manufacturing.

"A transfer from engineer to manufacturing worker? Who ever heard of that?" His supervisor was baffled.

Darwin replied, "It pays by the hour and I'm easily replaceable when I have to leave. It gives me more freedom to go whenever I'm called."

The story of the engineer with a brilliant reputation who had asked for a position on the assembly line circulated the company like wildfire, many heads shaking in wonder, but now Darwin had the freedom to serve ECKANKAR as completely as he wished, and still earn the little money he needed.

During one of his many summons from Paul, he had the chance to meet Paul's wife, Gail. Paul often wore blue tennis shoes, and so, when Darwin walked into the room wearing blue tennis shoes, Gail said jokingly, "What are you trying to do? Walk in the Master's footsteps?"

"Yeap!" he replied.

More and more, Paul relied on Darwin to aid him in many things. At every seminar, Darwin was the only one welcome in Paul's room at any time, and often Darwin would look in to see if there was anything he could do for Paul.

Darwin became aware how much his training was speeded up and that he was constantly being tested and watched not only by Paul, but by many of the Masters of the Vairagi as well. One afternoon, during a seminar in Salt Lake City, Darwin went to his hotel room to lay down and get a few moments rest. A man appeared, dressed in a short maroon robe tied with a rope. He was powerfully built, stocky, dark eyed and bald. Darwin immediately recognized him as Yaubl Sacabi, the ECK Master who is the head of the spiritual city of Agam Des in the Himalayan Mountains. He looked about thirty-five years old, but he had been the Living ECK Master during the high period of civilization in ancient Greece and sustained his body mainly by spiritual energy, partaking directly of the ECK

Life Current rather than physical food (although he did drink herbal teas). It was a meeting in which no words were spoken. An enormous amount of information was passed on silently, and Darwin came out of that experience knowing that Yaubl Sacabi had been assigned by the Nine Silent Ones (Silent Travelers, who are directly responsible to the SUGMAD) to speed up Darwin's own training.

Paul's health was not very good; he had been poisoned a few months earlier in Madrid, had barely survived, and only partially healed himself enough to keep up his responsibilities as the spiritual leader of the world. An assassination attempt had been made on him right here in Salt Lake City, which had only marginally failed. Paul was being exhausted by writing down the tremendous amount of knowledge that was pouring through, and his extensive travel and lecture schedule. Darwin's compassion for Paul grew to be a strong force in his life. As they became closer, Darwin knew there wasn't anything he wouldn't do to help Paul with his work. He was thinking of becoming a missionary for ECK, going to other countries on the globe to open them up and help people meet the Living ECK Master.

In Oregon, Darwin saved every penny he could by moving to a cheaper apartment, turning off the heat and eating very little so he could maximize the amount of money he had available for ECK activities. He even sold his electric organ, although he would miss the music a great deal. He drove all over Oregon, Washington, Idaho, Utah, and Montana, spending many hours on the road. His horizon of responsibility was ever widening, and he was consumed by his service to the ECK, yet not losing his head but using common sense in his every day life, such as keeping clean and eating.

Around the beginning of the year 1971, a spiritual event of great momentum took place that was to determine the entire future course of his work for ECK. The years of his training and testing had finally reached a point where the spiritual hierarchy put a decision before him. Darwin relates the incident in this way: "...I was approached, not by Paul or anyone in the physical, it was above time, space and matter in the Soul body—here I was in a circle with the Nine Silent Ones and the MAHANTA, the Living ECK Master of the time, and I was in the middle and they questioned me, not like a drill, but asked me point-blank if I wanted the responsibility [of being the Living ECK Master], and I didn't hesitate. I said, 'You must know what you are doing, I'll accept the responsibility and also I know I'll need some help.'"

"Of course, they realized that and I didn't breathe a word of it to anyone," Darwin continued, "because that's one of the biggest tests. When the time was right, Paul knew it, and he checked out when he wanted to. He said things to make people question, deliberately. He made it hard for me. Don't make things easy for the next guy, in that sense. But it doesn't come easy and as one learns to really work for that which one wishes to gain out of the spiritual life— not whether it's a new status in the sense of a title, but the knowledge of God—then it's up to the person that reaches that area, whether he becomes adept, a Master on this path; it's truly up to the individual."

Working with Paul Twitchell, the Living ECK Master, wasn't always easy for Darwin, as working closely with any Living ECK Master isn't easy for his immediate aides. Darwin remembered Paul telling him one time:

"It's difficult to work with a Master. Everything he says or does has meaning. You get very frustrated if you try to rationalize a Master's actions. Trust your inner voice. Remember, as a person I'm no different than anyone else, and you'll think I've let you down at times. You have much to learn. It is the knowledge of God that makes the Living ECK Master to have the edge on the rest of the world. Yet to the uninitiated, as well as some initiated, it seems as if the Living ECK Master is just another human being who may make an error. However, everything you do, every place you go, you will work for the good of ALL, for in ECK (spirit) there are no errors."

A month later, Darwin was asked to a youth planning conference in Las Vegas, where several of the leaders in ECKANKAR were invited to discuss special plans for young people in ECK. One of the participants of the meeting was Millie Moore, a lady who was one of Paul's first chelas, very direct and outspoken, who had helped a lot with the administration and organization of ECKANKAR in the early days in Las Vegas. Looking around at the people gathered in the room, Millie saw a young man she had never noticed before. "My God," she exclaimed to herself. "I've seen him in my dreams. That's Paul's replacement."

She went over to Darwin after the meeting. They greeted each other as if they were old friends. Later, she found out other ECKists, quietly and without saying anything to anyone else, had come to the same conclusion.

After one of the sessions of the meeting, Paul called Darwin to his room. During the course of their conversation, Paul pointed at a stack of newly printed blue posters that had Paul's picture on them. "See those new posters over there in the corner? Take one, and I'll autograph it for you." Darwin took one from the stack and brought it to Paul who wrote something on it and gave it back. It read, "To Dap Ren Gross, with spiritual love, Paul Twitchell."

Darwin said, "You know, you looked just like this when you appeared to me one night on the inner during my spiritual exercise!"

Paul looked away bashfully without answering. Darwin rolled the poster up carefully, but the different name didn't register with him until he unrolled it at home to look at it again. Dap Ren! After a moment, he rolled the poster up again and stored it away in a container. He told no one of his new name. However, in his own consciousness, it grew in significance. It finally dawned on him what had happened at that moment in time when he received that poster.

The Master had given him his spiritual name. He had received the Ninth Initiation and that meant his entry into the Ancient Order of the Vairagi and unusual spiritual responsibilities along with Silent Ones, the ECK Masters, the instruments of God in this universe and beyond. After his answer to the question by the MAHANTA and the Nine Silent Ones a little earlier, Darwin wasn't shocked by this revelation, but as is frequent with individuals of high spiritual development, he didn't see himself as such. He asked himself: "Whyame, God?"

In May, 1971, Darwin received a note from Paul asking him to go on a trip to London, England, with him to help in giving consultations and initiations.

> I have made reservations for you to fly to London, England May 18th, arriving on the 19th, with hotel reservations at the Grosvenor House, where Gail and I are staying! You would be leaving there on May 23rd for states!
> Is this alright with you? I'll give you a phone call soon on it. Don't think the Iceland trip is going to materialize! But will need you in England with me on this trip. You'll hear again from me soon! Thanks kindly for all you're doing for ECK.
>
> Affectionately,
> Paul

Darwin spent five days working closely and almost constantly with Paul, learning much as Paul let him participate in the work he was doing as a Master. It was like a treasure of experience observing Paul giving consultations, gently separating the emotional entanglements from the real spiritual problems that people came to him about. At the end of the trip, Darwin said to Paul:

"Thank you, Master, I'm on my way back to Oregon ... to keep things going there."

"Sure, Darwin, that's where the future is, the Satsangs, the ECKists, the field. We'll never make the mistake of putting anything or anybody between the ECKist and SUGMAD."

Back in Oregon, people noticed the changes that were occurring with Darwin. He was becoming much more confident, his talks came less from quoting the books but more out of his own authority, his hesitancy and shyness disappearing, the light shining in his eyes. In response to questions about his London trip, Darwin answered, "A curtain has been pulled. I'm receiving a lot on the inter guidance—something is going on."

On May 26, 1971, Darwin heard from Paul again:

Dear Darwin:

My deepest appreciations for coming to London and giving a hand of help with all the people who showed up. I am quite sure that your experiences in London gave you an added depth to an already rich background in ECK. I missed giving you this pix in London which Patti Simpson had sent!

We will be together again soon in the physical. I am adjusting my schedule to be with you at the Oregon Seminar, at least for one day, if not for the two days. You can count on this and let the word spread about.

Gail joins me in sending our love to you and all the chelas there.

Affectionately,
Paul

Darwin took up his extensive lecture travels all over the northwestern United States again, having two successful highlights with the opening of an ECKANKAR Center in both Portland and Eugene, Oregon, in July. He went to the Youth Conference Seminar in Chicago and again enjoyed the company of Paul.

A spiritual experience following the Chicago Seminar was both terrifying and exhilarating. Darwin laid down to rest, but couldn't sleep. Suddenly, he was aware of the presence of Rebazar Tarzs and Paul. "Do not be afraid. I am going to disassemble you, atom by atom, and reassemble you as you were." He felt his whole body being disassembled and dismantled into separate atoms. Rebazar, in his crisp, clear English voice whose sound raised Darwin beyond the ethers, boomed out to Paul, "I've built him with a straight back." There was a deep sound, deep blue light, then Golden White Light. When he was aware again of his body on the bed, he felt that it had been rearranged, each atom changed and all his organs and body systems completely restructured once more just as they were. Except in appearance, he was a different person, spiritually.

As Paul had promised in a letter the year before, he attended a Seminar in Oregon. Darwin was the seminar director and set the event up, working together with the local area chelas. Paul gave talks on love and the importance of daydreams. He looked thin, almost gaunt, his face lined with dark rings under the eyes. He seemed more weary than people had noticed at any other time. The seminar was a success, and Paul was pleased but seemed very tired. He had another seminar coming up in Cincinnati, Ohio, in September.

To this seminar Darwin had been invited to speak on the program. Usually, Darwin wouldn't ask Paul if he should go to a seminar, but this time, he asked him as Paul was leaving Portland.

"Paul, should I go to that seminar in Cincinnati?"

"No, you don't, you stay home. You have other things to do."

Paul knew what was to happen at the time of that seminar and arranged it so that most of the people he was close to did not attend. Even his wife Gail was told to remain at home to bone up on her studies for school on the following

Monday.

Darwin didn't question the Master's decision, but set up an introductory talk in Boise, Idaho, instead. By this time, he had given up his job at the electronics company to work full-time as a missionary for ECK. It was September 17th, 1971, when heading back from Boise his car suddenly stopped running without any apparent reason. As he pulled into a gas station, Darwin felt on the inner that something had happened. He tells of what happened then, in the following words:

"The moment that Paul translated, my car had broken down a few minutes before that. I was on my way home from Boise, Idaho. I'd pulled off the road, off the side road at a combination gas and store there. The station was closed, but the store was open, and I tinkered a bit there and I felt the presence of someone. Also, at that instant I knew that Paul had translated. I cannot explain how I knew, but I knew. I turned around and looked and here's the outline of the whole order [of the Vairagi Masters] and Paul with a smile, and I knew without a doubt the task at hand. I didn't tell a person, I couldn't. I didn't call Gail, try to approach her or anything because I knew if she was going to know, Paul would have to tell her, which happened, I guess, a few days after that when she learned and she tried to get in touch with me."

Darwin hadn't counted on this responsibility. He had still been thinking of doing some missionary work for ECK as his future, and when the whole order of ECK Masters appeared to him on that road from Boise, he still could have stepped back. But he chose to take the responsibility. On October 22, 1971, he stood in Soul Body in the Valley of Shangta, Tibet, near the ancient Oracle of Tirmer, to receive the Rod of ECK Power as the 972nd Living ECK Master in the line of the Vairagi Adepts.

CHAPTER 5

Understanding
The Law of Silence

The Master has been with every chela since
the beginning of time upon this Earth, and with
the other planets and the beings on those worlds.
He has assumed another embodiment with each
life spent in these worlds. It has always been the
ECK which has brought about the existence of
the living Master upon this planet and other
worlds. It has only changed forms and handed
down Its power from one departing Master to his
successor.

— *The Spiritual Notebook*

As the 972nd Living ECK Master in the unbroken line of
spiritual adepts known as the Ancient Order of the Vairagi,
Sri Darwin Gross reflected upon his roadside meeting with
the Nine Silent Ones on the occasion of Sri Paul Twitchell's
translation from the physical arena:
"They all smiled, raised their right hands and the Baraka
Bashad* was given. With it came a silent communication
never to be forgotten. It was as if all the orchestras of
heaven and the sweetest violins in any world gave forth
music which was too great to describe in man's limited vo-
cabulary. With a smile on their faces, and the Baraka
Bashad given as if on a cloud, they whisked off into the
morning sunlight beyond this world.
"From that moment on, each of the Vairagi ECK

---

* Baraka Bashad: An ancient person saying "May the blessings be."

Masters, including Sri Paul Twitchell (Peddar Zaskq), has been a great help and have never left me, for an ECKist on this path of ECKANKAR is never alone. The Living ECK Master of the time has a protection no one else has. That person that steps on the path of ECK to receive this magnificent teaching of ECK which only can be realized by the individual, also has a unique spiritual protection.

"In about 1965 I was having quite a time. I was being tested. I can see the pattern starting in the latter '50's on up to receiving the Rod of ECK Power.

"It was hard! When I came into ECKANKAR I had no inkling that this would happen. I was being prepared. I knew that ever since I was a child and a young person, a young adult, because of things that happened around me, things that I saw and knew and understood.

"As a youngster, teenager and young adult there were things I couldn't talk to anyone about. These travels that I was taking into the heavenly worlds, I was assisting people actually. Even in my young adult life, I helped and guided, because I was working towards the mastership and had certain functions as I grew older, that became very apparent to me that I had some responsibility spiritually, but I didn't know precisely what it was, and I didn't ask. I only did what I could, and I always did the best I could, whatever I took on.

"Things changed drastically and swiftly in ECK. My initiations were speeded up very swiftly from my 5th in Las Vegas, October 1970. This occurred about a year before Paul's translation [death]. The ECK Masters made me aware that this was going to happen. After I accepted, Paul started turning over much of the responsibilities to me while he was here, and I couldn't speak of it.

"I was healing, assisting with the various spiritual guides. The healing can be up to anyone, but there were things that Paul was doing that he turned over to me to do, and there's different ways and things that I can't begin to tell the public, because first they wouldn't believe it; second they'd say, prove it, and I can't, because they can prove it to themselves; third, some of the things if I could prove them, they'd want to lock me up or throw me off this planet."

On October 22, 1971 at the Fifth ECKANKAR World Wide Seminar in Las Vegas, Sri Darwin commented on his becoming the Living ECK Master:

"I was slated to do a little missionary work within this world and I knew the time was coming fast, starting with January of this past year, and other seminars, and even holding and being in on consultations with Paul over in Europe and a few here in the United States. I was not aware of this happening. He was training me to go out into the field. Little did I know, because I didn't want this. I have been here before. I was to have a particular mission to assist the MAHANTA in getting out the word of ECK, which I learned just recently, but I didn't think it was going to be this way. All of a sudden I was getting only one, two, or maybe three, sometimes if I was lucky, four hours of sleep. Very few people realize the demands on the physical body of this current, the responsibility of it flowing out to each and every one of you with love. This is all that it takes.

"Those of you that have been initiated under Paul have been greatly blessed. It is very difficult and hard at times getting through these lower worlds while in the physical body. I have seen it a number of times assisting my teacher and some of his pupils who have translated, as well as those that are presently on this physical plane of existence, into the Soul plane and planted their feet there. From there that individual is on his own, but as he progresses into the next plane and above, sometimes the fear even becomes worse, because that individual has not learned how to shift his state of consciousness. He is still dwelling in the lower worlds.

"Learning how to balance your vibrations and situations as they arrive while in the physical body is something that you learn once you reach that Fifth plane of Being. I had a little problem at one time that my teacher handed me and I immediately approached a goodly number of past learned men—spiritually learned, I might add. They wouldn't help me. They said, 'We do not descend.' Most of the people aren't aware that these great teachers that have been on this planet—they are in another field of work, you might say. They have their duties to perform. Those of you that have the ability to be with your teacher, your Master, or the MAHANTA, are very fortunate. Those who have not gained this yet may have a few things to work out.

"Every teacher that has taught the true teachings of ECK and ECKANKAR that have been on this planet, has taught the Light and Sound. Some of the offshoots have taught it but they can only go so far. They still approach the MAHANTA to have their Atma lit to get into the pure positive God Worlds. Regardless of what path they come from, if they have reached that state of unfoldment they will get into the Soul plane. But that's as far as they go. This is where you are fortunate. Those who have been initiated under Paul and those who are being initiated today that are new, that are coming into ECKANKAR, there is nothing held back, nothing other than your own state of consciousness. Expansion of this, though, without the use of anything but your own energies is up to you. You are given help. If you should get off into a negative direction, a sidetrack you might say, this is up to you to ask for guidance back to the path."

Sri Darwin's acceptance of the Rod of ECK Power was commemorated in a painting entitled "The Passing of the Rod of Power" by ECKist Diana Stanley who attended this sacred ceremony in Soul body and later rendered the experience with oils on canvas exactly as she had perceived it.

As Darwin explained: "The Rod of ECK Power is not a physical rod, as we think of the 'staff' here. It is invisible. There's quite a change that takes place in that individual's body, in not only the Radiant Form, but physical body too. I've had more changes happen. I've had plenty before accepting it and since I've accepted it, many physical changes as well. It is directly from God. It's hard to describe — it's invisible, yet it's very real and it is a 'staff' I cannot misuse. It's used for the good of all mankind, to lift in consciousness.

"Paul didn't leave anything in writing, didn't have to. But he appeared to Gail and told her. She was in San Diego when he translated. I was out on the road giving a lecture over in Idaho and was on my way home. Most of those who were very close to him weren't there. Gail was in touch with Paul in the dream state and still is. I meet with him occasionally. It wasn't his choice, and it wasn't Gail's choice, the choice of the Living ECK Master. Even though it is stated in the Shariyat and he's mentioned it in the writings elsewhere, some people didn't understand it, which is their prerogative. If they don't accept it the way it happens, that's their level of understanding and state of consciousness. If they get upset, it's their own fault. If they think they've been passed by, maybe they have but there's always another chance for that person. We are always tested from day to day.

"For the outer part of the structure, or appearance you might say, a very interesting thing happened when Gail called me up to the stage and gave me that flower [a blue carnation] after she read that poem [The Golden Hour].

"It was like a transition there too. All the electricity went off, the cameras, nothing worked, even the recorders. It was noticeable to me, there was a whole shift and it happened so fast that even the electricity that was supplying the building went out, but basically it was more noticeable on the video, on the 8 or 16 millimeter, and the battery-operated equipment plus the microphones.

"It was kept quiet until the time was right. Of course, the question was why me, why was I chosen, but they didn't say I had to be quiet about it. The interesting part, I knew I was under a great test and so if it happened, it happened; if it didn't I had my goals set for what I wanted to do in this

109

physical world. And being the choice of mine to do what I wanted after this life and beyond eternity, I had already made my decision. But I hadn't counted on this responsibility!"

Although Darwin had not been told to remain silent about the responsibility the Vairagi ECK Masters had offered him, he remembered the admonitions of keeping silent from the many ECK writings by Sri Paul Twitchell, one of which appeared in *The Shariyat-Ki-Sugmad*, Book One, as well as the individual home study: "He shall practice not only the Kamit, the Law of Silence with his secret [Initiate] word but shall practice the silence in his own affairs with ECK, and whatever is given him in the secret teachings.

"Whatever the MAHANTA, the Inner Master, gives him in secret through the channels of the inward self, he shall keep secret and not speak of to anyone else. He shall practice this Law of Silence with others who are not to be told any of the deep secrets of ECK. He will not speak about the MAHANTA and their inner relationships, nor of his affairs in the works of ECKANKAR. Those who do are violating the very heart of the works and shall have to pay in some manner or other. . . . Divine love comes through the practice of the Kamit, which is the Law of Silence. No one can enter the state of love until he knows loyalty, devotion and love for the ECK [Spirit]."

Darwin also knew that by sharing these inner secrets, they would lose some of their power for there were some who would scoff and misunderstand. Then too, changes become a way of life for the ECKist and the tests presented moment by moment could alter an overall plan depending on the manner in which the tests were accepted and passed. But Darwin had long been accustomed to keeping his inner experiences to himself and this one was sufficiently stunning to make him wonder incredulously. He had been accustomed to working on the sidelines while bringing the teachings of ECK to the uninitiated. As the Living ECK Master he would stand alone as the spiritual leader of ECKANKAR, the focal point for the chelas and the public as well, although he knew he would have the continuous support of the Vairagi ECK Masters in any way he might need it. It was the greatest way he could act as a vehicle for the SUGMAD.

Whereas most of the ECK initiates and the world awaited the announcement on October 22, 1971 as to who would be Sri Paul Twitchell's replacement and assume the spiritual responsibilities as the 972nd Living ECK Master, many chelas actually had an awareness of who this would be. This from their own personal inner experiences and knowingness, or through the dream state.

When asked by an *ECK World News* reporter how she felt about having the opportunity to serve two different Living ECK Masters and if she remembered her first meeting Sri Darwin Gross, Millie Moore (one of Sri Paul Twitchell's first chelas) responded:

"It was hard for me at first, not that I didn't know that Darwin Gross was the MAHANTA and the Living ECK Master. I knew this the first time I met him. I had heard a lot about Darwin Gross. As you remember, we had a Youth Training Conference that Paul called, and at that time, we sat across from Darwin. Many chelas in my class kept asking me who was going to be Paul's replacement. I honestly didn't know, because Paul never told us—only that he would be with us about five years, six at the most.

"So when I looked across the room at that conference and my eyes gazed upon Darwin Gross sitting across from us, I thought, 'Gee, that's Darwin Gross from Portland, Oregon,' and I recognized him. I knew who he was; I'd had much experience with him in the dream state, and as I was sitting there looking at him he looked at me. Well, there was the Darshan, the gaze of the Master!

"I had kind of gotten used to this piercing eye of the Master and I thought, 'There's Paul's replacement. I wonder if he knows yet.' Paul had told us about how hard it is to accept this in yourself, and it was very difficult for Paul to bring the message of ECK to the world and say I am He [the MAHANTA]. I also thought of the shoes Darwin was going to have to fill, and I wondered if he was aware of what his mission was going to be in this world. I said to myself, 'I can hardly wait for the meeting to be over so I can go up and introduce myself to Darwin Gross.'

"Well, as it turned out, the minute I approached him I didn't need to say a word, because Darwin knew me as well as I knew him. The same love that emanated from Paul emanated from Darwin. We just put our arms around each other and let the love flow. I wanted to say something to him so badly, but the opportunity never arose, and, of course I could never mention to anyone that I knew Darwin Gross would be the next Living ECK Master."

Another ECK chela later wrote to Sri Darwin: "We could not help wondering, especially those who heard our beloved PAULJI tell us at the Fourth ECKANKAR World Wide Seminar, there had been some thought of an older man to follow him as Living ECK Master but that a YOUNGER MAN was being groomed. How pleased we were to hear you say Paulji had told many of the chelas who would be the chosen one. Darwin—he told my daughter. He told me DARWIN. I must admit to you that we had talked among ourselves and we said, even before Paul told us, that we just could not conceive of it being anyone but DARWIN.

"The day PAUL translated I was visiting my daughter's home, and my sister called me there to tell me. Goodness gracious for one who knows better I began to cry. I got in my car, backed out of her drive—smack into the back of a parked car across the street, breaking a tail light. That really didn't stop the tears though because as I was driving along PAUL suddenly was with me, he was laughing and he said, 'Edith, what are you crying for? You didn't cry when your husband Bill translated. Stop crying. Why cry? Haven't I told you I am with you always.' I was ashamed to have to have him tell me but truthfully I was unspeakably happy that he spoke to me."

To clarify a few points about Paul's translation, Darwin commented on Paul's general state of health and some other circumstances surrounding that event as well as an earlier situation:

"Paul had gotten a little poison over in Spain and this was about a year before he translated. Not all ECKists had this ability to break the connection between Paul and Darwin. It's like an umbilical cord, and there's much written about the blue cord, the silver cord, the silver cord being the lesser than the blue cord. The silver cord is the astral body, the lower bodies; the blue cord is the mental bodies. The gold cord is the Soul body, unbreakable. Now you can't break that, and Paul chose the time and place in which to translate. He was not sick, ill or was not poisoned at that point of time. I'd like to straighten that out for a lot of people have got that all wrong. He stated that he was going to test all of us on the path of ECK. Those that are unable to take it will step aside.

"I was slated to go to Cincinnati and at the last minute he said, 'No, Darwin, I don't want you there.' So, I went to Boise. I had that set up anyway because up to that time I'd been to every seminar to assist him and help him, and some he invited me to and others he helped me to, but most of them I paid my own way. He didn't want me at that seminar and I didn't question it. Paul was not poisoned in Cincinnati. That happened in Spain. Gail was with him in Spain and she brought him home, hurriedly, and got him under the proper doctor's care. He came out of that all right and he held a great number of seminars after that."

When Paul did leave this physical arena the circumstances, this was of his own choosing. Even in this did he carry out one last responsibility and as a gift of love in fulfilling a mold one fifth initiate had made sometime earlier when she told Paul she wanted to be there in his arms when he left.

113

Paul had arrived at the Sheridan Gibson Hotel in Cincinnati a day early. On Friday evening he had a light supper with a few of the higher initiates, more of whom he joined again later that evening in the coffee shop. He had a late meeting in his room with several people which lasted until about 12:30 a.m. on September 17th. Around 1 a.m. this fifth initiate mentioned earlier started back to Paul's room. She knocked on the door. He had already retired for the evening, but in a few minutes opened the door. As he greeted her, he collapsed. A nearby seventh initiate and the house doctor were called immediately. Paul had left instantly. The seventh initiate reported he had observed Paul leaving in company of the Vairagi ECK Masters. The attending physician reported death by heart attack. And the fifth initiate's mold had been dutifully, if lovingly, fulfilled.

Naturally many chelas were shocked by the suddenness of Paul's departure, but they gradually adjusted, some sooner than later, to his leaving the responsibilities to a new Living ECK Master. There are no secrets in ECK and some even had immediate perception that Paul had transcended to an area where he could serve the SUGMAD with even greater freedom. Bernadine Burlin, several years before becoming Sri Darwin's personal secretary, wrote the following in her dream diary on the morning of September 17, 1971:

"Greg [son] and I were with many others in a large room. Paul was walking around, chatting and smiling, looking wonderful. Gail was with him. I began washing dishes and remarked how sunny the room was—part of the roof was glass. Dream quite lengthy. I came up to Paul, touched his arm and told him how marvelous he looked. He hugged me and buzzed around all of us informally. It felt like a great celebration. When I awakened it was 1:00 a.m. the morning of September 17, 1971. When a friend called me, in tears about Paul's translation, I told her my dream and knew the celebration of life continued for us all."

Having begun her studies of ECKANKAR with Sri Paul Twitchell and continued under the spiritual guidance of Sri Darwin Gross, Bernadine (BB) was not only present at the Fifth ECKANKAR World Wide Seminar for the announcement of the new Living ECK Master, but also aware of some of the differences and, more important, similarities between these two spiritual giants:

"In December 1968 I signed up for the ECKANKAR Discourses and set sail upon the cosmic seas of ECK, an urging for which I am forever grateful.

"I first met Paul Twitchell in February 1969 when he spoke to a group gathered in Los Angeles, but I had grown to love him through his written words, the monthly discourses and the ECK books. His words struck home with me time and again, and I knew that my search was indeed over...once and for all.

"While my relationship with Paulji [Paul Twitchell/ Peddar Zaskq] on the outer was restricted to hearing him speak at lectures and occasionally shaking his hand, the inner relationship was a totally different story. This inner rapport developed slowly through the disciplines of the spiritual exercises of ECKANKAR, and in the dream state. He was warm, affectionate, responsive...we ate together, walked together, worked together... I sat at his feet, the Master and the Chela, on the velvety green hillsides of some distant plane, while he discoursed on many subjects. In visions, his presence reassured me countless times I had nothing to fear. And trust I did.

"Paulji continues to visit me from time to time in the dream state with warmth and affection. I am very grateful for his guidance and acceptance, and I know our paths will continue to cross throughout eternity. Incidentally, I felt it rather prophetic that he, the 971st Living ECK Master, chose to translate September 1971—9/71.

"When we gathered in Las Vegas that eventful October 1971, to learn the identity of our next Living ECK Master

115

of ECKANKAR, the air was electric with excitement. We had seen Darwin Gross many times at various seminars, a handsome, friendly young man who expressed his love for the ECK through his beautiful songs and piano. He would greet us warmly whenever he'd see us, so it was natural to call out to him that evening in Las Vegas as he was leaving the hotel. The idea was to invite him to join us for dinner. But he grinned, waved and hurried on his way. Three hours later he was announced by Gail Twitchell as our new Living ECK Master. I actually jumped up and down like a kid!

"Although I still identified for awhile with Paulji's presence, it was not difficult to give love to this new Master, and once I realized that the Inner Presence was STILL the same, that it had not changed no matter who the outer Master had become, I truly placed the attention and support where it needed to be for ME to grow...upon Sri Darwin Gross, the MAHANTA, the Living ECK Master of ECKANKAR."

Another ECKist, living in a more isolated part of Canada, was soon to recognize the same important Truth: "When Paul translated, there was a period of confusion for many of his chelas who were rather newly on the path of ECKANKAR or who were isolated from chelas with the understanding needed to carry them through this period. I was one of them and during this period Paul continued to appear in my dream states to give me counsel and love. Then one day it was Darwin who appeared and I knew that they were one and the same, the ECK, even though they outwardly in their physical bodies exhibited different personalities and mannerisms."

This same chela was aware, however, that even in the physical expression in the presentation of the message of ECK to the world, Paul and Darwin were curiously similar: "They both taught ECK in much the same manner—no grand orations or gestures, no special voice inflections which would have provided them with an 'attention-getting' device. Nor did they wear fancy clothes or insist on dramatic settings in which they could be 'framed' to show how exalted they were and are. Indeed, neither Paul nor Darwin were or are 'showmen.' Paul was and Darwin is a quiet speaker, making pithy statements, wearing simple, subdued clothing. Each talked without notes, with a feeling of being unrehearsed and straight from the Soul and each revealed themselves to have a gentle sense of humor, able to give as well as to receive."

Reflecting on the evening of the historic announcement of his mission as the 972nd Living ECK Master, the MAHANTA in this and all worlds, Sri Darwin said: "That night I was put on a stage in Las Vegas, I was scared. I didn't know what I was going to say. I didn't know how the people would accept me, not so much the personality, because the personality doesn't have a thing to do with it. Some people stepped off the path of ECK, when I took the ECK Rod of Power, because they didn't like me, my personality perhaps. It was different from Paul. They were attuned to his personality, which Paul stressed all the time he was here, not to look at that part. Let that be.

"It's like jumping into the ocean without a lifesaver. But knowing that you're going to be taken care of.... Even on this path, the initiated—take the person who was initiated by Sri Paul Twitchell, and then he takes off, translates, and the next Living ECK Master came along, which happened to be me. I still have a spiritual function to perform with some of his initiates in this physical world, but in the spiritual world, those that are initiated by him, he's taking care of part of their spiritual growth and unfoldment. They'll reach a point where I must assist spiritually."

One ECK chela, a seventh initiate at the time, took several months to come to this very important realization. When she did, she wrote it down and her comments were published in *The Mystic World*, August/September 1972 issue:

"Since the World Wide Seminar in Las Vegas last October, I began having problems, not real major catastrophes,

117

but minor changes in attitudes, health problems, distractions during my periods of contemplation, jealousies and resentments began creeping in and I really didn't like myself. I felt like the ECK which I'd loved so much was slipping from my grasp and I was powerless to stop it. I knew that the Master would never leave me so it must be I who had separated myself from the ECK Stream and I was not happy. I realized what I was doing wrong, and all I could get in contemplation was 'physician heal thyself,' and then one day it happened.

"As I stood dressing one morning, not feeling well at all and really thinking of climbing back into bed because I hurt, Dap Ren [Sri Darwin Gross] appeared and stood beside me and I saw him in the mirror. In a very simple and humble manner he asked, 'Why have you refused my help? Why won't you let me heal you?' I started to reply, 'because I know it is my own fault. I created it and,' but then I couldn't finish, as the wondrous realization and understanding flowed through me and healed me, and I thought, 'Dear God how could I have neglected my Master so.'

"We have to have the Outer Master. The only way to the SUGMAD is through him. There is never a time in the history of the world that the Living ECK Master is not here. Those of us who have been fortunate to serve under two Living ECK Masters in one lifespan must accept the truth of this. It doesn't mean that we love Paulji less, but we must let the personality go. The only way to reach the ascended Masters or the SUGMAD is through the Living ECK Master who is the GODMAN. As I contemplated on the importance and meaning of all that had befallen me, I was guided to Chapter Twelve of THE SPIRITUAL NOTEBOOK and then I realized how I had neglected one of the three main principles of ECK. I was practicing the Presence of the wrong Master. Forgive me Dap Ren for now I can seek no other as you are he: the Sat Guru, the Mahanta, the SUGMAD of ITSELF."

The job of the Living ECK Master is not easy. It is the

most thankless job in the world as well as underpaid, yet in other ways it is the most rewarding. A chela wrote to Sri Darwin: "The one big lesson for me was the magnitude of the sacrifice of yourself and Paul, and other Great Beings, who have voluntarily come back to earth during this grim Kali Yuga to help the rest of us to find our way back to SUGMAD. And we, through our ignorance give you a bad time! But we do gradually learn a little. Thank you for your love and patience."

In *The Shariyat-Ki-Sugmad*, the sacred scriptures of ECKANKAR known as The Way of the Eternal, it is stated that the Living ECK Master "is the transformer, the divine channel for the ECK." His purpose is to show those Souls who are ready the way back HOME into the reality of the pure positive God Worlds: "The Living ECK Master is above time and space. He is God's essential expression and is never separated from the source of true wisdom and reality. He is able to see the past, know the future and to give healings, happiness and create miracles for those whom he loves, and those who believe and can accept his gifts. For all those who have reached the state of consciousness of the knowing level shall realize who they are and shall be ready to receive the gifts as dispensed by the Living ECK Master.

"The work of the Living ECK Master has already been finished with every chela who comes to him to be lifted up. He knows what the chela is ready to receive before the petition is made. He gives all to the chela in advance but if the chela is not ready, there is no recognition that he has already received his gift. When the chela is ready, the gift shall be recognized and received with the joy and blessings of the Living ECK Master."

In this, their spiritual function, Sri Darwin Gross and Sri Paul Twitchell, his predecessor are one and the same, identical. Their spiritual message is the same, that the pillars of the Light and Sound of ECK lead the way back to God and the end of all karma in the lower worlds. The more specialized missions of Darwin and Paul in this world, their personalities, their ways of fulfilling their missions express unique individuality, with Darwin's major objectives being a natural expansion and evolution of the foundation established by Paul.

Paul had presented the message of ECK to the waiting world as ECKANKAR, the Ancient Science of Soul Travel. Some attention was put on achieving awareness beyond oneself through Soul Travel, movement of the inner consciousness as Soul through the worlds of duality, of matter and spirit, through the physical, the astral, the causal, the mental and etheric planes to the first step of Self-Realization on the Fifth plane of consciousness known as the Soul plane—the awakening into "Consciousness Five," Paul called it, and even wrote a guide book through these planes he called *The Tiger's Fang*.

Darwin accepted the challenge and took ECKANKAR the next step, into Consciousness Five, presenting the teachings as ECKANKAR, the Path of Total Awareness. Placing the attention on moving beyond the lower worlds of duality into the pure positive God Worlds of BEING, KNOWING and SEEING. From this 360 degree point of view there was no need of "travel," but simply being aware of what was wanted at any given point, shifting emphasis beyond Self-Realization to the next step of God-Realization, to those limitless areas beyond the Fifth plane. Some individuals tended to intellectualize this and missed the point. A little later to more simply and directly present the message of ECK, the timeless teachings of Soul, Darwin focused on presenting them as ECKANKAR, A Way of Life, so that individuals from all walks of life and all backgrounds could understand what ECKANKAR has to offer them as individuals.

Paul was an intellectual who had studied history and other paths extensively. He was a writer by profession who appealed to all levels of consciousness through his writings on practically every topic. Darwin is a man of scientific orientation as well as a musician, a man of song, of feeling and intuition, who appeals more directly to Soul often bypassing the mind to lift the individual beyond the mental realms of the lower worlds of creation into the heights of pure consciousness. Both came from small towns, were primarily self-educated men of common sense and unlimited potential, multi-faceted, multi-talented, rugged individualists entirely devoted to SUGMAD and Spirit. Paul was the Master from the beginning and established as the Mahanta Consciousness. Darwin was first a chela in this life who quickly matured into the Living ECK Master and the awesome responsibilities associated with that state. The first few years or so of the ECK Mastership he was working into and establishing himself as the Mahanta, reaching into that state of highest consciousness—the ultimate spiritual challenge, privilege and responsibility.

On the physical level, as well as the spiritual, Darwin committed himself wholeheartedly with single-minded devotion and service to the SUGMAD, the ECK and the chelas of ECKANKAR. Paul had established the core of the ECK writings through many books and discourses, enough for many hundreds of years to come, according to Sri Darwin. Consequently, Darwin initially focused on initiating and delegating programs and projects to strengthen the physical, as well as the spiritual network of Arahatas, Area Representatives and Mahdis in the field. Many times he has stated that it is the ECK chelas who are the organization of ECKANKAR, that the physical office exists only as a base to provide the books and discourses, provide information to that individual who is seeking to take the next step, to provide materials needed in the field in presenting the message of ECK in a pure and simple manner, and to provide guidance in certain areas needed to maintain this objective.

Darwin commented: "It's been a hard role, physically. I've had to kind of watch what was going on, otherwise things could have gotten out of hand. Now I'm fortunate,

121

we have a very good Board to help with guiding the physical part. I'll only make suggestions and help guide it. They have the daily work on the business side so now I can get off into the discourses and other things more spiritual."

Paul had had little interest or experience in organizational matters and was not so much involved in that aspect than what was absolutely necessary. Darwin had had executive positions in the business world and more interest in leadership of this kind. Serving as President of the ECKANKAR Board of Trustees, he took the helm in welcoming those aboard to guide them and train them as required in their assisting to get out the message of ECK. Commenting on the opportunity to assist the Living ECK Master in this regard, a staff member at the ECKANKAR International Office said: "I'm the luckiest person on earth to be working with a man so full of love, devotion to an ideal and a sense of humor."

Darwin established a system of teamwork in the Office and in the field. He spent the first few years of his Mastership traveling extensively throughout the world to meet with the ECK chelas and to talk with those at seminars and introductory presentations of ECK about this most ancient spiritual teaching and what it has to offer the individual: "Preservation of the individual Self throughout Eternity as a conscious co-worker with God." He traveling tirelessly to meet the newcomer, to give the Darshan, to ignite the Atma of the initiate, to shake the hand of the newcomer, "to bring Light and Love into the worlds." In Montreal a chela brought a fresh red rosebud to give the Master. Although the physical meeting did not occur, it was given with the heart in divine love, and it was received and acknowledged by the Master. At the end of Darwin's sixty-minute talk, the chela noticed the edges of the perfectly red rosebud had become streaked with iridescence as if dipped in silverdust.

In Jacksonville, Florida the gift of spiritual love was passed from Master to chela as Darwin stood at the front of the stage to shake hands with each and every one in the audience who came forth. The long line formed down one aisle to the stage, and one by one, one after the other, each came up the other aisle transformed within themselves, many with tears of gratitude and joy flowing from their eyes spontaneously. After so many lifetimes of wandering, searching through lifetime after lifetime, they had earned the opportunity to again meet the Godman, the Vi-Guru, the Lightgiver... and this time recognized him and accepted the gift of liberation as Soul. And the same scene repeated, with infinite variation appropriate to each moment, to each Soul... in Zurich and Milan, in London and Oslo, in Lome, Africa, New Zealand, Australia, Mexico, Greece, New York, Los Angeles, Seattle, San Francisco, Chicago, Houston, Miami, British Columbia, Central America, Peru, Hawaii, Japan, India, Singapore, Chattanooga, Syracuse, Beaver Bend and on and on and on in all the levels of Heaven.

At the same time Darwin devoted himself to presenting the message of ECK through the written word as well as the spoken word. He writes a special monthly "Wisdom Notes" to the ECK chelas, articles for *The Mystic World* (a bi-monthly publication for members which now includes the "Wisdom Notes"), the *ECK Mata Journal* (an annual magazine of chela experiences with the Light and Sound), the *ECK World News* (currently discontinued), *Leadership in ECK* (a periodic informational bulletin for the ECKANKAR leadership), the *Leaflet* (a publication to higher initiates), and many other pamphlets and articles. He completed *The ECK-Ynari*, *The Secret Knowledge of Dreams* discourses and the *Satsang III* discourses both begun by Sri Paul Twitchell. He wrote a series of discourses for the higher initiates *ECK, The Sacred Way*, a pamphlet "ECKANKAR, A Way of Life," and the book *Your Right to Know*, and is simultaneously working on several manuscripts, one of which is an introduction to the Shariyat-Ki-Sugmad, the sacred scriptures of ECK from the Golden Wisdom Temples.

And all of this while establishing special spiritual training programs and introductory talk and seminar systems that place responsibilities on the local leaders in ECK as a foundation for growth in the field. And while attending as many seminars as possible himself in the physical and *all* seminars, talks, Satsang classes, etc. on the inner in his spiritual body on all the planes of God.

CHAPTER 6

A Year Crammed into a Day

To all appearances, Sri Darwin Gross is a splendid version of the average man. He stands 6' 1" tall, carries his weight well, is athletic in build, ruggedly-handsome with blue eyes that piercingly penetrate. In a crowd he moves along with the flow of people seemingly undistinguishable from the rest, but those who have walked with him notice how he draws the quick glance of the passerby as though he were a magnet of some kind, a magnet of love.

The average man certainly does not carry the weight of the Living ECK Master's spiritual responsibilities, nor would his day-to-day workload be considered average. Those who work closely with Darwin are acutely aware of how conscientiously he oversees the business activities at the ECKANKAR International Office in Menlo Park, California, how he smoothes out situations with personality conflicts within ECKANKAR, as well as outside of ECK, how he attends and guides meetings, many regional seminars and ECKANKAR events, as well as the three major ECKANKAR seminars: the World Wide of ECK held on the closest weekend to October 22nd of each year, the International Youth Conference, held annually around Easter weekend, and the Creative Arts Festival, held mid-June to commemorate Children's Day.

Wherever and whenever Darwin Gross enters the scene, things hum into smooth action at top-speed. The physical whir of action is visible to all who are a part of the moment, but the spiritual side is no less affected and felt by the worlds and planets and universes under the

125

Living ECK Master's spiritual care.

Interspersed with his twenty-four hour a day responsibility, Darwin contributes introductory talks, is interviewed by well-known television media and radio station personnel, travels extensively to all countries, and finds an occasional hour or two to play his vibes, walk in the woods or soak up some sun. His heavy schedule is bruising and fast-paced and not in the least "average," yet he takes his time.

A typical day will begin around eight in the morning; however, he's been up since five or six o'clock. He will be at the ECKANKAR International Office twenty minutes before anyone else, if he's coming in. Whipping around the main office, he'll collect bodies like magnets:

"BB, Mike, Janice—can you come?"

They move out to the Production Department of the ECKANKAR Office, where he meets with the Production Manager. The secretaries take notes, Mike adds some comments, and gradually Darwin peels the threesome apart:

"Janice, you can go." In a moment: "You too, BB."

And he's off to another part of the building.

One day Darwin's personal secretary, Bernadine Burlin (BB), was scouting the building for him. "I found him standing in the warehouse gazing intently at the ceiling. I watched him watching the ceiling for a moment and then learned that he was figuring out ways to utilize the space under the roof as shelves for ECK books. Another time when I couldn't locate him, he was up on the roof assessing where to put up an antenna. I never know where he'll turn up. But what impresses me is that no job is ever too menial for Darwin to tackle."

He holds meetings all day long and often into the evenings as well. In the midst of one meeting, held in the auditorium at the ECKANKAR Office because of the number of people involved, Darwin was discussing an office policy but stopped abruptly when two staff members were observed whispering to each other. "Speak up! Don't ever whisper or talk behind my back. Say it out loud so everyone can hear it." The whispering couple complied, embarrassed, yet aware that a lesson had been learned and all those in the room made mental notes as well.

Around 30-45 days prior to any ECKANKAR seminar, Darwin feels the pull and tug of those planning, participating and attending these important events. Regional seminars are handled primarily from the field, overseen by the Area Mahdis, while major ECKANKAR seminars are handled from the ECKANKAR Office, working with ECK leaders in the area of the seminar site.

To the ECKist, a major seminar may be the only opportunity for them to see, hear and possibly meet their spiritual leader, the Living ECK Master. With every major seminar, the mail increases. Posters and brochures are sent out. Preregistration heightens the excitement. ECK books are packed to go to the seminar, along with art work and newly acquired items like tapes, new book editions, etc. The Office buzzes between exhilaration and exhaustion!

Decisions are made by Sri Darwin as to program highlights, themes, speakers, and placement of Office personnel in areas of service at the seminar site. Flight reservations are made, hotel rooms relegated to personnel and a suite with bedroom and parlor set aside for Darwin, for meetings as well as spiritual consultations. As the seminar date draws closer, excitement mounts both in the ECKANKAR Office and in the field. The pace gallops for all concerned and Darwin's ability to sleep gets less and less.

Usually Darwin travels to the seminar with one or two of the staff members. Occasionally he will sleep or doze throughout the flight, but more than likely he will conduct business with either or both of the individuals with him.

At a recent stopover in Chicago, between planes, Darwin enjoyed two hot dogs with mustard, without the buns. He topped them off with strawberry yogurt, reboarded the next flight and divided the rest of the journey to the seminar between reading magazines and pacing the plane in an effort to stretch his legs. Already the ECK current flowed through him so intensely bumps and welts appeared on his feet and his heels itched. Now and then he'd massage the calves of his legs or pound his legs with his fists.

Met at the airport by the hotel limousine and another staff member, Darwin and his crew moved quickly through the city and to the seminar hotel. In the lobby he was whisked to his suite, but not before a plump, middle-aged woman spotted him, whipped around to her friend, "It's him! Madge, look, it's him!" She gave him a hearty hug. He tried not to wince from the discomfort he still experienced from back surgery, to remove two inches of a rib, which he had undergone less than four months earlier. The staff members, Mike and BB, readied the elevator and tried to unobtrusively usher him in, but they knew better than to interfere with the Master's association with his chela and Darwin's consideration of them all.

Once in his room, the bed was tested for firmness. "It's soft!" He prefers a hard mattress or often sleeps on the floor. When other rooms and firmer beds were offered for his use, he declined wearily, "No, I'll take what Spirit provided."

It was a relaxed evening with club soda and grape juice, fruit provided by the seminar people, and nuts passed around by Darwin. He reviewed the seminar schedule, the type of microphone he'd be using, the stool available to him on stage and the props he'd require, such as a God Worlds Chart or the sketches of the ECK Masters. Propped up on the bed against a pillow, Darwin was left alone to watch some television, his favorite shows being Star Trek, Battlestar Galactica, Buck Rogers, good mystery stories and westerns. It was one o'clock in the morning.

This particular seminar was a regional on the east coast and the overall atmosphere was relaxed and friendly. The people had come from surrounding states either by car or air. When Darwin appeared in the lobby they would approach him singly and shyly, reach out to touch his hand, their faces bright with love; then they'd step back, almost overwhelmed to have been that bold with him.

After a light breakfast, Darwin took a walk. He spoke with BB about his travel plans which would include some European countries, possibly Russia. The spring air was brisk and invigorating but he had to use caution in regards to chills that assaulted the still tender areas from the back surgery. On the walk he was aware of a couple following him at a respectable distance. He bought a pair of light blue slacks and an extra undershirt as added warmth, once again aware of another couple who watched him from a distance.

In the evening Darwin gave a talk, very basic in its simplicity, describing the levels of heaven to the audience and using the God Worlds Chart to implement the talk:

"Those of you that are new to ECKANKAR and its teachings, as well as the ECKists, go slow! There is no hurry and I'll ask you not to believe me! We deal with Soul Travel, not the movement of bodies. In the ECK discourses as well as in the ECK books, you learn to keep the various lower bodies intact. The teachings of ECK take up and make up all walks of life and all teachings. We are not saying it's the only path to God but the one direct path to God."

Many newcomers attended, even people from the hotel who were fascinated by the care and preparation that had gone into Darwin's visit by the personnel from the ECKANKAR Office.

A leadership meeting, led by Mike and Lynne, followed Darwin's talk in the auditorium. He had gone to his room to have a private meeting with four of the Higher Initiates in ECK. An important issue needed resolving and the principals were visibly upset. "I need to know WHY you are doing this, Darwin," one stated heatedly.

"I don't have to explain my reasons for doing any-

129

thing," Darwin replied evenly. "The decision by the Living ECK Master should be respected. I don't owe anyone an explanation. Sounds like you are attached to the chelas in the area, the area itself and this situation here." The spokesman reluctantly agreed that might be so.

The half-hour meeting ended with feathers being smoothed and problems resolved, hugs exchanged and sincere declarations of love for the Master. At no time did Darwin raise his voice or indicate censure of their anger and frustration. The Higher Initiates are the "Right Arm of the Living ECK Master," the vehicles of Spirit used to spread the message of ECK in their communities, vehicles who are open spiritually to the ECK flow and who are to make the word of ECK available to all who wish to return to the Godhead. These vehicles are dear to Darwin, he loves them with a divine love, and they love him deeply.

His feet had swollen and were itching him from the ECK current surging through his physical body. Darwin accepted an offer of a foot massage, his physical vehicle fatigued and drained, yet too keyed up for rest and sleep. By midnight he was ready for some dinner and a cab was called. The cabbie referred to his garden that sadly needed rain. "It'll rain by tomorrow," Darwin winked at a staff member. The cabbie was impressed. "Them's m'eats, y'know, I need to have 'em grow." He turned his head toward Darwin. "You sure it'll rain?"

"It'll rain tomorrow," Darwin repeated.

It did.

Back from dinner, Darwin entered the hotel lobby as a small group of ECKists were softly singing ECK songs. As he approached they eased into "Oh, How I Love Thee, Blessed Sugmad," the words and music composed by Darwin in admiration of Sri Paul Twitchell. Darwin leaned against a railing and sang with them, his voice rich and vibrant. Lingering a few moments, he thanked them for their music and their love. Then he headed for the elevator and his room.

At a major ECKANKAR seminar, thousands of ECKists and hundreds of new people throng to see and hear the Living ECK Master. At the Creative Arts Festival, Darwin delighted the audience by playing his vibraharp sometimes as a solo, often with a selected group of musical performers. Occasionally he would sing one of the many songs he had composed for love, life and of the Supreme Being he served in a totality few could know or understand.

On one occasion on stage, he wore a leather vest, cowboy hat and thumped a handmade instrument that consisted of a stringed broom handle in a bucket. He was joined by a couple of guitarists in ten-gallon hats. The audience loved the delightful ECK songs delivered with a "hillbilly" flavoring. Darwin's fingers required two bandaids following this performance.

At the ECKANKAR World Wide Seminar in Baltimore, October 1979, Darwin's accelerating back pain made it difficult for him to stand for any period of time. In January of the following year, he would undergo a second surgery to correct a frozen rib joint under his left shoulder blade. But no matter how his physical body was hurting, his responsibility to the chelas of ECK came first.

During one talk he drew a large and beautiful conch shell from a small bag he had brought on stage. "I brought it from Hawaii. Its sounds remind me of the sounds of HU one can hear in all things. Would you like to hear it?"

Indeed they did! A moving silence followed the hauntingly beautiful tones.

He had stood for an hour throughout his talk and then invited the chelas from Africa to join him on stage. About thirty-five or forty Africans, from Nigeria, Togo, Ghana and the Ivory Coast, huddled shyly around Darwin, their eyes glowing with happiness, their hearts joyous. Through a French interpreter, Elena Favale of Milano, Italy, Darwin conversed with these people, having them introduce themselves and tell something of the adventures that had brought them to the seminar, as well as to the path of ECKANKAR. It was the first trip for most of them and the obstacles had often been great, but nothing was going to stand in the way of their coming to this World Wide Seminar of ECKANKAR and meeting their Living ECK Master.

Every one of them began their story with "Merci, Mahanta!" Gratitude was evident in every word and the audience heard hair-raising tales of how they met resistance in their efforts to come. Several of them sang ECK songs in French and the youngsters presented Darwin with a special gift.

Now Darwin had been standing for three hours. He had been offered a high stool by concerned staff members who knew his back pain must be excruciating by this time, but instead he had quietly requested that chairs be brought on stage for the African ladies.

"Why doesn't someone get him off the stage?" a member of the ECKANKAR Board of Trustees muttered.

"Because you don't interfere with the Master and his chelas," BB answered. "I wouldn't presume to do a thing beyond what we've done—offer him a chair. It's the Living ECK Master up there on stage, the physical body doesn't matter to him at this point."

The African chelas left the stage and Darwin ended the morning's session, but his day was just beginning. He moved slowly through the crowd to a back room where he met for another hour with the chelas who had come from countries outside of the United States and Canada. They did not often get to attend seminars where they could meet the Outer Master. He drank distilled water and leaned against a high stool at the front of the room. He chatted with them informally, masking his fatigue with laughter and listening to each as though they were the most important individuals in the world. Finally he eased himself toward the door.

Four staff members flanked Darwin on all sides on the slow walk back to the hotel. One murmured, "Boy, you sure gave the African chelas a lot of time on stage. It was incredible, the love that comes from those devoted people. But we could see it was hard on you."

"I was OK," Darwin smiled weakly, but his eyes sparkled. "I wanted the audience to see how some chelas in the world learn to rely solely on the Inner Master for their spiritual guidance and protection. They don't have access to the Outer Master but their devotion and gratitude to Spirit brings them through every situation no matter how difficult. We have things easy here by comparison and it was important that the African chelas share their stories and their love for the Master."

A Higher Initiate massaged Darwin's back and announced that he was dozing. But before too long, he was at the Secretary's door, looking surprisingly refreshed.

"BB, how many consultations do I have?"

"About 40 have requested consultations, Darwin."

"Let me look them over. What time is the next meeting?"

"Around two o'clock if you're up to it."

"Good. Tell them I'll be ready." He moved out of the doorway but called back, "Oh, BB, I want to call a meeting of the Higher Initiates tonight after my talk."

BB, Janice and Lynne looked at each other incredulously and shook their heads. "Isn't he something?" They marveled at the resilience of the man, how swiftly he could rally his strength so as to move forward as a vehicle for the SUGMAD, the Supreme Deity.

Now their work began in earnest. Mike was notified to ready a large room in the hotel to hold over 600 Higher Initiates who might be attending the World Wide of ECK. An announcement of this meeting was prepared to precede Darwin's evening talk. Lynne notified the Board Members that Darwin had OK'd their meeting later that afternoon, and as Darwin reviewed the consultation slips, he placed those he had accepted on the secretary's table.

Each of the three seminar assistants got to a telephone to

notify the consultees that Darwin would see them at a set time and place. Generally, Darwin gives consultations only to members of ECKANKAR; however, he has seen many uninitiated as well, those in specific need, such as a spiritual uncertainty or a pressing situation that they felt needed the Master's guidance. The consultations may run 10-15 minutes or as long as 30 minutes with a donation requested at the time of the consultation for the ECK Message Fund.

Three of these consultations were completed before Darwin's next meeting convened, and several more consultations were lined up to follow the meeting. Then Darwin was reminded he did not have much time before his evening talk.

There was a brief respite for him to have a glass of juice and a shower before he was ready to walk over to the seminar site with several of the Staff. Backstage he shook hands with performers and stage personnel. He sat quietly waiting his turn, occasionally glancing at a few notes in his pocket. A young man was improvising an ECK song on the piano and Darwin lifted his eyes as though listening, but he seemed preoccupied. BB and Lynne sat nearby.

Spotting Mike in the wings, he motioned him over. "I want to visit the Children's Room tomorrow, maybe after lunch. Have Joan there with her camera. BB, tell Harold I'll need some feedback on the Sedona property before the Board meets in the morning. I want Harold to be there too. I have some higher initiations to give following tonight's Higher Initiate's meeting. I'll begin the meeting and you three run through the Mahdis Training procedures with them. If there are any questions you can't answer, get back to me on them."

The emcee announced that a HU chant would precede the Master's appearance. As the HU, in harmonious tones, filled the arena, Darwin moved slowly onto the stage, removed his suit coat and loosened his tie. The lavalier microphone was secured around his neck. The HU became fainter and fainter.

"Ladies and Gentlemen, Sri Darwin Gross, the MAHANTA, the Living ECK Master."

Some of the subject matter Darwin used in his talk came from situations he had read in the consultation slips. If he couldn't see these people personally, he could relay answers to them from the stage if they were aware enough to spot them. It usually assisted countless others who had similar experiences:

"We have to use common sense in our relationships with others. Communication is important between mates but if an atmosphere is emotionally charged or the principals are tired, they should wait and talk their disagreements out at another time. I'd just remove myself from an environment that was emotionally charged. I wouldn't want to be a part of it. People judge situations without knowing all the facts about them.

"One time during a seminar I went into a tavern to get a six-pack of club soda and someone saw me go in. Before long it was all over that Darwin had been in a tavern. They didn't even know what I'd gone in there for; they were judging me due to a stigma in their minds. Prejudging is a very negative thing; it's one of the claws of maya, illusion. That's where the word 'prejudice' comes from. I just laughed at it and didn't say anything to justify my activities. I didn't rebel or try to explain anything. Later on I straightened it out from the platform when I gave a talk. We are watched constantly, not only by our own people but by other groups and religious orders. However, more than that, from the invisible side at all times."

He took his watch off and laid it on the table before taking a sip of water:

"Sometimes I feel this body's 300 years old. Other times, I feel like I'm 21 or 16. It depends on the situation. If you talk about age, it depends on where you're coming from. The actual physical age makes no difference. I know people are curious, but age has nothing to do with one's spiritual unfoldment. Yes, I've changed. When we take on more responsibility, you allow a certain amount of this ECK current, the life force, to flow through you. I have to regulate it, otherwise it would burn my body up. The Higher Initiates will find this happening also; they'll change drastically as their responsibilities increase. Working out problems, healing people, guiding them, assisting in so many ways, physically it affects me. I may not take on karma, but I help them work it off. If they have a specific function for us on the spiritual side of life, here in ECK, I'll help them. I don't have to, but there's no where else they can get this help.

"I had to be shown. I became a believer by being shown. In order to bring about a greater understanding, not only in this country but in the world as a whole, and in other dimensions, other worlds, it is very necessary for me to do this. I have chosen to do some of that sort of thing.

"There are spiritual principles in the pure positive God Worlds which exist and are spoken of throughout the *Stranger By The River* by Sri Paul Twitchell, which is the Testament of the ECKist. There are spiritual laws and if man understood and tried to practice these, things would be different. Before a seminar, and after I go through a great physical stress, in the physical realm alone, sometimes as much as a month or two, down to a couple of weeks before that seminar, I'm out of commission. The body takes a beating in many, many ways.

"I am a vehicle for Spirit, the ECK Current. Some people get to see the shaft of current coming down into the aura and body, then flow out. Sometimes others can see the current emanating out of my hands into the outer, from my body out. This does happen but I don't do it deliberately; I don't have to. Some people will see some of the ECK Masters for they do appear. None of us are ever alone on the path of ECKANKAR. We have a line of communication with Spirit to God.

"I moved on to a much greater communication with

meetings with my spiritual teacher, Sri Paul Twitchell, receiving initiations into the ECK Itself more directly. As a younger person, I could only go up to the mental plane, no further. When a child cries during sleep, it isn't a nightmare. Soul doesn't want to come back to the human state of consciousness. With that understanding, those people who have frightful dreams are being shown what existed in the lower worlds and going beyond themselves, such as astral projection. If they knew this, they wouldn't be afraid, for they always have a spiritual guide with them. Some of the techniques are given in various ECK books. They explain what takes place. A marvelous road map was brought forth in Paul Twitchell's *The Tiger's Fang*. It details Paul's journey through the many levels of heaven, from the physical, astral, causal, mental, etheric and Soul planes, including the pure positive God Worlds."

When Darwin finished his talk, he moved down into the audience, several Staff Members making a way for him. He grasped outstretched hands from every direction, no one particularly pushing towards him, just content to be in his presence.

On the way to the Higher Initiate's meeting, a few ECKists trailed behind Darwin, reluctant to lose sight of the physical Master they loved so dearly. He was tired and his feet were swollen.

"Mike, I'll slip into the Children's Room before I have that television interview tomorrow. And I'd like to look in at the Book Room for a few minutes later on tomorrow and maybe sign a few copies of *Your Right To Know.*" Darwin's new book was just off the presses and already garnering much interest from the public, the press, and the ECKists.

He entered the room where the Higher Initiates were awaiting him, slipping out 30 minutes later with those who were to receive their higher initiations. Then he went out with a couple of friends for a late-night snack, returning around 2:30 in the morning, his day and theirs, finally coming to a halt—on the physical anyway.

* * * * * * *

In putting this book together, BB asked Darwin what his normal day was like and he was quiet, really didn't want to talk about it. He likes to be alone, likes to walk and swim, enjoys the sunshine, the song of the birds. As you have read earlier, he loves all life, including animals, birds and children, not necessarily in that order. His usual day begins with his arising quite early and going to bed quite late, with walks in between during the day and sometimes at night, more than likely in the evening with or without the stars out bright and shining.

There are always Initiates' letters to read, occasionally one or two to answer, for it is virtually impossible to answer all of them physically. There are interruptions which seem to come constantly from either the ECKANKAR International Office, about a situation in some area of the world, or from individuals spread around this world and their situations which are usually emotional difficulties and personality conflicts which he doesn't care to get involved in.

In his cheerful living room, Darwin went on to say: "As one progresses spiritually on this path of ECK, the individual learns to rely on the inner communication, keeping the day to day life in perspective using common sense. It is called a balance.

"The Living ECK Master needs time to do his spiritual work, to assist via that vehicle of God known as Spirit, ECK as it is called in ECKANKAR, only when asked. This is an area where the various groups have banded together, religious groups primarily, as well as some eastern ones, in an attempt to do away with ECKANKAR and those who follow its teachings.

"I'm straying from what I do during the day, yet it involves it. Individuals cry out for help inwardly because of either a physical or verbal attack from a complete stranger, friend or relative. When I'm at home alone, I eat sparingly due to not only the fact it's good healthwise, but also a shortage of food in some parts of the world, hoping it will assist and be helpful to others in less privileged countries. It is rare for me to get more than a couple of hours sleep a night because of my spiritual responsibilities, and if I feel the need to rest in the afternoon, the physical duties are such any rest is short-lived.

"As ECKANKAR grows in this world and the Living ECK Master's time becomes more devoted to assisting individuals in the dream state, as well as the awake state, they draw energy from the Radiant Form which affects the physical.

"I like to play the vibes occasionally, or the piano, but rarely have time. Sometimes I feel I'd like to do as Paul stated, go out to the ocean and just keep walking, but there is someone who has been helped and this continually gives me the courage to know that one is working for the good of the Whole. I read a number of magazines and newspapers to keep abreast of the negative world news and local activities. I do my own laundry, mending, and iron my own shirts.

"There is a constant observation of various individuals' spiritual growth which must be attended to. There is also a constant and continual planning of the various seminars, not only helping guide the physical and spiritual part but getting involved in those areas that tend to go negative and straighten it out."

At the June 1980 Creative Arts Festival in Las Vegas, Nevada, Darwin commented from the stage: "Funny things happen to me when I get before a crowd especially trying to sing or play an instrument and I think I'm going to give it up! Because someone over in Africa, Europe, or it could be on the other side of the United States, or up in Canada or the North Woods, Yukon or Alaska, they're pulling at me, asking about this or that, and my attention, when it comes to this [playing the vibes], I am unable to devote time to music totally. I know most in ECKANKAR understand that.

"There's a way for those of you who aren't ECK Masters that if you get to the top of the mountain, you don't have that kind of trouble, but once you reach that area and start working beyond five bodies and in six, then you start having those difficulties down here on Earth. It's like some of the early men of this world have usually built their homes or abodes high on a hill or in a mountain, on the highest spot on the plains, so they could see what was coming, and in their limited vision, or some unlimited, were able to reach the top of the mountain by going to that temple within."

CHAPTER 7

Reaping the Whirlwinds

"Modern religious teachings conceived that God would take care of the good and send wrath upon the wicked, that anyone who obeyed the moral laws would receive God's grace, abundant health and prosperity. The whole key to this sort of teaching lies in a failure of consciousness of those who are striving for the material end alone, for SUGMAD cares little for the physical and material embodiments which exist in this world. IT is interested only in the preservation of the individuality of Soul, not the astral and mental laws of morality," stated Sri Darwin Gross in *The Mystic World,* July-August-September, 1979.

"However, those who work as leaders in the field or in the ECKANKAR Office as management or a supervisor must uphold the law of this world of morality," Darwin has commented. "There have been those that feel they can be discreet and still play people games of this world but they are only kidding themselves." As pointed out in *The Shariyat-Ki-Sugmad,* Book One, page 149, by Paul Twitchell:

"Moralistic power is the only force by which Kal Niranjan can operate. The Kal has no other force in this world than what we call the forces of nature. But it works best in man because of the consciousness of human nature. Man lives by this moralistic power which builds churches, civilizations, and societies; he makes laws and enforces laws by it."

In his book *Your Right To Know,* Darwin covers issues that are considered unpopular and controversial by many of today's standards: Abortion, Drugs, the Occult, Morals and Ethics, False Teachers, and the Illusions of Death. His simple, precise truths show these issues to be traps laid by those in "authority" who play power games. Keep the masses fearful through guilt and tradition or submissive through drugs and pleasure-seeking devices and the material worlds are kept under control and run the way the negative forces wish them to be.

When a maverick spirit does not conform to the patterns of behavior set by the government and the church, that individual is in for trouble. There is even a proposal afoot to make Christianity the national religion which virtually ignores the freedom of religion clause in the Constitution of the United States.

"Even though America was spiritually established for all people, to worship as they choose, individually," Darwin commented, "it's interesting how Christian-oriented the various groups have become and have joined together to try to make everyone else a Christian. That is no better than the Moslems or the Communists trying to dominate the whole world to make everyone a Communist. Today, as a whole the consciousness of the people in the United States is much broader than those that have a narrow viewpoint."

Society's rules and regulations are necessary to maintain a semblance of order in the lower realms. There is order in all the universes of God, maintained and overseen by the Vairagi ECK Masters assigned to that particular responsibility.

"All philosophies and teachings derive from this one source of ECKANKAR," and according to Darwin, "One can prove this for themselves. The teachings of ECK don't put down any other religious or philosophical teaching. It is recognized that they are a branch, an offshoot of the mainstream. There are those like the Christian Coalition (Spiritual Counterfeits Project) and various organized religious groups and eastern ones as well that are trying to throw dirt at us, to do harm to some of our people, but they misrepresent their own principles. They'll get some part of the teaching and twist it around to make it sound like ECKANKAR is an occult teaching, the works of the devil; they haven't really taken a look at the teachings of ECK, the psychology of it. Just that book by Sri Paul Twitchell, *The Flute of God,* is the psychology of Spirit.

"I understand why they do that sort of thing, for they have not learned to work beyond the emotional level. We don't pull people off their path or from their church. The individuals that step on this path of ECK are spiritually hungry, they want something more spiritual in their lives, that succor that they can't get where they're at, and they can get it here. But yet they have to earn it and work for it. These people that are throwing rocks at us, it will go back to themselves and they don't know that, for all the great teachers taught that one reaps that which one sows. When you throw something out negatively, either thoughts or in words to another group or individual, and that group or that person is heading up that group, such as myself for ECKANKAR, I'm the one that's being attacked. It goes back to them, sometimes twice as hard. For some it is immediate, others it may take time, months, even years. This depends upon the individual's spiritual unfoldment. No one person or group is immune."

For quite a time, Darwin held off public comment about a Baptist college group in southern California who distributed a badly written paper full of innuendoes and untruths about Darwin. They were approached, refused to withdraw the paper or refute the untruths, so ECKANKAR took legal steps. The litigation was settled out of court when they saw ECKANKAR meant business.

Several offshoots of Christianity have tackled ECKANKAR, calling it "black magic" and "occult," neither accusation being true. To clarify issues, ECKANKAR took out full page ads in newspapers and magazines explaining what ECKANKAR was, that it did not proselytize or criticize other religions, and it pointed out how the Christians' monies were being misspent.

Surprisingly, the reaction from mail received at the ECKANKAR International Office was positive with many people suddenly interested in ECKANKAR. Jewish sources commended ECKANKAR for the ads and wanted to be included in the next run which had been addressed "Open Letter To Christians." They wanted it to read .... "To Christians and Jews."

When it was learned that the Spiritual Counterfeits Project group were putting out a journal against ECKANKAR, Darwin, two members of the ECKANKAR Office Staff and ECKANKAR's legal counsel went directly to the SCP headquarters in Berkeley, California, and asked to see the material before it was published. They were assured a copy, no later than two weeks from that day, would reach Darwin before publication, but this never happened. SCP obtained private mailing lists of ECK Centers and ECKists throughout the country and mailed copies of their journal to them. The journal was filled with untruths about Darwin, Paul and Gail, as well as the teachings of ECKANKAR, deliberate attempts to malign and slander the individuals and the ECKANKAR movement. Legal action was not taken against SCP, an offshoot of the Christian Coalition. "They gave us a lot of publicity that they did not realize," Darwin said.

"The tragedy of this type of attack," he continued, "is its effect on the millions of innocent people who will find the very fabric of their spiritual lives distorted and damaged subconsciously, and ultimately will affect them emotionally. I'm not going to punish anyone, but it is a violation of spiritual law to attack anyone's spiritual path, and Spirit's reaction is swift and can be terrible. When the person attacked is dedicated to the spiritual growth of those who are sincere, the retribution is quick and disastrous at times. They are so ignorant of what they do to themselves and those they influence. They will reap the whirlwinds they sow.

"Man must never attack others because of their beliefs, their spiritual actions, except in self-defense. In ECKANKAR, every person, ECKist or not, has the right to practice, to believe, to experience Spirit and God, in their own way, without interference from anyone else, whether through mockery, police, fear or ridicule. An example of what some of the various religious groups are responsible for and many do not know it, nor are aware of their action is, as I pointed out to a major newsperson two to three years before the Watergate crises, that those groups in Washington, D.C. and across the country praying for others, for Senators, Congressmen and the President would result in a lot of negative reaction. Why? Most of the leaders of this country did not ask to be prayed for, these groups did not have their permission.

"Another example, various evangelists going to countries like Iran, and Central America, etc., and attempting to convert them to their way brings about many negative repercussions."

One of the points brought up in the SCP journal dealt with plagiarism. It was claimed that Paul Twitchell took passages from other writers. "I don't have to defend Paul," Darwin stated. "Paul told us we would be tested moment by moment and many ECKists are finding these doubts hard to handle. Each must overcome the slavery of the mental plane and learn to depend not on logic and reason or metaphysics but upon the Spirit of ECK and the spiritual exercises."

Paul had stated that the book in question had been dictated to him by the great ECK Master Rebazar Tarzs, a previous Living ECK Master. Rebazar Tarzs appeared to Paul on a nightly basis to dictate the material that the ECK Masters wished brought out to the world. Darwin continued, "The effect of this charge of plagiarism has hampered the spiritual growth of many that were on the fence, too naive, too unsure of their own spiritual experiences to trust

145

the works of ECK. Such charges will only turn on them and dismantle their efforts, for in essence, they are attacking the life-giving force, Spirit."

As Darwin pointed out: "ECKANKAR does not convert or ask for donations. In fact, a person is required to study for two years before becoming a member and an initiate in the Second Circle. This is to build a spiritual foundation and be sure they are ready spiritually and choose, themselves, to take the next step on the spiritual ladder to the Godhead, for the choice to return to their home, their Source, is always up to the individual, for where is there proof unless you see and/or know within yourself where you are going and what you are going to do? I had to know for myself."

A Christian group "in the name of Christ" disrupted an ECKANKAR regional seminar in Portland, Oregon, broke windows in the ECK Center there and threw paint all over the building. A similar occurrence took place in Las Vegas, Nevada. Police protection was obtained in both cases. These people do not realize that actions like these affect the world as a whole.

In 1979, the followers of the Rev. Jim Jones who lived communally in Jonestown, Guyana were forced to commit suicide. When the Jonestown massacre hit the headlines, Darwin stated publicly:

"It was never mentioned by the news media that the Jonestown group were Christians, and that their full name was People's Temple of the Disciples of Christ. Such a thing as Jonestown could not happen in ECKANKAR. The Mahdis who is a higher initiate in ECKANKAR, and is the arm of the MAHANTA, the Living ECK Master, assists in spreading the message of ECKANKAR in its simplest form, without any mental or emotional control and pushing the teachings on anyone. We do not have any sort of commune and the effect of communal life is detrimental to those involved as it has always been. This is one of the reasons that ECK Centers and Reading Rooms should be run by the vote of the majority of the ECKists and not controlled by one individual."

Darwin has evinced concern that our basic freedoms are being eroded by those who seek to control. The relaxed universal acceptance of drug use caused him to send letters to state political officials to "not support any measures introduced to the legislature which would legalize or encourage use of marijuana. Drugs destroy the user's spiritual and physical ability to function as a truly complete human being.... Should the use of marijuana be legalized this country and the world as a whole would become passive and weakened. This is especially dangerous because the user does not see that he has been deceived. Marijuana is a misdemeanor-type drug that is more than a misdemeanor in its effects."

In a press release that was scheduled for the fall of 1977, Darwin stated:

"Nothing is more depressing than to see the misguided using drugs to reach higher states of awareness. These people claim to have had a God-Realized experience, but nothing is further from the truth. What the user does not understand is that he has deceived himself and has had only a small experience in the astral world, the first level of heaven. He has become a victim to that destructive mental action, lust. If allowed, lust develops into an abnormal demand of becoming destructive and degrading. The chief function of lust is to pull the user of drugs down to the common level of animals and keep him there."

As Darwin pointed out another time:

"The Communists want to dominate the world in an attempt to bring the free world to its knees. They have been using the negative influences of marijuana, heroin and cocaine to do it, not only in America, but in Canada and the free parts of Europe where people can move around freely. Even *Newsweek* magazine pointed out in an article 'Where The Poppies Bloom' that the Russians are trying to dominate the areas where heroin is grown, such as in Iran,

Afghanistan, Pakistan, Burma, Mexico, etc.

"The religious groups of the world don't seem to see this. If they did, they wouldn't be fighting amongst each other to see who can gain the greatest number of followers, again for control. These people do not understand the divine holy spirit, let alone God."

A young man experimented with Kirlian photography, photographing his fingers while he was in two distinct states of consciousness. The first picture was taken when he was in a normal peaceful condition, the colors brilliant, sharp and clear. The second picture was taken two hours after taking hallucinatory mushrooms. The young man's finger was totally different in the photograph, with diffused coloring, red blotches, no corona to speak of, virtually a dead negative force. This was related in the April 1978 *ECK World News,* complete with colored photographs of the experiment. The young man stated: "A drunk person will produce a photo similar to the #2 photo and the same with a person on the effects of pot [marijuana] and very well the same for a person who is angry. All more or less depending on the degree."

He went on to say: "... when I heard Sri Darwin Gross at the ECKANKAR World Wide Seminar in Seattle say how drugs break the aura and one is out of protection against negative energies ... I knew it was true, because I photographed the effect of it."

Personal experience is often worth more than a thousand words. Darwin receives hundreds of letters of gratitude from those who have found a way out of their drug addiction, from those who want help. They have received the assistance from the Living ECK Master who is a clear vehicle for Spirit to flow through because they were sincere in their desire to rise above this negative quality and because they initiated the healing themselves.

"It's the attitude," Darwin explained. "One word—attitude. It boils down to that one word, attitude, because you think the world is down on you and owes you a living. A lot of people feel that way. That's why our poverty, our welfare lines are long. In New York, in one of the largest distribution places for welfare checks and food stamps, there's a lot of fraud within the structure of the city government or the government of the people who are supposed to be issuing out these things. They are issuing out false I.D., and they're getting caught. It'll get straightened out. Ultimately, you don't get away with those sort of things. There would be far less of welfare and poverty, not only in this country but in the world, if it was taught in the school or taught in the home that the positive powers of thought are good, but they're limited. If one has the proper attitude about one's self and his relationship to the world and to his fellow man, he wouldn't have this 'world owes me a living' feeling."

Darwin continued: "I'm hoping that the American man doesn't become fat and lazy as predicted in *The Shariyat-Ki-Sugmad,* Book One, by Sri Paul Twitchell and let the yellow man walk in from the northern borders and take over. We as individuals, when things of this world are given to us in great quantities, the easy way of life as stated in commercials today, and don't take care of our physical responsibilities, whether it's the exercise that one should have, such as walking, or the negative foods that we put into the body, but again it isn't up to me to say what a person should eat nor drink. If it makes them feel good, and it agrees with them, that's up to that individual.

"At one time the world was ruled by the blacks over in Africa and Egypt in the biblical days and before that actually, around 3,000 B.C. I don't believe the Egyptians and the Judeans know that they derive from the black race. Then the white race came into dominance. They were being dominated by the black race at one time in which a lot of black magic was used. The powerful forces were destroyed by their own doing. But this was after man had been seeded, you might say, from other universes. Much of this is discussed in *The Shariyat-Ki-Sugmad,* Book One.

"It is possible to travel physically from one universe to another but not with the present vehicles. ECKANKAR has been established in all the universes everywhere, not the way we'd like to have it, but the Living ECK Master operates in all of them via Soul. The Living ECK Master does the same thing on other planets as he does here. In the Soul body you are unlimited and capable of being on all planes simultaneously. This all boils down to one phrase: states of consciousness.

"Even though man's scriptures speak of man being put on Earth in the beginning of time, that is partially true, but it goes back far beyond man's scriptures or recorded in time, whether it be the Shariyat-Ki-Sugmad, or various bibles. You'll find there is the black race here, the yellow race there, the white race, some are the Polynesians and there's a total of seven different colors, seven major universes, many beyond that.

"There is in the physical sciences, physics books, astronomy, astrophysics, chemistry, but basically astrophysics, where it is referred to as The Red Shift and the sciences are being concerned about it. There's really no concern needed. It is true that this planet, a lot of people were born and raised here, and have reincarnated many times. Some have been planted here too, from the other universes, other worlds. As Sri Paul Twitchell stated: 'Earth is the ash can of the universe!'

"I'm subject to all the laws and rules, both of this society and of this universe as the next man, even though I can rise above them in a state of consciousness and not be affected by them in Soul as others are. But there are also spiritual laws which I must obey and these are laws that man doesn't understand and much of which has not been taught by various religious teachings. There are a few rules in ECKANKAR. Certainly if someone is smoking, I'd prefer that they didn't in my presence, and I'll remove myself from them. When you deal with the physical level of this world, this universe, there has to be some sort of structure whether it's a large or small business or this universe. Common sense is the word. Take the universe, this world and the galaxy it's in. Everything as far as the planetary system is concerned, the heavenly bodies, everything is precisely in order, where they belong. So is each person this moment of time, where one should be.

"Those who have eyes to see will know that the huge clouds of hydrogen that occupy the vast reaches of space and which lie closely to the earth's surface within the electromagnetic fields, when stirred by a powerful thought-force established by a prayer group or a master mind or through the lords of this world, start cause which must have effect somewhere, somehow, even though it might be the creation of new worlds. This is often the beginning or cause of wars, great prosperity periods and other cycles of mankind. The thought or mind power is so established upon this earth plane that it will be some time before we will have enough positive vehicles for the ECK in order to clear it out through the education of the races for true spirituality. Occult powers in the past have destroyed many continents and land areas.

"An example of this appeared in *The Shariyat-Ki-Sugmad*, Book Two, by Sri Paul Twitchell. Atlantis became the great capital empire when Lemuria submerged from massive earthquakes and tidal waves. Of Scandinavian types, the Atlantians were great sailors, trading abroad, and governed by kings. Gradually sage kings [wise men] took over, to be followed by tyrants and dictators who posed as sage kings, and who leaned upon the corrupted priestcraft to manage the masses. This 'super civilization went down under a tide of water created by terrible earthquakes and upheaval of land masses, because of its morals, corruption and degeneration of sex.'

"Mark this forever in your mind! Every present thought solidifies into a future condition!

"In ECKANKAR, the individual learns the only power in existence is Divine Spirit which is the essence of God.

The teachings of ECK are caught by the individual on this path to God. ECKists are taught to be a clear vehicle for IT (Spirit) without directing IT in any way.

"Those religious groups that sit on the steps of Washington, D.C., to lobby for some program of their church are hampering this nation for the two do not go together—religion and politics. I for one am very much against the religious orders that have primed, promoted and placed Senators, Congressmen and lawmakers to govern this country in an attempt to make it a Christian nation, for this country was established, and is, for all religious beliefs for the individual. You may not believe this, however, George Washington was shown how to form the thirteen colonies by the ECK Master Fubbi Quantz, as George knelt to pray.

"America was founded by our forefathers who came to this country looking for religious freedom, without persecution, as my grandparents did. All of the colonies were organized with that main purpose in mind. Furthermore, the American founding fathers put that into the Constitution of the United States that all men had the right to freedom of religion, of their choice and belief.

"This has come down through the courts of America and many other nations and down through the years. The ECKANKAR spiritual leaders are being ridiculed by a large group of individual religions as well as churches banding together to attack others and their principles, just exactly the opposite basis upon which all free countries were founded. I for one would not like to see North America become like Iran or East Berlin and I have been there.

"In order to combat that, we must recognize that these groups are using psychic means. Each person and each group has the right to have their own religion, and there's no one who has the right to come in and tell them they cannot have a religion as long as that religion follows the laws and does not get into any other person's space, or does not belittle others or interfere with their own religious beliefs. Those that gather together with guns to destroy one another or tear down this country or others must face the end result.

"ECKANKAR does not ask for trouble, and, in fact, seeks to be good neighbor to everyone, but we don't let people walk all over us either. Everytime someone tries to step between the Living ECK Master and the chela, there are difficulties, situations, and they wonder why. It's a spiritual law that none are to step between the Master and the chela [known as a student] for there should be no barriers between himself and the chelas of ECKANKAR.

"For it is said in ECKANKAR that whosoever puts his hand over another to govern him is a usurper and a tyrant. The ECK [Spirit] declares him an enemy. This is not understood by most people of this world.

"Collectively we don't try to change society, we don't get involved unless it's on an individual basis. If anyone has an ax to grind, they will have to write their own congressman or on a local level get involved with the city function there. We're not here to change the world we live in or society as a movement. The ECKists have a culture all their own, in music, poetry, crafts, etc., many recognized international talents.

"We can show the world that different nationalities, people of different colors can get along together, can work together. Just visit a World Wide Seminar of ECK or International Youth Conference sometime. There's a movement down in Texas that's trying to change our currency and take the words 'In God We Trust' off. I'd be very much against that personally as an individual. If we left that on but keep the eagle on one side, take the human personality off the other side and put the dove on, then we'd have more power in our coin or our exchange for services rendered; that's all money is for, whether it's in paper or silver. There's a little too much emphasis placed on that and some people actually worship money, that's their bag.

"Some of these people in the material world, that have made it, whether it's in movies or business, even those that are preachers, ministers, evangelists, they know that the

153

coin and our money is an exchange for services. Some of these people worship it and that is worshipping the Kal force (known as the Dark Force). There is too much emphasis put on gaining stature in life, to gain a high degree of salary and having the same things that Mr. Jones down the street has. This sort of pressure gives an individual a real hassle in the spiritual life because he's working and striving to sustain and take care of his responsibilities, and if the pressure is put on by the husband or wife to climb that social ladder, materially, and one doesn't want to, arguments come about and feuds, and they go into debt just to keep up with others.

"Spirit might know more completely what that person truly needs. I have to go back to my own experiences. I have set into motion certain things I wanted to be, such as my life's work or certain physical things I wished to have, and Spirit turned it around in another direction. I'm on stage now, helping many people. 'The whole world is a stage and we're all actors in it'—an old Shakespearean line. And many other people have voiced it, wrote about it, stressed it. And there's a lot of good young players out there and older players who play their parts well. All that a person is really looking for is recognition. That's what it all boils down to, but in the end if they are recognized by another human being and not recognized by God, and don't have that communication properly with IT, God, there's something lacking in that person's daily makeup.

"This sort of work is never easy. It's very difficult, very hard. Hard on the physical being. I could treat my physical body a little better, by going off to some mountain retreat in a cabin somewhere, just write, lay the body down from time to time, I could keep it very young for as long as I wished. If you look at my pictures, I stayed about the same age, until about 1972-73. I started aging very rapidly. Working from another area, such as the Soul plane and beyond, I had to let go. Once I step aside as the Living ECK Master, I'll retain the MAHANTAship until the next man works into it. It is not for me to say who he is going to be or when that takes place either.

"We had one older man, a doctor, who was very upset because he thought he was supposed to be the next Living ECK Master. He quit and stepped out of the outer teachings because he wasn't chosen as the Living ECK Master. He was upset with Gail, Paul, and upset with me. Neither Gail nor Paul had that much to do with it. Paul was only present when I was asked the question from the Circle of Nine. I didn't really want this position, I wasn't looking for it. I was looking to go out in the world and spread the message of ECK as a missionary, you might say, and just being a vehicle in whatever country I could, to bring about a greater awareness of the heavenly worlds and the factors of survival beyond this physical universe, what we call death, that you can visit the heavenly worlds during this lifetime. So I had set my sights on that.

"Lo and behold, this came along and not only had I aged overnight, even though I'm a young person, young in heart, and there is no age as we think of it; ultimately I may have a long life, perhaps as we think of long. I've been around for awhile and am still young.

"It is true that the Living ECK Master has various abilities, but usually always used for the good of the whole. I was in Kashmir, India, and there's a mixture of various religious followings there, the Moslems, the Hindus, all kinds of yogis, Christians; there are those that pray and those that meditate, or use some form of worship and just begging God to do this or that for themselves and somebody else. Coming back from Asia, I was sicker than a dog. I bought a camera over in Japan and neglected to declare it. I didn't fill out the sheet on the plane, so customs gave me one and I didn't fill out the back side.

When they went through my luggage, they found the camera and I had a receipt for it. I would have been happier to translate, because I was that ill. I was fined for almost as much as the camera cost but it was my fault since I didn't fill out the form properly.

"There's much that man will learn. We're a little slow at it, partially because of the ignorance of some people. We have an enormous amount of technology that we aren't using to help mankind, which I believe is a far greater evil, in a sense, as we think of good and bad. Our automobile could be electric and, having a range of cross-country and back again, without having to even recharge the battery. But because of the politics in the automobile and oil business, it's not allowed. For instance, I've read about individuals who, back in the twenties and thirties and forties, developed carburetors that would allow you to have mileage of 80 to 100 miles to a gallon of gas, and the oil and auto industries wouldn't have it. Another example is the man in Vancouver, Washington, who had a hydraulic motor in each wheel; he and his prototype disappeared. Times had it that an oil company bought him out. His car did not require gas. This was in the late 40's.

"We have had several films that we would like to show but we don't have the funds and it's a very difficult task getting the ECK message out. We've been turned down by the major networks. Even if we could come up with the funds, they wouldn't show it nationwide. I was trying to get 'ECKANKAR, a Way of Life' shown nationwide and couldn't get it done, so we're going to every little station that we can. It's prejudice. Because they're either funded or the president of the station who may be a Protestant or Catholic or some other belief. He's got his faith, which he's afraid the board or religious leader will give him hell, and it's turned down. Some of these may not even reach the president, but the program director. We haven't been able to buy time on the national networks. The goal was just to present the message of ECK. The interesting part of it is we are not far out and do not use the emotions nor mind controls or no psychic control. It is an individual path, interesting and very balanced. At all of our functions you will find not only youth, clean and groomed, but youngsters from the arms of mothers, to the grandparents as well.

"Many of the evangelists are truly harmful to the masses because of the guilt factor that they are constantly impressing upon mankind. I'm sure they aren't paying the top prime-time dollar. I'd like to see some ECKists appear with their music, some poetry, art work, etc., and have some time myself to voice my opinion about certain spiritual laws and what is happening. Yet it is not necessary, for I do not want people flocking to ECKANKAR. Those that read a bit or hear a talk will make that decision within themselves to take the next step to read another book or look closer at the teachings of ECK.

"The music of the youth today is very destructive. That harsh beat, which is the beat of the jungle, influences individuals to do things they don't want to do normally. Subconsciously, it works on the person, and ultimately it comes out. The music of the Beatles, the rock groups in general, punk rock, with their devilish or clownish makeup, funny clothes, they just want attention, to be recognized. They are using the music to excite the youth, and in many cases in the music of the world, whether today or in the past, various individuals have been somewhat responsible for it. One person back in California was killed. He was quite a promoter of rock groups and the karmatic burden that he had set into motion due to his actions caught up with him and he's no longer with us on this Earth plane.

"In an article that appeared in the newspaper entitled 'Rock Music Can Upset Your Body Rhythms,' Dr. John Diamond of New York City's Mount Sinai Hospital concluded from his research: 'There is no doubt that loud rock-type-beat music can upset the delicate balance of the natural rhythms of the heart and blood vessels.... Many rock songs have a totally different beat which conflicts with the natural rhythms.' Dr. Diamond tested 20,000 rock records during his research, and says 'the different impulses in loud music can throw the heart out of synchronization, weaken the body and make it more vulnerable to disease.'

"These musicians presenting discordant music are conscious of what they are doing, but they're ignorant of the spiritual laws. There are a lot of people between twenty and thirty years old, when you speak to them, they don't hear you. Their hearing drops off at a very early age from the hard and loud music played at discos. Take the early blacksmith, learning his trade, pounding on that anvil and iron, his hearing went to heck in a very short order.

"Man knows this in science, but hasn't taught it to the children in school. The audio level is crucial, it can be very detrimental, it can kill a person. Eighty decibels of sound can wipe one out. And if you put another component along that sound wave, like light, it could be used for the good of man or it can be disastrous. Medical men, science, audiology men know that at a certain decible level, to expose a human being to it, he is gone. The children should learn that at a very early age. You can listen to good music, and this is the individual's choice if he wants to listen to rock, but do it on a low key. Don't turn up the full volume of that amplifier. The softer sounds are able to do more for man than the hard, harsh sounds.

"Man is born with inner happiness. We are taught as children so many negative things, negative words like 'can't' and 'don't.' There is a whole list of negative words that should be eradicated from our childhood vocabularies. Even as adults we can say 'please excuse me' rather than 'sorry.' Don't downgrade yourself. Every time we downgrade ourselves, we subject ourselves to a little bit of hell. These are things that should be taught to a child. The consciousness of our children of four and five today exceed the consciousness of the ten to fifteen year old some thirty years ago.

"We're not using television properly to teach these young minds. TV is a terrific influence. Over in Japan, they have educational programs that the children watch, as well as being taught. Maybe adults are being educated at the same time. They show travel films all day long, and of different countries, different parts of the country. They go into the sciences and various subject matters that are necessary and pertinent to them today. It is a great medium, such a tool for education that we, in this country, as advanced as we are supposed to be technologically, are behind some of the other countries that we have helped bring along.

"One out of every ten people have mental/emotional problems and there is definitely an answer in ECK. I usually give that individual a specific spiritual exercise to use. If they know where their difficulty originated from, whether it's a lack of understanding or something impressed upon them from someone else, it can be resolved. One young lady was bothered greatly by her mother. I don't get into family situations or even people problems, but she came to me very distressed emotionally, and of course, her mother was praying very hard for her. The young lady, a college girl, was studying while trying to put herself through college and also interested in her own spiritual development. Her mother thought she was being misled, going to the devil.

"I told her to stop, drop ECK, but it bothered her that she couldn't study in school, and also the prayers from her mother were interfering with her life. I asked her to step aside until such a time that she was old enough to go out into the world and work. To finish her schooling since that difficulty existed with her parents.

"The children are basically under the guidance of their parents until they are old enough to go out on their own, but the girl didn't follow the advice. She tried, in essence, to ride down two streams at the same time, which is not advised. So it tended to tear her up emotionally and she had to seek professional help. It wasn't due to the study of ECKANKAR. It was partially due to her mother's prayers for this young lady, and her drive and willingness to continue, for there was a hunger for her spiritual unfoldment.

159

"A person who comes into this life with an emotional problem at times can be helped, but not in all cases. If it's drug-induced, and if there's some brain damage, I wouldn't make any guarantees. I've seen people help themselves overcome some very difficult situations with emotional problems through the spiritual contemplative exercises of ECK.

"This is one of man's greatest ills. I don't care what nation he's from or what nationality or what color. We are not taught as youngsters, and this is one of the teachings of ECK that the ECKists get from their parents and the teachings themselves, not only from the parents but from the youth discourses—not to look back, not to hang onto the past moments or past days or years. If it was a negative, forget it; any accumulation of positive events are necessary to retain, because it helps build one's character but also gives him and allows him to develop himself in a 360 degree viewpoint.

"Those who are not getting a thing out of their philosophy, religion or faith will ultimately find a book on the shelf somewhere about the teachings of ECK, or hear a lecture or talk to a friend, and they'll wonder about it. They'll either be for it or set it aside and wait, or be against it.

"In my youth when I was being taken to church, I felt then if Jesus could walk on water, I can, and I can do better things, not only because he said so, I felt it. Those who are waiting for Jesus to return to Earth will never see this happen, for the year 2000 will come and go and we as human beings here on Earth will still be struggling with prejudice, misunderstandings amongst each other and possibly even have to battle people from another galaxy to retain Earth for man's own propagation. My father told me not to believe everything you read or hear. Even though I love Jesus as a man and teacher, he did not write one word. That which is in the Bible has been handed down many years after he had left the planet Earth. The level of heaven he works from, he cannot hear the prayers of those who pray to him. Each man and woman is a child or Son of God. It is the Divine Spirit which is known as ECK that is the essence of God and assists some through prayers.

"I'm finding that some of the higher initiates are—not just myself—performing miracles daily without publicity, without broadcasting it, as well as prophecizing and setting up predictions for themselves, however, not for others though. There was a psychic here on TV making predictions that President Carter was almost going to break down through the emotional stress and strain, and other people were going to have ill fate. A person like that who might be a vehicle for Spirit is actually setting up conditions for these people and may actually have to live them out. It's a very negative psychic thing.

"Not too long ago, I was in New York City. I was going to a show and I took an acquaintance with me. We got to the show and all the tickets were sold out. My guest was somewhat disappointed, so I walked up to the box office. They told me they were sold out and I turned around and this party overheard me. You might call it coincidence, but he said, 'Do you want my tickets? I'll sell them to you.' I said, 'Certainly, I'll buy them and even give you a few dollars more for them.' But he refused. 'Oh, no, I want only what I paid for them.' That is a true story. What happens is the ECK takes care of us if we let IT.

"Another time I was a guest speaker flying out of Portland, Oregon. I had reservations but when I got to the airport, that particular flight was cancelled and everyone else had been transferred to another carrier. It was full and there was no way I was going to get on it. So knowing that if I was to be a guest speaker, I'd get there, I went over to the counter. I gave the man my ticket and he told me I couldn't make this flight. I said, 'I believe I can, I'm sure that there'll be room for one more.' And there was.

"These things I sort of knew, but again, the individual if they trust Spirit and know that if it's to happen, it will happen for the good of all. You'll go right up to the edge of the wire and if it doesn't happen the way we think it should, then we are trying to interfere with Spirit. If it doesn't happen the way we think it should, we become upset. But if you don't become upset, and it's 'OK, if it happens, it happens, if it doesn't happen, why, there's a reason,' we should accept it. This is what I'm talking about. There are many ways that Spirit works in the ECKist's life, if they'll let it!"

In the Canadian magazine *I Am.*, May-July 1980 issue, the editorial page carried the following article entitled "The Counter Culture":

"There are apparently 3,000 so-called 'cults' in North America alone. The Spiritual Community Guide lists hundreds upon hundreds of these organizations ranging from covens to UFO groups through back-to-the-land enterprises to spiritual communities, new age thinkers, and research foundations.

"The word 'cult' has been a sensational headline grabber, especially since, but even before, the Jonestown horror. Bandied about by the media, it has been used as a blanket statement to cover all marginal organizations with the dreaded brand of the Beast. It has been an easy means to titillate and raise viewer or reader attention at the expense of fair and thorough examination.

"This is not to say that some organizations might not have run afoul of the law. Like many big corporations, some of the larger groups have been investigated by the government. Reverend Sun-Myung Moon's Unification Church has been closely watched; eleven members of Scientology have been indicted. On the other hand, other legal and governmental investigations, state-wide and province-wide will now have exonerated many of these infamously tarred by the media.

"Still these government operations raise unanswered dilemmas. In one Canadian province, Quebec, for example, organizations cannot get a teaching permit unless a recognized psychologist or psychiatrist is one of the principal directors of curriculum. Which gives a monopoly in the mind-awareness area to those university educated and approved, not withstanding the fact that there are many other wise and learned persons who have come by their happiness and knowledge of life through years of selfless work, self-examination, discipline, and overcoming frailties to which most of us, including doctors, succumb.

"So these individuals, unless they have a bent for instant pop-celebrity via the pocket book best-seller industry and the talk shows, are forced to walk the way of 2,000 years ago when the Nazarene stumped the dirt roads of Palestine talking to anyone who would stop to listen. Excepting the Doctors of Law (law was then a very spiritual thing) who didn't appreciate this cultish clan of fisherman talking parabolic heaven. The Roman government didn't interfere, until the Doctors managed to brand him a 'revolutionary,' a word as detested by Rome as 'cult' seems to be today. Still it was individual indecision (Pilate's) that got him crucified and not a Royal Commission of Inquiry into strange behavior modification: after all, the Nazarene preached leaving family behind, giving up your belongings, putting all your faith in him, preparing for the millenium, being a messenger for God, etc. Sounds familiar? Sure! 'Cults' are saying the same thing today.

"Believing in the freedom of speech and religious or philosophical beliefs as accepted in Canada and as protected by the 1st amendment in the U.S. Charter, *I Am.* has written to literally dozens upon dozens of known 'cults' offering them the opportunity to state and proclaim who they are, their reason for being, and their role in the spiritual unfoldment of planet Earth. We did not deal with the mainstream religions — those groups which, over the years, have passed from 'cultdom' to establishment figureheads. We feel those responding offer a quite complete picture of the different currents of spiritual awareness in North America. The Book of Cults is their statement."

163

While ECKANKAR is not a 'cult,' they did respond to the request for material about ECKANKAR, and in the May-July 1980 copy of *I Am.,* Darwin's article on "The Spiritual Body of Man" from his book *Your Right To Know*, appeared on page 60 of the magazine, and page 62 carried excerpts of Paul Twitchell's *The Flute of God*.

CHAPTER 8

Individual Experience

"Love is often considered the most important commodity, but so many individuals misunderstand the love because they put it into the human terms, terms that they can physically relate to. Divine love is something you can't hold in your hands but that can flow through you. This is a part of the tree of God or the river of God, whatever one wants to call it. It's that life-giving force but there is something beyond that, when you get into the pure positive God Worlds, you'll find that that love that you knew on the physical plane, astral, causal and mental plane, is an aspect of God but the other side of that is another face, known as the 'two faces of God.'"

According to this statement by Sri Darwin Gross, the love flowing from the SUGMAD (an ancient Chinese name for the Supreme Deity) as divine life-sustaining force is different from the love experienced by the human consciousness on the physical and emotional up to the mental planes of being. Instead of being expressed in the lower bodies of man, the divine love uses the highest form of consciousness as a vehicle to reach every man, creature and plant in all the universes of God.

Every individual, being Soul, a spark of God, has this God-consciousness as a potential within him. It is his link to the creator, the Absolute. But at all times there is only one fully realized manifestation, an embodiment of the MAHANTA on all the planes of creation, and he becomes known as the MAHANTA, the Living ECK Master. Thus Darwin's full title is Sri Darwin Gross, the MAHANTA, the Living ECK Master.

When Sri Darwin, the Living ECK Master, worked into the MAHANTA state, he, like all beings of supreme attainment, had the choice of remaining in the pure positive God Worlds of eternal bliss and freedom, or to return to the lower worlds of limitation to serve those willing to listen to the teachings of ECK. Darwin chose to return, the divine love that flowed through him like a great torrent filling him with compassion for all those still struggling for their own fulfillment in God. In his own words: "When this is experienced, the flood of joy and happiness is overwhelming. One wants to go out into the world and shout from the highest mountain top or from the tallest building or jump upon a cloud and let the whole world know about God, for they have reached the first level of the true God Worlds. At this step, one must learn how to keep in balance the emotions. Why? Should you move Spirit through the emotions, as an evangelist has for years, he is not sowing good seeds for the true works of God, but negative ones.

"Man has always identified God with Light and Sound, yet has forgotten how to use It for the good of mankind. The Light and Sound of God is spoken of in all the scriptures of this world and only in the scriptures of ECKANKAR [*The Shariyat-Ki-Sugmad*] explains how it can be used."

Darwin teaches that the goal of the student on the path of ECK is to become a co-worker with God, yet, it is up to the individual. He explains: "This is the individuals's own choice should they wish to become one with God, to accomplish God's purpose, a miracle worker and perhaps to become a Master. But one must completely surrender to the God-consciousness, the Inter Master that is within you. We don't become a god, we become Spirit, a vehicle for IT, retaining our individuality throughout eternity.

"After I became the Living ECK Master, I chose to work with the MAHANTA consciousness. It took three to four years of additional tests and hard work to become a vehicle

166

for that great state of consciousness which is beyond the God-conscious state. For the individual that would like to know more about and understand the meaning of the word MAHANTA, you'll find a greater explanation in *The Shariyat-Ki-Sugmad*, Book One, and the function of that state of consciousness and the individual who has worked to allow that state of consciousness to use him for the good of the Whole."

Darwin took up his assignment as the MAHANTA, the 972nd Living ECK Master in an unbroken line of teaching Masters, to serve in the many roles this omnipotent, omnipresent, and omniscient vehicle of the SUGMAD gave him the capacity for. In eastern terminology, he is known as the Supreme Master, the Sat Guru, the true Master, or the Vi-Guru, the Light-Giver. In ECK, he is referred to as the Light-Giver, Vi-Guru, Inner Master, or the Spiritual Traveler.

One of the main duties of the Spiritual Traveler is to assist those persons who are able, consciously or unconsciously, to separate themselves in the Soul body from the physical state of consciousness and travel in any of the realms of the universe of universes. Whenever someone practices Soul Travel, be it in a spiritual contemplative exercise, the dream state, or in any other circumstance, the Spiritual Traveler is beside them for guidance and protection. "The experience of Soul traveling or flying in dreams is very exciting," states Sri Darwin. "As one continually expands their consciousness and gains more knowledge about himself, the world around himself and the heavens, the experiences of flying in your dreams becomes a new dimension. You'll find all the physical sensations of the act, the closest waking life experience, you might say, would be a parachute jump or hang glider."

The benefits or transcending the physical state through Soul Travel are numerous and often unique to the practitioner, but in general it can be found that it results in the loss of the fear of death. In one of the many letters Sri

167

Darwin receives attesting to this fact, one student of ECKANKAR writes:

> Dear Darwin:
> When I first experienced being beyond the physical body—moving out of my physical state of consciousness into a higher state of consciousness without the physical body—when I actually experienced that for the first time in my life, I knew without doubt that there is life beyond the physical body, that life is a continuing thing—through this world and into many other worlds of planes of consciousness. This awareness had a tremendous effect on my whole attitude from that point on in my everyday life.
> The fear of death is gone. The pressure of feeling there isn't enough time, that there is only so much time to do something, all of that's gone now. I live in the moment, in the here, in the now...
>
> M.
>
> (Above letter on file)

Darwin notes: "This victory over death is the greatest triumph of Soul. It is Its privilege to have this knowledge and grace of God bestowed upon It while living in this physical universe."

As the ECKist learns to go beyond himself and becomes more aware of the subtle worlds outside the range of the physical senses, his dream state becomes more and more important in his unfoldment. His training never stops. In fact, when the student is asleep, it is much easier to teach and show him certain truths, because the waking mind with its limiting conditioning is no longer in the way.

The chela may be taken to one of the seven Temples of Golden Wisdom that exist on the various planes, to study the Shariyat-Ki-Sugmad, the ancient scriptures of divine knowledge, put together by the Adepts of the Vairagi down through the ages. All of man's scriptures and philosophy derive from this set of ancient scriptures. Or he may be trained in a skill necessary in his day to day living. On occasion he will be brought to the causal world to view some of his past lives or future events. After becoming a member of ECKANKAR enrolled in the discourses, within four weeks to six months, the chela receives his First Initiation, his first link-up with the ECK current, in the dream state. From then on, much of his karma will be worked off in dream experiences.

In all this, the ECKist is never alone. When working with individuals in their dreams, the Living ECK Master is referred to as the Dream Master. He appears to the dreamer just as he would in the physical, only illuminated by a great radiating light. In his company, and only then, they are admitted to the Golden Wisdom Temples. He works to uplift them to a point where they can have an objective view of their day to day troubles and problems, and many times the individual wakes up to find he has gained a solution to something he has been unable to resolve with his intellectual faculties.

Most ECKists keep a dream journal by their bedside, and the many thousands of letters and reports Darwin has in his files bear witness to the impact these dream experiences with him have on his followers. Here are a few examples:

> ...One of the most memorable and remarkable dreams experienced to date was with Darwin. I was exploring the grounds of a beautiful large estate surrounded by green shrubbery. I noticed Darwin's form appear in front of me like an apparition. Slowly, Darwin approached me. The joy and exhilaration at seeing the Master was so intense that I started repeating "Darji, Darji." Upon reaching me, Darwin put both

169

arms around me and kissed me on the cheek. He then turned around without saying a word and walked back to the spot where he had appeared. His form gradually faded. For days after this I felt happy. Whenever I get down or feel negative, I think of this dream and it lifts me up. This must be Darwin's way of reassuring me that he is watching over me on the inner and demonstrating his words, "My love always surrounds you."

B.

...Tonight, for example, the Inner Master helped remove the almost paralyzing anxiety I was feeling about the upcoming National Board medical examinations which I will take this coming Tuesday and Wednesday.... With much love,

K.

...I returned to Nigeria on the first of August. That very night, in my dream state, I had again a very wonderful experience, my first Soul Travel. I went to a far place in the dream; I can't clearly describe it. I saw the MAHANTA with two ECK Masters, Rebazar Tarzs and Lai Tsi. They did not talk to me. I was requesting you to help me to talk to them. I was able to identify them by their pictures...

I felt I was in another world, higher; I was conscious of the place I was. I...asked to be taken to the Temple of Golden Wisdom. I awoke and discovered that it was in the dream.

A.

Dear Darji,
...I am not always aware of my dreams but following the seminar one night I apparently

170

lifted my head in sleep and laughed, saying, "That would be fun, wouldn't it, Darji?" You can't believe how those simple words uplifted and encouraged me. I knew then without doubt that Soul has experiences irregardless if the little self is aware of them or not...I honestly can't remember a time when I was more fulfilled than NOW. Life is no longer a dismal burden but full of promise and adventure. Deep questions have been answered. My personal life is being quietly dealt with...I've changed my ECK responsibilities to being the treasurer for the local ECK Center. Before, I would have been terrified to take it on...How subtle, how perfect, how beautiful. The gift from the Master is knowledge of your existence.

Baraka Bashad,
K.

The MAHANTA, the Living ECK Master is the embodiment of the Light and Sound of God. He is the ECK manifested as form, but to many this is visible in the inner as a blue or white star or globe of light. In one publication for Higher Initiates, Darwin described this star in the following words: "You have read much in the ECK writings about the Blue Star of ECK, yet many still assume it to be a five-pointed star; it isn't. It is the six-pointed star, that which appears in the spiritual eye when one crosses over from the psychic worlds into the Atma Lok (Soul plane). This is the star of the East, seen and followed by the Magi in the biblical story of the birth of Jesus, and known as the Star of David as well as the Seal of Solomon."

Therefore, the inner form of the Inter Master is perceived according to one's own level of unfoldment and awareness. For some, it is a feeling of a presence, of warmth and love; others see a star or field of light, and some may hear silent words spoken or feel a wordless

171

communication. It is not the appearance of the Inter Master that changes, but the individual's perception of him as their inner senses are gradually unfolded.

When I see the blue star I can't help but smile. The physical body even responds to the presence of the Master. I feel a warm glow about me. It's such a happy experience.

R.

I continue to be constantly blessed by your presence in the form of a field or globe of blue light inwardly and even occasionally on the outer.

C.

One of my greatest experiences happened the other night. On the inner I saw a blue light which changed to a flame and took the shape of yourself.

J.

(All of these letters on file.)

While the MAHANTA is the Vi-Guru, the Light-Giver, and appears to the seeker to bring him divine illumination and pour forth the heavenly knowledge of all things, his main objective is to connect the individual's consciousness to the Sound Current. The Sound is the vehicle Soul uses to travel back to the God Worlds of pure Spirit, and the basis upon which Soul's relation to reality is measured.

"We can do without the Light but the Sound we cannot do without," Darwin says. "Sound is the vehicle through which all things are manifested. One can do without the Light but the Sound, this pillar of God, is the most important factor to develop in one's own spiritual unfoldment."

In the works of ECKANKAR there are a number of spiritual exercises to develop the ability to hear the Sound, see the Light, or both at once. For some chelas it is easier to see the Light, while others may tend more towards hearing the Sound. But gradually, the two aspects of the ECK current will balance out, and the chela will be able to distinguish between the various planes of existence and the sounds heard on them. Here are two examples of chelas who are aware of their linkage to the Light and Sound through the MAHANTA:

Darwin, MAHANTA,

It is as if you were always standing beside me. When I close my eyes the blue light is there, the star, the music and nothing in the world can then shake me. The stronger the attacks from the negative are, the stronger becomes this inner security, that I have reached, for what I have always been looking: The Living ECK Master, and with him the opportunity to return to the SUGMAD...

Darwin, I am unable to describe how gradually all life becomes sound, and love, which is the love for the MAHANTA, for you. You are so near and I see you in all others and my love for others is the love for you.

My life is yours, has ever been and will ever be yours.

B.

Me and Darwin went to a palace and it was made out of silver and gold. I saw a house and it was made out of the same kind of gold, and then we went to talk about the gate because it had bells out of the same kind of gold. The silver was pretty and it had all kinds of decorations. Me and Darwin travelled around. We floated around. All the houses were pretty. The bells dingdonged and rang. It made a beautiful sound. I

felt good.
I like Darwin a lot. He talked to me. His voice
sounds like my father. I saw a lot of different
colors. It was a pretty world and I like it a lot. It
was like a dream of a life and I liked it a lot.

K. Age 6

It can be stated that all sincere students practicing the
spiritual exercises of ECK have spiritual experiences at
any age. These experiences take place in the Soul body,
and often the individual in the physical consciousness is
not aware of them. This may be because the person's low
perception level does not allow his experience to form a
memory pattern which may be recalled by the physical
state of consciousness; on the other hand, it can be a deliberate action by the Inter Master to obscure physical memory so as to protect the chela from becoming upset or im-
balanced.

Sri Darwin states, "The teachings of ECK are very subtle.
A person will say, in a consultation, 'Well, gee, am I progressing spiritually?' Then when questioned, in a spiritual
consultation, they hear the little click, they're gone, but
they don't have recall of it yet. But they're aware that they
are going out beyond themselves. They see the light coming and going. They become impatient. They are having
spiritual experiences and aren't aware of it or don't feel
they are. It's not so dramatic, like my coming up there and
kicking them in the pants or jerking them out of the body.

"We're not in for that, and it's not going to happen that
way. It's subtle; Soul is very gentle. I am gentle, the ECK
Masters are very gentle with people. We're going to take it
one step at a time, because of its seriousness, and what is
gained. If this knowledge of God is misused, a person
could harm himself, as well as other people."

The physical presence of the Living ECK Master may
cause an opening of the spiritual senses in those fortunate
to be near him. The strong ECK current flowing through

174

him, especially at large gatherings such as seminars, has an effect on many people that may be described as mild spiritual experience. When shaking hands with him or being embraced or touched by him, it isn't uncommon for that person to feel something like a slight electric shock running through their arm or whole body. They are uplifted into a different, more positive and survival oriented outlook on life, divine love within them is ignited, and for many the connection to the Inter Master becomes much stronger after such an experience.

This report by one young chela may serve to illustrate this:

> ...Then, as I touched Darwin's hand, I had my first "naturally produced" experience of expanded consciousness, of Soul experience. I was conscious of a great flashing light between the Master's eyes and my own. Physical consciousness disappeared as I experienced a feeling of great lightness. It may be described as a shock.

> As I turned into physical consciousness, I felt as if I were floating, descending, back into the physical body. I knew that, finally, here was a true spiritual Master. I knew it with all my being and awareness, not because of particular related experiences of phenomena.

> In the days that followed, I knew that life would forever after be different, that my "old self" was fading, a new life beginning. This was illuminated to me in very definitive ways, as I knew the changes in myself.

> As the days progressed, little changes manifested as I began my new life. The long hair and beard came off. I was faced with the shocker of the necessity of being self-responsible at all levels (practical, physical level at which I had

maintained a personal illusion).

...I consider it a joy to work with Sri Darwin
Gross. I appreciate the Master's love and guidance beyond expression. I know that opening of
the awareness to the 360° point of perception is
my task to do and up to no one but myself.

M.

There is no worship or adoration of any kind for
Sri Darwin Gross. He has disciplined himself to where he
is a perfectly clear channel for Spirit, the Word or Voice of
God, and it is to IT that the chela must look. Darwin has
stressed many times that the ECKist should go to the temple within as his starting place for experience beyond himself. When he becomes trained at this, it may no longer be
necessary for him to be in the physical presence of the
Master:

...Thank you also for your visit on the inner to
say goodbye to me on the morning of the evening
that you had to fly out from N.Z. I awoke at five
a.m. to see your beautiful presence by the side of
the bed and I remember stretching my hand out
to you as the words "Baraka Bashad" and the
most incredible Sound and Light filled the
room. I knew then that I would not be seeing you
in the physical...

From your newest and littlest leaf, much ECK
love.

In ECK,
M.

The seeker asking for proof that Darwin is indeed the
MAHANTA, the Living ECK Master, need go no further
than to the temple within. Here, he is raised to a plane of
knowing where the knower and the known become one—a
plane beyond any possibility of doubt. He is not merely a

believer, his conviction is born out of actual experience and trust in his inner spiritual senses. He is not asked to accept anything without proving it to himself; however, one must earn it and work for it. Out of his own experience comes true satisfaction and the step beyond being a seeker. One chela writes:

> ...Soon I was to *know* Paul Twitchell was writing the truth because I met the Inner Master in all of the majesty of a Divine, omniscient and omnipresent Being. It was an overwhelming but ultimately satisfying experience. I had finally found all that I was searching for, and much more than I had ever dreamed could exist in the way of fulfillment.
>
> In a series of visits, the Inner Master opened up a flood of recollections, waves of understanding, administered an initiation, and pointed out the Path that I was to walk and the direction of my very own spiritual mission in life.
>
> B.

Sri Paul Twitchell stated in his writing that it did not matter whether the MAHANTA, the Living ECK Master had fifty chelas or fifty million; he could be with each and every one of them. Both Sri Paul and Sri Darwin have told their audiences and readers many times: "I am always with you." One of the main reasons why people feel lonely, Paul writes, is because of their feeling of isolation from God. One can be in the middle of a crowd, and still be lonely. An ECKist, however, need never be lonely, for he has the divine presence in the form of the Spiritual Traveler with him at all times. As one letter to Sri Darwin expresses:

> Dear Master,
> ...At times, during my contemplation, I have experienced the love of the MAHANTA, which

has lifted me in an area of BEING, a feeling that I have never experienced and no words can properly describe. No longer do I have that lonely feeling, and am ever so thankful to be on this path and accepted by the MAHANTA as his chela. With love in ECK,

D.

To his followers, the ECK Master is a teacher, spiritual guide, way-shower, and a constant companion. The Love of the SUGMAD flows through him to uplift all living beings, and often contact with him on the inner or the outer will harmonize the disruptive vibrations within an individual's body, his emotions or his mind commonly known as sickness, or ill health. The MAHANTA as healer doesn't use methods like aura adjustment or the laying on of hands, but simply lets the ECK flow out to that individual without directing Spirit as to any specific result. It is up to Spirit and the consciousness of the individual, whether he is ready to receive the gift of healing.

But when the person is ready, the ECK will act swiftly and in ways that the average man would term "miraculous" or "unbelievable." Or such healings are dismissed with the words "coincidence," "accident," or "illusion." According to Darwin, "The whole of man's experiences are limited by what he observes with his senses and understands with his mind. We should keep in mind that in ECK there are no coincidences, that those working in the lower levels of heaven look to and think of miracles, freaks, accidents, intuition and coincidences due to the lack of spiritual unfoldment."

Most of all, it seems, the individual desiring a spiritual healing has to achieve a detached attitude towards his condition. If he clings to his illness, emotionally or mentally, if he wishes for healing but only hugs his ailment all the more to his breast, the healing will not take place. He must be willing to let go of the cause for his suffering, to give it over to Spirit to handle in the way IT sees fit. The MAHANTA, the Living ECK Master will never force a healing on anyone, nor will the ECK lend ITSELF to the wishes of the lower consciousness.

There is the story of the young woman who underwent nose surgery to correct a deviated septum. Shortly after the operation, the weakened structure of the nose collapsed and fell to one side, giving it a horribly lopsided and deformed look. Her appearance meant a lot to the young lady, especially since she was an actress and depended on it in her job. A second surgery was performed. The bandages came off a week later to reveal the nose even more shockingly deformed, with a deep dent running down the middle.

She broke into tears. Already she had not been able to work for months, and now her appearance was worse than ever. The surgeon scheduled her for a visit a week later to see if the condition corrected itself. It hadn't. The young woman despaired at the thought of a third operation, but the doctor saw no other solution. A date was set.

The following day, she received a phone call from Darwin to discuss the television appearance she was setting up for him. When he asked her how she was, she answered, "Not so good."

"What's wrong?"

She told him all about her troubles, including the fact that she had been unable to work for five months now.

"Describe the area exactly where the problem is," he asked. She did, and added that she was doubtful another operation would be much more successful.

"Can you let it go? Do you want to go back to surgery?" he said.

"No way," she sobbed. "I can't go through with it emotionally."

"Don't worry. Just give it to the ECK. In the meantime, please set up the interviews. I'll be in New York Wednesday."

The next morning, she awoke from sleep feeling great.

"Almost like it's Christmas," she thought. The bathroom mirror showed the reflection of a nose that was perfect. The deformity and dent was completely gone. The nose looked just like it should have looked, had the first operation been successful. On her next visit to the doctor, he was baffled. "This is unbelievable," he mumbled. Six other doctors were called in to look at the pictures of how the nose had been and to see the sudden change. They were all very much surprised. One said it must have been a miracle that caused the healing.

Being able to let go and surrender the problem to the ECK may be viewed as an indication that the individual has learned his lesson from whatever experience he is going through, and no longer needs it. He is ready for that next step, letting the Spiritual Traveler guide him out of an area of difficulty or pain to a level of greater beingness. The feeling of being punished by fate or the hand of God—the concept of sin—has no place in the ECKist's life, for has it not been said that you reap what you sow? The purpose of experiences are for the unfoldment of Soul, as explained by Darwin:

"The measure of a person is often taken in times of adversity. One learns in ECKANKAR that Soul resides within the physical body for some; however, it is up to the individual to separate Soul from the body as pointed out even in the Christian scriptures as well as *The Shariyat-Ki-Sugmad*. We as human beings are here on Earth to be tested and purified in Soul to earn our way through the difficulties of the lower worlds back to God. Man's true purpose here is to experience life and gain the understanding of God and the growth of Soul."

The ECKANKAR teachings give many techniques for turning a problem over to the divine Spirit. One is forming the problem and everything involved with it into a "snowball" with one's mental hands, and then throwing it into the ECK stream. One can visualize the ECK current as a shining river, and see the snowball melting away into it.

Another technique is writing a letter to Sri Darwin Gross, and either putting it on the nightstand, in a drawer, or sending it to the ECKANKAR International Office. In any case, the MAHANTA will have read the letter as it is written. Sri Darwin receives many notes such as these:

Dearest Darwin,
...I know you heard me the first time (as you note) because before I reached the Post Office with the letter (two blocks away) my shoulder was better and not painful and throbbing as it had been. There is still some slight discomfort and a grating (like a calcium or mineral deposit) when I move the shoulder, but this is nothing to compare with the previous discomfort and inconvenience...
Love and blessings!
M.

...Before I close this letter I must thank you for the immediate help I received in the emotional problem which I wrote you about between this report and the last. As I dropped the letter in the mailbox, I seemed to be instantly relieved. Thank you. Love, peace and happiness!
L.

Practicing the presence of the Master can itself be a healing technique. Knowing one is taken care of helps relax the state of anxiety or worry that tends to interfere with the natural healing process. Putting the attention on the Inter Master is like tapping into a secret source of strength that carries one through circumstances which otherwise would have been unbearable:

Beloved Master,
I wish to thank you for always being with me.

181

During my stay in the hospital, I felt your presence constantly. Your love surrounded me...

I had a beautiful time in the hospital. I was guided to help a woman who also had a mastectomy but wasn't doing as well as I. I stayed cheerful and happy, and my physical body responded rapidly to healing....

Dear Darwin,

...For in the many problems that I have had during these last six months, you have continually showered me with love and strength that I never knew was possible.

You tell us that your love and protection always surround us. Until this summer, these were only words with little meaning. But during my mother's illness this summer, you showed me the meaning of those words. There were many times when I thought I could endure no more, and then you would give me the strength to go on. When I asked you to help my mother, you answered my call, and helped her live through the numerous complications that the doctors feel should have killed her. How can I ever thank you enough?

...Beloved Master, how can I express how grateful I am to you? You have helped me lose weight that years of will power couldn't remove. You have taught me that love is not possession and jealousy. I know I have much now to learn, but knowing that your love and affection are always there is a great knowledge to possess. Thank you.

Affectionately,
R.

So many of the problems human beings have can be directly attributed to their own detrimental actions towards themselves. These actions, whether they are destructive or self-destructive ways of thinking, negative emotions or physical abuse to their body, are repeated and tend to form habits that the individual has an increasingly hard time to break. When the harmful effects of their actions begin to make themselves felt, they cry out to the Master or God to be saved from themselves.

Rarely will the Living ECK Master take on the karma a person has earned for himself. Instead, the student is advised to practice the spiritual exercises of ECK and be patient, for the purpose is to lift him above the necessity for self-abuse and fill him with the sense of his own divinity and purity, rather than a temporary removal of the symptoms. Sri Darwin comments:

"Take, for example, those who abuse themselves with drugs. Drug addiction is an affliction of the body and mind. It requires professional and medical help and advice. I receive letters every day from people who have dropped the use of drugs, alcohol and tobacco after being in ECKANKAR only a short while. It is not that the ECK prohibits their use, although initiations are not given to anyone abusing drugs. It is because such habits drop away naturally as one progresses on the path of ECKANKAR. At some point, their use is not compatible with the spiritual being. A chela must choose either the habit or the spiritual path. When this becomes apparent there is no contest. No one will give up the ecstacy, the joy of the spirit, the positive force that grows more vital each day."

The letters that Darwin receives on the subject of negative habits almost uniformly emphasize the ease with which they are given up when the ECK infuses the consciousness of that individual. As one awakens in his spiritual understanding, the things holding him back drop away:

My attitude has really improved during the last couple of months since I haven't smoked

183

"dope." It is such an enticing and disguised TRAP. The enigma is that the clean, drug-free consciousness is the highest of all. The marijuana trap is so very subtle because I was convinced that it really wasn't a "drug" and even appeared to be beneficial. The only way to quit is to really want to. Fortunately, the ECK led me into situations where the negative aspects of the "stoned" consciousness were forced into view ....when viewed from the clear consciousness of the Truth, the "stoned" consciousness becomes just another limited area on the path of realization.

Love,
H.

I had smoked pot for 7 years before becoming an ECKist, but dropped it completely when my Satsang instructor told me several months ago that you said not to smoke at all if you are taking the discourses. It was as easy to do as walking out the door, much to my surprise. I'm sure the ECK and yourself assisted me with this.

M.

Last October at the World Wide Seminar I was very sick. I had developed a degenerated disc in my neck and after a year of wearing a neck brace and 3 months of traction I was resigned that this painful problem was here to stay at 20 years old. I accidently walked into you as you were leaving the auditorium, and you raised your hand over the both of us and said, "May the blessings be." My neck problem is gone now. But you didn't only help me get rid of that, you also helped me to stop smoking pot, too.

After the World Wide I felt great. My neck felt better. But every time I would smoke pot, it would hurt like the dickens. Gradually, I smoked less and less. And now I can say I don't think I will ever smoke again and my neck is fine, too!

B.

Unfavorable negative conditions of any kind can be traced back to one single cause: imbalance. Be it mental illness, subconscious pressures, emotional suffering or physical pain. Emotional attachment, for instance, to an object which is temporary will eventually cause pain because that object will inevitably be lost at some point in time. The ECKist learns to have and use material objects without undue attachment to them, he learns to avoid the strong preference of one thing over another, one idea or argument over another. His balance is found in being a channel for the ECK, serving ITS cause in the sense of "being in this world, but not of it."

Sri Darwin stresses that the teachings of ECK teach that, "Soul and Its separation from the physical body has been stressed in not only the writings and teachings of ECK but by all the great teachers down through history, before Jesus and during Jesus' time. I have always stressed that while you live you must live a balanced life with Spirit and living in this world.

"In fact, that balance which is so vital to survival is pointed out in *The Shariyat-Ki-Sugmad* as well as the ECK discourses and other ECK writings. This also means that once the Living ECK Master is your spiritual guide, by keeping your thoughts on him your daily life is improved."

This does not imply escape from the world. The ECKist does not seek refuge in a mountain cave or live in a secluded ashram, but masters his life in society by not being the effect of things he does not desire for himself. Control of thoughts and emotions are part of the teachings of

185

ECKANKAR, but time and again Darwin has emphasized the need for common sense. At one seminar attended by Darwin during a period of questions and comments from the audience, a woman told of how Darwin had saved her daughter's life—not by healing the child but by making the mother realize that her daughter needed proper medical attention and surgery. The child had been dying under the treatment of a naturopath who had prescribed only natural foods and herbs. Common sense should be used by the individual to determine when it is perfectly all right to take advantage of the benefits civilization offers. "Man has not learned to live only on air and sunshine—yet," Darwin said to the audience of the seminar.

The trick is to let the mind be used by Soul as an instrument, rather than be subject to the conditioning the mind has undergone from childhood on. Often the imprisonment in his own set ways will hinder the adult to do Soul Travel, because his mind will tell him it's impossible, or because of the fear of the unknown. Children, on the other hand, still have a much greater randomity of mind. They are not so sure, as the average person in his adult years, that the physical world is the only reality, and all else is illusion. To them Soul Travel is natural, and it is equally natural to have a spiritual guide with them. ECKist parents are often amazed by their children speaking of "Darji" or other ECK Masters with the greatest familiarity:

> Dear Darwin,
> First, I wish to discuss my son, David, age 21 months. David was in the children's room at the seminar. This morning, David woke up and I went in his room and talked to him for awhile before I got him out of bed. He said, "fly like a birdie" and I said, "Did you fly like a birdie?" He said yes. He then said, "window" and pointed to the window. I said, "out the window?" He said yes. He then said "Darji." I said,

"Did you go with Darji?" He said yes. We have never taught him the word "Darji." We never told him of soul travel in any way, nor have we ever told him anything that he would associate flying like a birdie with the word, "Darji." My hope and my chosen belief is that David is soul traveling with you, Darji, and there is nothing more we could ever want for him.

L.

One evening, my 4-year-old daughter and I were lying on the bed in the spare bedroom draped among the extra pillows and blankets, listening to a number of ECK songs. She was squirming around and chattering to herself in an almost undecipherable language.

...Although her chattering continued, I could tell instinctively that her eyelids were getting heavy. Then, she was still for a moment, and I heard her say clearly, "Good night, Darwin; God bless your heart." In that precious moment, I could feel the presence of the MAHANTA sparkling like a million diamonds, and all from the mouth of a 4-year-old ECKist. She rolled over on her side, face on her hands, looking at the wall with wide, pretty eyes, and gradually went to sleep.

D.

One parent reported a dream her 8-year-old son James had told her:

I was dreaming I was in the Land of the Lost, all alone. There were ape people with sharp sticks who were chasing me. I wasn't an ape man, I was a normal human. Then dinosaurs started chasing me. I was afraid and started say-

187

ing, "Darji, Darji!" Then Darwin was there. He made the dinosaurs little like lizards and petted them and put them in his pocket. Then he said, "Nothing can hurt you when I'm with you."

B.

Dear Darwin,

Thank you that I am in ECK. I appreciate all what you have done for me. I am very scared of the dark because I see ugly white faces and when I say "MAHANTA" or "Darwin" they go away. So, thank you for helping me. I love you very much.

R.

Protection from harm is one of the most frequent subjects related in the thousands of letters Darwin receives a month. "My love and protection always surround you" is a statement he often uses to close his written communications to the chelas of ECK. The teachings of ECK state that every man is surrounded by an aura, an electronic field; that outermost sheath is the astral body. The aura acts as a protective shield and cannot be pierced from without, only from within. This happens when the individual has negative or detrimental thoughts, emotions or actions against himself or others. Then his aura is weakened from within and harmful influences can affect him. However, should the individual not be aware, a person with strong mental powers can penetrate the astral body.

The unique protection the MAHANTA, the Living ECK Master offers to all who are aware of his presence is that the love of the SUGMAD flowing from him to each individual fills the aura and heals the openings or holes that make the person vulnerable. To those whose inner sight is developed this protective force is visible as a mantle or curtain of white light completely enveloping the individual's whole being. It works on every plane of heaven the person might be endangered on—the mental, causal, astral, and physical—and makes him virtually untouchable and invulnerable.

Dear Darwin,

I would like to thank you, in this letter, for the time my life, or at least my physical vision, was saved due to the protection afforded each chela by the Living ECK Master.

I work in construction as a carpenter with my brother and we use pneumatic nailing guns. On this occasion my other brother was also working with us. He was nailing the studs to the plates on the ground with our big spiker and I would align them on the layout marks. In this particular instance, he fired a nail; it just caught the corner of the 2x4 plate and ricocheted off, heading directly at my face. The nail stopped in mid-air, about twelve inches from me. I observed it spinning for an instant, and then it fell harmlessly to the ground. I was stunned. Those nails have 100 pounds of air behind them and it shouldn't have stopped—according to all the physical laws. I myself have shot nails that have just nicked a corner and observed them travel for a great distance like a dart and stick through aluminum siding into wood on a neighboring house.

...Thank you for this protection.

F.

Dear Darwin,

On Friday, February 17, 1978, in the men's comfort station downstairs in the Greyhound Bus Terminal, here in Washington, D.C., two burly black men accosted me in the middle of the afternoon. I was the only person in the men's room when those two came in, threatened me. . .I was at their mercy; I had no defense; one man had his arm around my shoulders.

But something swiftly happened around me, I know not what. My personality changed; I had no fear, and suddenly the two would-be robbers backed off pretending it was a joke, but it was no joke. . . I can only describe what took place was due to the invisible presence and protection of the MAHANTA, the Living ECK Master.

Sincerely in ECK,
J.

At least several times a week, Darwin receives stories of road accidents where people were protected from severe harm or death. He is often aware of acting in the Soul body, his hands on the steering wheel of the endangered car, guiding the vehicle out of situations that should have ended in fatal collision by all laws of probability.

My Beloved Master,

This fall, I was going along the expressway. My girlfriend was in the car with me.

As I was telling her that I had no fear of death anymore, a truck that was in front of us dropped a large piece of steel off the back, which came right for the car. We were in the exit lane of the expressway. The steel hit the right front tire of my car. The car spun around, going the other way. All my physical eyes saw were cars and trucks coming straight for us. All my spiritual eye saw was your face. For no reason known to me, I floored the gas pedal. I did not realize that had happened until I hit the guard rail. It seemed as if my foot was in slow motion as I took it off the gas to the brake. We had crossed four lanes of traffic, and neither of us were hurt. Thank you, Master, and I say that with all sincere gratitude and love. What topped this all off is that I had just put a small picture of you right behind my steering wheel just a few days before this happened.

Thank you again, dear MAHANTA, for your protection.

M.

The primary job of the MAHANTA, the Living ECK Master, as assigned to him by the supreme SUGMAD, is to gather up Souls to take them back through the lower worlds of duality to their true home in the pure positive God Worlds to become co-workers with the Deity. To do this, he guides them on the inner and outer, teaches them, protects them spiritually and helps them work out their karma, but perhaps his singular most important responsibility is to initiate them into the audible life stream. Only the MAHANTA, the Living ECK Master can give the true initiation into the ECK for he alone is the representative of the SUGMAD, the Source of the Life Current. There is a different Circle of Initiation corresponding to each plane of existence, i.e. physical, astral, etc. up to the God-conscious plane. The initiation of the First Circle is generally given in the dream state via the MAHANTA, and constitutes a preliminary linkup with the Sound Current.

"It takes place when one is ready, usually in the dream state and with conscious awareness, although some do not remember this initiation," Darwin says. "It is entirely between the chela and the Living ECK Master. With some individuals this takes place on the inner planes, with others it takes place in the heavenly worlds or beyond time, space and matter. But it may be reflected in the form of a vision during a spiritual exercise. Others will have a knowingness that a significant occurrence has taken place."

The Second Initiation is both an outer and inner initiation, and for the chela, this is one of the most important

191

steps in his unfoldment. It is his actual linkup with Spirit, demanding of him a sincere commitment and dedication to serve as a vehicle for IT. This decision is not thrust upon him, for in ECKANKAR each step is up to the individual. The Inter Master never interferes with the decisions of the chelas, giving them complete freedom at all times. If, after two years of study, the student wishes the Second Initiation, he may request it. Sri Darwin explains:

"The chela should study for two or more years with the discourses of ECKANKAR as well as the ECK books to build a spiritual foundation to become a member in ECKANKAR."

The initiations from the Second through the Fifth are given by the Mahdis, an Initiator appointed by the Living ECK Master who serves as the right arm and vehicle for the MAHANTA to work through. An Initiator is an Initiate of the Fifth Circle or higher. The transformation a person goes through after an initiation is documented by thousands of letters and reports in Darwin's files. One new Second Initiate writes:

Dear Darwin,

I know that you are aware that I was a Catholic priest for nineteen and a half years. However, I can now say that the priesthood never gave me the love, confidence or security that I now know. I must also state that I now know more about SUGMAD and I am beginning to understand life and living better.

Since my second initiation I have noted within myself a richness and depth which can be described as "profound." I feel better spiritually, emotionally, and physically and I know that the promise I made through your hint is giving me untold benefits.

In summary, I am changing, and I am aware of it, and I'm sure of it. I'm a spark of SUGMAD and I like it.

W.

All in all, there are twelve initiations that an individual receives to become an ECK Master in ECKANKAR. An ECK Master, however, is not necessarily the Living ECK Master. In Sri Darwin's words:

"The Living ECK Master is always a man because of that positive atom of structure. A woman can become a Master but not a Living ECK Master. There are a total of twelve initiations that one has to go through or take in order to become an ECK Master. You can take nine here physically but the rule is bent occasionally; ten, eleven and twelve took place while I was here in the physical body, but they weren't given physically. They took place in the Soul body.

"I do the initiations from the sixth on up. Anyone who has an initiation from the second on should never ask for initiations and that includes the higher initiates. If someone asks for one, I'll turn a deaf ear for awhile. The only initiation in ECK that one can request is the second."

The MAHANTA is constantly watching the chelas, observing how they go through the tests and trials of existence in the lower worlds, how they are progressing spiritually. Their spiritual unfoldment rests in his hands, and he knows exactly when they are ready for their next initiation. Instead of seeking to gain advantages or a greater title or status for himself, the chela might progress to a faster degree by serving as an agent for God or IT. An ECK Master gains his stature mainly by his overwhelming desire to surrender to the Divine Spirit and be wholly consumed by IT. From this experience comes a deep sense of joy, one of the principal survival factors in the heavenly world. Darwin says:

"The most distinguishing facet of the ECKist's existence is the sense of joy, a joy which arises from his or her own knowledge that death is a myth, that the word 'life' has a reality that encompasses a state of existence beyond man's imagination and that the only thing which holds man from the realization of these states is his own self, his limiting concepts."

Once the chela has gained mastery over his own consciousness, his own universe, he is free to explore the worlds of God on his own. This is the most beautiful part of his journey back to his original home. He has gained spiritual maturity and freedom.

Darwin continues: "One can unfold spiritually to see and experience the SUGMAD (God) in all things, as well as in every person, when you've reached the Source, the one God that all deities of the various levels of heaven look to, including the devil (in ECKANKAR he is called Kal Niranjan, also known as the dark force), which is under the guidance and direction of that one Source. There is no beginning nor ending as one learns, and learns to live in the present moment of time, in living life to the fullest with common sense and keeping a balance in daily life.

"Beyond the level of heaven, plane or level of existence or dimension, whichever way you wish to think of it, very few are able to go into these areas and explore them. In order to do so, one must know God, have the understanding of God and have reached a level of spiritual evolution.

"In ECKANKAR, one learns not to pray for the Divine to give us something as individuals. Instead, we ask for that in the positive manner which would benefit all in our receiving. By so doing, we are lifting ourselves above the level of self-involving thought and giving greater significance to helping ourselves by doing for the Whole of all Life."

CHAPTER 9

Attitude and Attention

As Darwin's responsibilities increased in his role as the Living ECK Master, it began to take its toll on his physical body, aging it rapidly. His health which had been exceptionally good prior to his acceptance of the Rod of ECK Power, began to give him problems, although he called them "mechanical difficulties." By 1973, two years into the ECK Mastership, and well on his way in accepting the added strength and responsibilities as the MAHANTA he felt increased pain under his left shoulder blade from the accident in 1961 which had entailed fifteen days in traction. With increased travel, the stress of long hours of work, the pull of seminars throughout the worlds of God, sleepless nights and his continued concern for those under his spiritual guidance, the pain steadily worsened. Yet the ECK teachings tell us that the Living ECK Master accepts only those burdens he chooses to accept.

"My whole being, every bit of my energy is for no person or no thing except to guide Souls to the higher planes of awareness," Darwin commented. "My lack of formal education is history. Like the ECK Masters before me throughout all history, my personal life reflects the times I live in, the clothing, food, lifestyle. With one very significant difference. Besides my spiritual role, I am one-centered in the essence of God, the ECK."

Darwin, affectionately known to the chelas of ECKANKAR as Darji, does not have a personal life, per se. All encompassing is his role as Lightgiver, Wayshower. Yet he has worked at many occupations, a basically happy individual who enjoys being around those who are cheerful and joyous in their demeanor. He has said: "These are factors of survival, not only in this lifetime but beyond eternity, including eternity. If you look at those people who are aged, who might be eighty years old but look like forty, that's because they have enjoyed life and like to fill their lives full of happiness or joyfulness. You have to keep a balance; if you go out on the street whooping in a very exuberant state of happiness, they'll think something is wrong with you. This is without the use of drugs or anything else; it's one's knowledge of life, spirit and heaven."

Those who have worked with him or have known him before and since he has become the Living ECK Master speak of him in glowing terms. He has kept the love and devotion of his son, Tim, and his daughter, Renee, even though he rarely has an opportunity to visit with them. Both of them are married with children; both, like Darwin, are musically oriented. They were born during his first marriage to Rae Baliff, a marriage that lasted seven years, with Darwin and Rae parting as friends.

He felt it was extremely important not to argue in front of his children: "I didn't want the children growing up in a negative atmosphere. At a very early age is when you form their character and the first six years are the most important years of that child. I don't like to argue and I never did. I've had enough of it as a child between the parents, and in previous experiences with women, they've tried to make me argue about certain points and I wouldn't. If two people can't sit down and talk intelligently and like human beings, you're wasting your energy."

Darwin taught his children the spiritual exercises of ECK and started them on the ECK discourses, but from that point on, they were on their own. Both of them have attended ECKANKAR seminars, and Tim accompanied Darwin to the Seattle ECKANKAR World Wide seminar in October of 1976. Darwin was still feeling the effects of a severe cold, as well as the back muscle and shoulder pain he had been troubled with from the old injury. Darwin and Tim were backstage awaiting Darwin's turn to speak before the evening's audience when someone brought to his attention a religious group outside the seminar entrance, blocking people from coming in.

Darwin walked out to speak with the individuals. They were seen detaining people from entering the seminar site, handing out their literature and attempting to block the entrance. Darwin explained they could not do this or disrupt the ECKANKAR meetings. He asked them to move away from the entrance. They refused. Darwin added: "You don't know anything about creating karma, do you?"

With that, Darwin took the literature from their hands and handed it to Mike. His eyes narrowed, his powerful gaze upon the individuals. "If you return, we'll call the police!" Then he whirled around and returned to the backstage area again, his talk just moments away. Darwin had wasted no time or words. It had been handled immediately! The individuals in question did not return. Darwin stated later that this should have been handled by Higher Initiates who had been aware of this instead of bringing it to him.

Tim stands ready at a moment's notice to be of service to his Dad, his love for him evident and strong. BB, Darwin's personal secretary, has witnessed Tim and Darwin on the telephone for a ten-minute period, where each says very little to the other. BB could see Darwin working diligently at his desk and since Tim was on the speaker-phone, she could also hear Tim scribbling away at his end of the phone. Every few moments or so, one or the other would interject a thought: "You feeling OK, Dad?"

"Yeap! Wife OK?"

"Yeah, she's in Ohio."

In the intermittent pauses, both men continued their writing.

"But as humorous as it seemed at the time," BB added, "there was something special going on here that I could savor. It was a silent communication, mindful of that which existed between Darwin and his own father, a divine, unattached love that still indicated a caring. I could see these moments between Tim and Darwin as the essence of divine love that Darwin often spoke of, so subtle, so fragile, like a bubble on the wind."

Tim remembers Darwin teaching him to drive while holding Tim on his lap, weekends on camping trips in California, joining Darwin on his sales trips down the Oregon coast, a summer they had together in the San Francisco peninsula area, a special trip they took to North Dakota and Canada, going with Darwin on talks he gave on ECKANKAR. It bothered Tim when few showed up for Darwin's talks. Tim was constantly amazed at the gadgets Darwin had at home, prisms, magnets, inventions. There was always the divine love between them, the respect, the admiration. Never dwindling, secure in its spiritual foundation between them.

Darwin tells an endearing story of divine love in a little Sheltie dog, a toy collie, that he bought when the children were very small. "I taught Topper to keep Renee in the yard. The love Topper and I shared was divine, yet detached. He was my dog and he would do anything that was asked of him. We went for many long walks at night and I knew that the dog wanted to move out with me when I separated from Rae. However, I was compelled to leave Topper with the children. The very next day after I moved out of the house, Topper went out into a busy street a block away from home and was run over. If he couldn't be with me, he didn't wish to live!"

On October 13, 1973, Darwin and Gail Twitchell were married by Helen Varner Frye in Sedona, Arizona. Darwin announced it from the stage at the World Wide seminar. The applause was thunderous! The general consensus was: What took them so long! They were a handsome couple, working together constantly and obviously respecting and loving each other in many ways. Since a mold had been set by a Higher Initiate for their Sedona wedding, it "happened" on a visit they had made to Sedona just before the seminar. Neither had consciously planned on it. Yet it seemed a natural event for both of them.

Gail had been acting as his secretary on their travels for ECKANKAR and she was an invaluable aide to Darwin since she, as Paul's widow, knew the demands upon a Living ECK Master. She helped Darwin in the Office; he drew upon her knowledge of Paul, his activities and goals for ECKANKAR. Gail respected and understood Darwin's total dedication to the spirit of ECK and the work of the Vairagi ECK Masters.

They had fun together. In Zurich, Switzerland, Darwin awoke Gail around 3:30 in the morning, suggested a walk and some hot chocolate. Rarely could he sleep much at night. Not finding any shops open, they opted for an all-night train, drinking coffee and talking secludedly. They watched as the charming Swiss villages, lakes and streams whisked by and learned that a cog railway at the top of a mountain above the city could take them to a restaurant for lunch. Gail marveled as Darwin had spaghetti and hot chocolate with real cream. Their romantic interlude lasted until early afternoon when they returned to Zurich.

Gail got some stationery from Darwin's briefcase to write a letter for him and was berated for going into his things without permission. He told her: "If it isn't yours, don't touch it! I would never go into your purse, dresser drawers or anything that did not belong to me. Would you like someone to come up to you and go through your pockets or purse without permission?"

Then he added: "One of the reasons I am so cautious of other people's property, their personal belongings, and wouldn't even go into my wife's personal things, emanated from an early teenage experience. While driving home from school one day, through the industrial area, I spotted a fire in this home, fire trucks, people gathering to see if they could help. Up to that time, I was never curious about

199

other people's business but there was one aspect where I needed to learn a lesson, which lasted a lifetime.

"They had carried furniture and appliances out of the house to save them from the fire and I walked in and opened up the refrigerator to see if there was anything in it. We call this being 'nosey.' Along comes the owner of the house and punches me right in the nose. From that day on, I never was inquisitive about anyone's personal belongings!"

For the next three years, Darwin and Gail lived and worked together out of suitcases and briefcases. Their travels included Africa, the Middle East, Australia, Europe, Central America, the United States and Canada. Now and again they'd take in a movie or spend some time on the boat Darwin had, but rest and relaxation were elusive visitors. He kept up with the negative world and local news via periodicals and television. Darwin enjoyed cooking and took care of his own ironing and packing. Their "big night out" was often a meal at MacDonald's for a fishwich or a hamburger.

Darwin encouraged Gail's graduate education, her growing independence and spiritual growth. He was neat and easy to be with and they were able to resolve any disagreements that entered their marriage. As time permitted, Darwin gave attention to a garden in the backyard, but muttered with disgust when they returned from a trip to find the vegetables gigantic misshapen mounds of inedibility.

One night while on a trip to New Zealand and Australia, Darwin awakened to find Gail taking notes. He had been giving a talk on ECKANKAR in his sleep and she had decided to take notes. "Don't you ever quit working?" she laughed. It had been raining most of the time they were there and Darwin had slept a lot. So they got up and washed their hair in the rain.

Gail became more absorbed in her responsibilities with the Illuminated Way Press, the publisher of ECKANKAR books (which Gail gave to ECKANKAR in the fall of

1976), and the Sunasu vitamins based on Paul's book, *Herbs, the Magic Healers*. Each was solicitous of the other as Darwin's back pain increased and Gail became ill for several months.

Tim spent his junior year of high school with them in San Diego and Renee lived with them for a couple of years before she married.

While he was married to Gail, Darwin's experiences with dogs continued. Gail already had Paul's "five dollar dog Teddy," also known as Theodore Von Dog. Paul used to tell audiences about his efforts to win Teddy over by taking the German shepherd-collie out for ice cream cones. Teddy soon found his home territory overrun by Duke, a miniature tri-color collie Darwin had purchased for Gail, and before too long by Ti Ling, a fuzzy ball of fur given to Gail by Ellie McLendon who raised Lhasa apsos.

Right from the beginning Ti Ling wanted to be king of the roost, but Teddy had run of the home and wasn't about to give it up. They fought periodically and one time Ti Ling lost his right eye with one chomp from Teddy's jaws. This never deterred Ti Ling who continued to dominate the dogdom household whenever he could.

One time a Mexican yard worker came into Darwin's yard ignoring the "Beware of Dog" sign on the gate. Darwin had earlier warned the man not to enter the yard unless he or Gail were on the premises, but the warning went unheeded. Half-way up the walkway, Teddy charged the man who fled in such terror he left the heels of his shoes implanted in the pavement, beside his hat!

It was not unusual for Darwin to take off in the middle of the night on his Harley Davidson motorcycle. Unable to sleep, he would head down the highway to an all-night coffee shop where he'd drink coffee, scan the newspapers and give attention to what was taking place in other parts of the world. He rarely wore his helmet, which concerned Gail, but in one instance when he had a helmet on, he spun out on a curve at 25 miles per hour. It was daytime. The weather was clear, no stones in the street or oil slick. But his bike slipped out from under him slamming him into the curb. Two other cyclists resting by the road came to help. They were surprised that he had escaped with no injuries and assisted Darwin while righting the bike. When the one remarked: "You've got God on your side," Darwin countered with, "Only I call IT Sugmad." They shook their heads and accepted the book Darwin offered them — *Stranger by the River* by Sri Paul Twitchell. Darwin was never without a book or two at all times. One of the cyclists joined ECKANKAR sometime later, crediting it for helping him stop drugs.

At the time of the accident, the electricity in Darwin's home went out momentarily. Gail immediately knew something had happened to Darwin and was relieved when he arrived home safely.

It had been Paul Twitchell's wish that his remains be cremated and the ashes scattered on the waters on the Pacific. One Saturday afternoon Darwin and Gail took out his power boat, then set out to sea to comply with Paul's last wishes. They stood silently for a few moments as the waves rocked the boat gently from side to side several miles out of San Diego Bay, spread the ashes on the water and returned to shore. Sharing warm reminiscent thoughts about Paul, they felt no sadness, for Paul was still very much a part of their lives.

"The ECK wedding ceremony is different. It's very enlightening," Darwin has commented. "It's not emotional but it's a spiritual event, a very lovely spiritual event that takes place. Each one that has been performed, the individuals involved have truly enjoyed it. In the ECK wedding ceremony, their marriage is a marriage of Soul. Not to be construed with the soul mate idea. Even in ECKANKAR, there are divorces, separations, and we're not saying that we have a cure for divorce. Two people that can't keep that flame going, for some reason or other, should not really live together. If there's children involved, that's one thing.

They have to think long and hard and twice about it. The ECK tends to hold families together and not separate them. Divorce can be on friendly terms, with no karmatic bond."

In the summer of 1977, Darwin and Gail agreed upon a divorce, as their ways in life went in different directions. Darwin and Gail have remained friendly, often communicating by letter or phone.

To those who are privileged to work closely with Darwin when he is in the ECKANKAR Office, an interesting phenomena presents itself. He is humorous, patient, hard-working, efficient, considerate. But they know that every word he utters has a meaning they should not ignore, for he expects immediate action on every request. His laughter generates smiles from all around him and his zeal becomes a learning experience for all within earshot. No matter what the situation, the personnel and staff work long hours and serve in any way they can to assist Darji, their spiritual guide and inner friend.

On one occasion, when Darwin had finished up some work at the ECKANKAR Office and was preparing to drive well into the night to Southern California, the Business Manager offered to help him drive. Darwin took him up on it. Mark jumped into the car and they took off. In the morning Mark was on a plane back to San Francisco, ready for another day's work at the Office. The fact that he didn't even have time to get his toothbrush or shaving cream did not phase him. Flexibility around Darwin is the first lesson one learns. And, like Mark, all those close to Darwin consider it a privilege to be able to be of assistance in any way Darwin allows.

It is difficult to draw a line between Darwin, the man, and Darwin, the Living ECK Master. The respect and love felt for the man becomes intensified for the Master. It also keeps the office staff in a state of awe and wonderment because casualness around Darwin can be deceptive when he is in the Office. There is a line that is never crossed with him and each comes to terms with this quickly or they aren't around him very long: that is, always be up front and truthful with him for he is able to see through the falsehood.

At a meeting at the ECKANKAR International Office, prior to the annual Creative Arts Festival, Darwin joined the group and immediately sat on the floor. He was relaxed and tired, asked if they had any questions and just generally enjoyed being with them. Another time, during a staff meeting, obviously tired and recuperating from past surgeries, he spoke of considering the possibility of stepping aside as the Living ECK Master. "Anyone want the job?" he quipped. No one volunteered! You might ask, why not? Those present who possibly might qualify knew that is something you do not talk about with others.

The man doesn't change when he becomes the Living ECK Master. He still likes to laugh, enjoy life, he does not become bitter. According to Darwin: "We as individuals are made up a little differently. Each of us is different. Paul might have a little lower threshold and get perturbed or upset easier than I, so he may have had a right to. He perhaps had had a harder life, and not all of us are going to come into this life with the same set of circumstances, so it varies. All of the ECK Masters have a great human side to them, all of those I've met and become acquainted with in ECKANKAR.

"I get instructions or ask for help from the other ECK Masters, and they are at my disposal in that sense," he continued. "The next Living ECK Master, when he's in this spot of responsibility, he'll have the Vairagi ECK Masters behind him. And woe to that person who misuses it, whether it's me or anyone else! The ECK Masters can walk among man and no one will know it. Quite frequently though, there'll be either a lovely scent or a great feeling of love. The ECK Masters do not tease. There is no time for that. Oh, on the physical level I will but I let the person know I'm teasing for I like to laugh, a little joy, there's so much sorrow as there is in the world, but this is in the human state. On the other side it's a more serious thing, it's serious here too. I don't keep track of what I do on the other side all the time. Maybe I do tease, but it's for your spiritual growth."

Six staff members joined Darwin in a round-table discussion involving a field project. For several hours he polled each of them for their input, why they would do this, how they would do that. Tiny tapes were kept of this material but when the meeting ended, the group realized that Darwin had summed up the entire exercise in a choice few words. "I felt that whole exercise wasn't really to get our ideas," BB interjected, "but to give everyone a chance to talk and sift things out so we could get on with what he really wanted done."

In one instance during a private meeting in Darwin's Office, a small tape recorder was used to take notes of pertinent information. Either Janice, the executive secretary, or BB, Darwin's personal secretary, were planning on transcribing the notes since both had attended the meeting. But through an error, the tape was given to another in the Office to transcribe and nothing appeared on the tape at all. It was completely blank! When brought to Darwin's attention, he indicated that he'd had nothing to do with it, that without his raising a finger, Spirit, through the vehicle, erased the tape.

When the pain in Darwin's back and left arm became unbearable, he visited a well-known clinic in Texas in an effort to pinpoint the problem. X-rays showed an inflammation in that area, but he was told he had arthritis and there was little they could do for him. They would not listen to his comments that it was a "mechanical difficulty" and not arthritis at all. Not until he visited a doctor in San Francisco was a bone-scan considered. A small tumor was diagnosed and surgery performed June 28, 1979, to remove a micro-scopic osteroid osteoma, called a "hot spot" by the doctors. The doctor reported that he had removed some bone tissue from two ribs and that the tumor was non-cancerous. Within eight months Darwin would be ready for action again.

The recuperative period was difficult for Darwin for he was restless, impatient, and all too aware of his continuous spiritual responsibilities as the Living ECK Master. Eight days following this painful surgery, he was holding an ECKANKAR Board Meeting in his apartment. Hot towels and gentle massage seemed to alleviate the immediate pain but he avoided medication whenever possible.

While the first surgery eliminated the problem from the cracked rib suffered in 1961, the old tenderness in his back and shoulder gradually returned to plague him, for "the negative force always attacks the weakest part of the body," according to Darwin. Dr. Hester Lewis located a spine specialist at the UC Medical Center in San Francisco who performed additional surgery on Darwin January 28, 1980. The second surgical procedure removed a frozen rib-vertebral joint which extended from an old injury from incorrect lifting years ago. The two incisions lay like a large "T" on its side, about one and one-half inches from his left shoulder blade.

Bernadine Burlin (BB) reported: "Darwin endured months of accumulated pain and discomfort from the surgery itself and muscle spasms that were helped periodically by hot towels and massage. It was difficult for him to take the necessary time to heal for his spiritual responsibilities never cease for him. He was subject to chills and colds that attacked his tender back. He is swimming where possible, jumping rope and hiking in small doses, in an effort to strengthen his back muscles. The warm sun helps. He who can heal others will not heal himself for it would mean calling upon the psychic forces and he will not do this for himself. It's been mighty rough on him but he's a remarkable man!"

Anne Roberts knew Darwin when he was an Arahata (Satsang teacher) in Oregon, before he became the Living ECK Master. She smiled: "The responsibilities and

206

spiritual burdens began to take their toll on him shortly after becoming the Living ECK Master. I was not prepared for the sight of him in Los Angeles at a seminar in 1972 when I stopped to talk with him for a moment in the hallway. He looked like he had just come out of a concentration camp. There were already new lines etched into his face and his weight was down. Somehow, I sensed the amount of karma he had willingly assumed, either for the chelas in ECK, or the world as a whole. I left him, turned a corner, found a quiet place to myself and burst into tears. I was to learn that his responsibility was no different than any other Living ECK Master who has ever walked the earth.

"This was a particularly obvious and isolated instance, because Darwin always takes great care in fostering a happy attitude and a zest for living, even in the face of enormous odds. He never parades his grievances before others to gain sympathy. Pity is something he would never bear from others because his spiritual strength and stature far overshadow whatever personal pain his spiritual burdens demand."

When the pain became too great and sleep impossible, Darwin would watch a late-late show on television and pop some popcorn. He is never without one to three ECK Masters around him at all times, and several ECK Initiates who witnessed his surgeries with an inner awareness, also noted that three ECK Masters hovered around Darwin's anesthesized body, watching the operation with Darwin himself.

In December 1979, Darwin officiated at his sister Adeline's funeral in Oregon. Walt Froeber, Adeline's husband, had contacted Darwin who was in England at the time. Darwin's dissertation followed the service given by a Catholic priest. Darwin read from *Stranger By The River* by Paul Twitchell, referring to his relationship with his sister, the silent communication they had together and how this had assisted throughout their lives to overcome situations and remain balanced individuals. Following the funeral, the priest patted Darwin on the arm and told him how much he had enjoyed listening to him.

Here, Darwin met once more with members of his family. Although he did not see them very often, he kept in touch with some of them. He had assisted his mother across the borders of heaven when she translated (died) in 1969, just as he helped his Dad in 1967.

As for his personal dietary preferences, since childhood, Darwin has been unable to tolerate rare meat because animal fat does not agree with his system. Onions and cauliflower never did agree with him and often make him ill if he eats them. As for ice cream, he says:

"While I was in training for ECK Mastership under Paul Twitchell, I went through a period of having a cone of ice cream each day, but as I unfolded spiritually, I was given a lesson. One day while having my ice cream cone I found it tasted like cow droppings. That did it for me! I was allergic to the processed sugar in the ice cream. I can tolerate real untreated sugar, pure maple syrup and all natural sugars from fruits and vegetables. Food and what one puts into their physical body has nothing to do with their spiritual unfoldment as some teach. Western man has been taught for centuries to eat meat; however, it is a discipline not to eat too much. Remember the statement Jesus made: 'Take due thought of what you eat or drink.' "

Those that work closely with Darwin must be clean in hair and clothing. "I don't mind long hair as long as it's neat and trim. I don't mind a beard as long as it's trimmed and neat and good-looking, but if it's scraggly and unkempt, I don't want them around me or representing ECKANKAR. That's true of women's clothes, hair and makeup as well. Heavy scents should be avoided, for the subtle, faint scents of sandalwood, roses and peppermint waft around us when various Vairagi ECK Masters are in our vicinity, but go unnoticed when masked by heavily perfumed products worn by individuals.

"In this position, the Living ECK Master can't say no,

208

nor could Paul. When Paul translated, he set the time, the place, the date, and did it. There was a young lady who wanted to be in his presence when he translated and she was there for he helped carry out that mold that was set. Somebody draws a picture or a mold which they wish fulfilled, and many times that is fulfilled. We must be very careful, not only how we say things or think things but how we conduct ourselves in what man calls 'body language' too. I don't pay any attention to the body language; many misuse it, suggestively. I overlook those things.

"Women have certain signs, men have certain signs, to attract someone or they want to shut a person off. You're talking to someone and they cross their arms, some think they're not interested or it might be more imposition for that person, or they cross their legs. These things are of the more mental and physical nature, astral basically, astral in the sense of trying to generate some enthusiasm in the emotional area, mental from the point that that person thinks to outmaneuver the other person or influence the other person. I overlook that. I don't pay any attention to that if some person or persons use body language. It goes right by me due to the negative qualities. A lot depends on how it's used.

"Anyone working with me has got to be honest. If not, there's going to be trouble. I want people to be honest with me because I am being honest with my fellow man. If they can't be honest, I don't want them working around me. They're not going to do themselves any good nor the Divine Spirit, for they become a vehicle for the dark force. I'm not saying that a person can't bend a little bit, or that you have to be as straight as a flag pole. When I ask things from people, I want it straight from the shoulder and an honest answer.

"I've grown up with having to tell the truth, although many times you tell the truth and people don't believe you anyway. I don't care to have people working around me who are unable to be truthful, because it'll catch up with them. One needs to keep a balance in life, in all the worlds of duality, and this is true of ECKists too. When one gives himself to ECK, they have to be prepared; they are going to be a vehicle and there should be no conditions on it. There are spiritual groups in this world that teach their followers how to lie. In time they must pay for it. As Emerson so stated it as compensation."

CHAPTER 10

ECKANKAR,
Its Place in this World

"I would like everyone to know the meaning of ECK," Sri Darwin Gross has affirmed. "In ECKANKAR the individual has always had the opportunity to journey to strange unknown worlds as well as levels of heaven in the Soul body. Today man has the ability through the teachings of ECK to open the door of traveling to these same worlds as well as unknown worlds which attract the imagination and stir the spirit within man."

Taking steps to fulfill this goal, Sri Darwin has appeared for interviews on radio and television talk shows throughout the world, a number of them major networks. In June of 1978 when asked on the Joe Franklin Show how many followers of ECKANKAR there are, Sri Darwin replied: "When we define followers, it's a person who has read a book, whether it's in this country or some other country. I'm not sure of the exact number, it could be in the millions. We haven't had the proper auditing of the books that were printed here in New York by a previous publisher. Throughout the United States and Canada, those who are truly followers that I'm aware of, there's upwards of 50,000 devoted people who are spreading the message of ECK. Beyond that, it could run into a million, two million people."

When asked by Joe Franklin if every person in the whole world was capable of following the ECK teachings, or whether there were some people who just couldn't or wouldn't fit into that, Sri Darwin answered candidly: "The person after picking up a book and reading it, is either for it

211

or against it. There's no middle path in that respect. Yet, there is something for everyone, whether it's a child or an adult. We have children who are just crawling or just barely walking, and they're very adept at going beyond this world in another body. It starts with movements of bodies, but they go directly after they adapt to that, in a state of Soul consciousness, above time, space and matter, where there's no negativeness. . . starting with the physical world up to the Etheric Plane, from there from the Soul Plane up into the various levels of heaven, such as the invisible world, the endless world, and the God-conscious plane of existence. You go directly, it's swifter than the mind can grasp. I'd say thousands and thousands of times swifter than the speed of light."

Explaining the concept of freedom in ECKANKAR, he continued: "Freedom in the state of consciousness to rise above time and space and matter, whether you're out here on the street in turmoil, and not being affected by it emotionally and mentally, but this is a spiritual freedom that we're talking about. In the physical we're limited. It's true that there are some of the ECK Masters that can come and go at will, and some individuals who are learning how to, I'll say, make appearances; in other words, utilizing the Soul body, and manifesting another body, but it's for the good of all. They don't do it mischievously. They will come and go, but they're a step to—you see man's consciousness today as a whole is ready for greater expansion. Throughout the world. I've most recently come from Asia and they're just spiritually very hungry. People who have studied not only Buddhism and Zen, but the various other religions that are over there in the East, and it's amazing."

More than three years earlier in January of 1975, on the nationally known Tom Snyder Tomorrow Show, Sri Darwin commented:

"I'm finding this, in different parts of the world a number of people have been seeking to understand more about themselves, the world they live in and the heavenly worlds. That person that has questions in these areas, that take up the teachings of ECK, they are answered for that person. I had not heard of ECKANKAR in my physical body until a book was placed in my hand, some eight years ago, perhaps as long as nine, maybe. And I learned that it was handed down very quietly from the Living ECK Master of the time to the student, on a one-to-one basis, until 1965 when Paul Twitchell started bringing it out openly to the masses, throughout the world.

"Reincarnation has its place, ESP has its place. Out-of-body travel has its place as well. A number of people have these experiences of being beyond themselves. Some are frightening, because they don't have the spiritual guidance, nor do they understand what is taking place. I am with that person on this path of ECKANKAR that is ready for that experience, so that they don't have this fear when they go beyond themselves, whether it be objectively or subjectively.

"The religious part is that the individual will go through a religious experience of Being and then go on and live his life the best way he knows how."

In response to Tom Snyder's question if ECKANKAR were a self-religion as opposed to a dogmatic religion where one would believe in saints and a savior and in God, and in heaven and hell, or if it were more concerned with just getting to know oneself, Sri Darwin answered: "It is more concerned with the survival of the individual self, throughout eternity. There is a part of the lower heavens, you might say a part of the astral world, that is set aside by man's religions as hell. It's a dark area, and it exists because man has put it into existence. There are superhuman beings — I don't call them Saints — they are very humble beings just as you might be or some other person that has gone through this experience while they're in the physical body and their neighbor would not even know it, or anyone else. An individual that goes up the spiritual ladder into the spiritual worlds, which there are many levels that are written about and spoken of in the writings and teachings of ECKANKAR—these are different levels of heaven. You can think of them as dimensions within time and space. But beyond time and space and matter there are still some levels of heaven that are known in ECKANKAR as the pure positive God Worlds. The Soul plane is the first plane or dimension in these heavens."

When Tom Snyder asked if Darwin had the Rod of ECK Power with him, Darwin replied: "No, but I carry it with me. I don't use it in the sense of a magic wand. Yet, there are things that I might do that I won't talk about, most think of as miracles, or the ECKists—they try in some degree, but they're not able to express what takes place and what happens. The average man cannot believe it." And when asked further if he used this Rod of Power to punish people in any way, Sri Darwin said: "No, I do not punish anyone. That's not my position. There are lords of karma that are in charge of doling out the positive or the negative karma. My only function is to see that those that wish to experience this called God or SUGMAD, or IT, and to expand their consciousness without the use of anything but their own initiative, during this lifetime, have that opportunity. I am only a guide and a wayshower, in a sense."

To the inevitable question—Are you God?—Sri Darwin answered: "No, not any more than you or the next person. I think the best way to explain this is that each living thing has a very small part of IT, or of God, and this is why man has that yearning to understand and know more about God, longs to be closer. The ECKists don't become one with God unless they choose to. It's a matter of survival throughout eternity—to retain your individuality. There's no other way. That is one of the reasons I chose to take up this teaching, but yet I found It chose me. I didn't really choose it. That small part of us is a part of God. You might say we're a part of It, yet for the ECKist the choice is the individual's every step of the way. What they want to do when they leave this life or during this lifetime, not just when they leave it, but the type of work—where they want to work from, whether it's from the physical plane, the astral plane, the mental worlds or the Soul plane, that's their choice on this path of ECK."

For that individual who is seeking and is ready to take the next step in unfolding spiritually within himself, the ECKANKAR International Office provides information brochures and pamphlets about ECKANKAR in more than a dozen languages, as well as several dozen books on ECKANKAR and various series of study discourses for either individual or group (Satsang) study. Many of the books and most of the discourses have been translated into other languages, the main emphasis being on English, French, German and Spanish. Most of the printed literature, excluding the high quantity printings of the English books, is produced at the ECKANKAR International Office, from where these materials are shipped to representatives and centers all over the world. It is generally advisable to read a few books before studying the ECK discourses, which are provided for study of one per month as a service which comes with a nominal yearly membership fee. Other study aids available include sound recordings (cassette tapes) of talks by Sri Darwin Gross, as well as his predecessor Sri Paul Twitchell, and some video cassettes.

There are presently some one hundred countries on the globe where members of ECKANKAR live. These range from a few individuals in countries such as Israel, Poland, Yugoslavia, the Philippines, and South America, to upwards of hundreds in each of the nations of Western Europe, West Africa and Australia, to many thousands in the United States and Canada. In most of these countries one or more Area Mahdis are present to oversee the Satsang classes and discussion groups taking place, conduct introductory lectures and see that the written material on ECKANKAR is available to the public.

The correspondence received by the ECKANKAR International Office from members all over the world mostly concerns administrative matters, such as membership requests, discourse mailings, etc. Questions pertaining to the ECK leadership in the field generally are resolved by the local Area Mahdis. The prime function of the ECKANKAR Office is as a focal point to provide introductory information, books, discourses, printed and recorded materials to the membership and to that individual who wants to know more about the ECKANKAR teachings and the ECK way of life.

In the free countries of the West, where ECKANKAR can be presented and studied openly, it is fairly easy to reach the interested public, compared to some of the countries under more restrictive government. In the case of the Warsaw Pact nations, where any doctrine that is different from the party line is looked upon with suspicion and persecuted, books and discourses have to be carried in personally and individually because of postal censure. In these countries there is a lot of fear and insecurity in those individuals interested in spiritual unfoldment, for the totalitarian regime will crack down on anything representing a striving for individuality. Yet, these individuals are in the true sense bold and adventuresome, meeting in secret in private places to discuss a teaching that brings them a freedom they had always dreamed of.

In ECKANKAR the sacredness of the individual's own consciousness and personal space is always respected and never violated with any kind of overt or covert pressure to influence or persuade. The message of ECK is simply presented to the individual; the choice is theirs and theirs alone. In this regard Sri Darwin has emphasized the importance of an individual's freedom of consciousness: "I've been assigned a spiritual problem, a guide that can assist them, ultimately whether it's in this lifetime or the next, and it'll be their choice whether they step on the path of ECKANKAR. If it doesn't take place in this lifetime, it sure will in the next. This is one reason why the ECKist doesn't hand out flowers or books to people on the street or drag them out of their church or off their path. The individual that stops seeking that understanding and is sincere, they'll find their way ultimately to a book on ECKANKAR and they'll make that decision themselves. Every step of the way is up to us as individuals.

"America is the most spiritually active area in the world. One of the functions of the Living ECK Master is to stimulate various religions; the push is on to win Souls by various denominations, but the ECKist way is not to interfere with people and let them choose themselves. Even *Newsweek* showed how the different Evangelists are misusing the dollars they've taken in. In order to gain a greater monetary way, they'll do certain things. It depends on how one chooses to take care of his responsibilities for they will reap what they sow.

"If a person says, 'OK, ECKANKAR is great, it's done this-and-such for so many people, I'm going to try it,' and the person doing that without even reading an ECK book or two is in for trouble, because they are still clinging to the faith they are associated with and wouldn't give that up, and we wouldn't ask them to in the first place. We don't pull them out of the churches or by the lapels off the streets, nor do we use a fear factor as the preachers do and the evangelists and the priests, that if they don't get right with Jesus or God, they're going to go to hell, they're going to be condemned. That's not true. I've had to help some priests and preachers out of the tombs of hell.

"There are people that think we are taking people away from their walk of life, and we're not. ECK is an individual path. I've heard it said from Catholics, Protestants, Jews, Moslems, Hindus, all the five major religions, but we don't take anyone away from their path.

"Many people bother others on television or radio, whether Sunday morning or some other day, there are programs that try to preach the gospel and in Jesus' time there was a great misunderstanding about what has been taught by many great teachers down through history. They've all

217

stressed to go to that temple within and not to build the stone temples, but there's a certain number of people that like to get together for social activities, to be seen amongst other people in their community and the church is no more than that. It is not giving forth any spiritual succor. It can't, they're not teaching the true Light and Sound, the pillars of God. But yet I'm not condemning them for that person attending a church or synagogue and is happy where he's at, I'm not going to disrupt and try to change that person's consciousness. Because I'd have trouble and the movement would have trouble and that's not my goal or aim, to disrupt the religions.

"There is a vast difference between the spiritual consciousness of the East and the West. We've had men from the East come to this country and lined their pockets with silver and gold, and they open up large accounts in Switzerland. In their country, they're looked upon as preachers, just like preachers are in this country. They really haven't come out with any great spiritual things over there. Meditation was good in its day. For the modern man of the world, it does not assist one hardly above the astral world. Yoga and its practices were good centuries ago, but today it's only physical exercise at the most. There's other ways to exercise the body, but it's again up to the individual. Had the various leaders of the past been able to take their followers into the high astral world, let alone the mental world or beyond, they would have progressed by leaps and bounds, compared to what they are today.

"Like my trip to India, Kashmir, people are still pulling wooden carts with wooden wheels, ponies draw them, or the women thrashing grain by hand, working the fields. America has the Living ECK Master, a wayshower, to show the rest of the world the people of the different countries of the world can live together and can get along and still be a modern country. Many of our people have gotten into the museum of science in the heavenly worlds, and had this happened by some of the leaders, spiritual leaders and teachers of the past, they'd been able to take their people into these areas, which they couldn't — nor didn't have the knowledge or power. Their function was to show that there are heavens, something beyond this physical plane: 'then it is up to those of that time as individuals to do something about it.' But have they? They formed religions around these past teachers. They really didn't progress, materially or spiritually. The past great mystics and spiritual teachers did not want to be worshipped, with one exception, Mohammed did. He set it up for himself to be worshipped, where neither Buddha nor Jesus wished to be.

"So many people down through history, including today, look to certain areas as holy land. They forget about the land, regardless of what country they are from, that which they are walking on. It's just as holy. One area is no holier than the next. The temple is within man. Until he learns to go there, he will always have questions. I'm not saying all of man's questions are going to be answered. He has to find out some of these for himself, by being bold and adventuresome, and gaining further spiritual enlightenment. Like this trip my friend took going to get some enlightenment, visit some of the lamas and priests and temples over in Little Tibet. He found most of them not operative, closed, decayed and dirty. The high priest or lamas were out looking for some political office. They are primarily Buddhists. Their teacher left many years ago, had translated. The followers who were here in his day, he was able to help and assist them, but whenever a teacher like that — Buddha, Jesus, Mohammed, or whoever, including Paul Twitchell — when they leave this Earth plane of existence, they can no longer help those that are left behind here on Earth. Those that are initiated by them while they were here, they can continue to help them in the heavenly worlds, but only up to a point. For a greater understanding about this, I suggest reading *The Tiger's Fang* by Sri Paul Twitchell, published by IWP Publishing.

"I don't want to try to convince anyone. We have had individuals step onto the path of ECKANKAR who have gone to the East, and some in ECKANKAR that have gone to the East to seek out a spiritual giant; however, they were maybe not unhappy with the Living ECK Master. They wanted to know for themselves if there was anything greater over there. Each one of them came back and said, 'It is right here,' because they could not find what they were looking for over there. It isn't there.

"The person doesn't have to go through the far corners of the Earth, if he goes to that temple within himself—I don't care where he's from, the U.S., Canada, Egypt, India, Africa, or Alaska, or North Pole or South; whether he's a farmer, a fisherman, a businessman or a banker. That has nothing to do, his status in life, with his spiritual unfoldment. Yet we have on the path of ECKANKAR, all walks of life are represented, all colors of mankind, all races.

"Those who are in the movie industry, or in the big business world, they have their niche in life. They're reasonably taken care of, in a sense. They're learning, or have learned how to take care of themselves. In some cases their forefathers gave it to them and will have difficulty, maybe, but don't understand the spiritual aspects of it. I don't aim this book, or the teachings of ECK towards that person. If they find it, and want to study it, that's their decision. There are more poor people than there are rich people, and I'm not saying that all the rich people have a spiritual understanding, but as far as making things easier for them in life, to allow them to get various books and read, have more free time, they have that. And it's up to them, whether or not they utilize it for their own benefit.

"I like to work with the person who hasn't got that great intellect. Once the intellectual person picks up the simplicity of it, they take off and run with it, as Sri Paul Twitchell stated in *The Flute of God* (IWP Publishing).

"They move very fast with it, but many times the intellectual person has a very hard wall to climb over and get around because the mind wants to pick at every little bitty thing, and some are so detailed, and the ordinary man who hasn't had a lot of schooling or hasn't developed that high degree of intellectuality will accept things more readily, of this nature. I see a lot of people come and go in ECKANKAR and this has helped them, not only to unfold spiritually, but helped them in their daily life, and are doing things that they have longed to do for finding a way to assist themselves, sustain themselves better, economically, and have a greater spiritual understanding in this world. For as man progresses technically, he will reach a point where he must gain a greater spiritual understanding or destroy himself.

"In ECKANKAR we don't go out here and preach the word as the preachers do, we just present and make available to those who have the ears to hear, that ECKANKAR is here. I don't think that we'll ever—not in my day, or for some time to come—have programs as various faiths have, as all the religions have, in bringing forth their message to the world via the radio and television media. We'll do some of that, but we'll do it differently. We're not going to be competitive, not going to try and win Souls or convert people. We want to just present it and let those that hear it make up their own minds—to take a look at the teachings. If they accept it, fine; if they don't, fine."

As local contacts for information and literature about ECKANKAR, there are ECK Centers, or ECKANKAR Centers, and Reading Rooms in various communities throughout the world, perhaps some 200 at this time, mostly in North America, England, Western Europe, Africa, Singapore and Australia. These centers and activities to make available the message of ECK are maintained solely by voluntary donations and voluntary work. All positions are without salary. The ECK Center further serves as the location for Satsang (study group that meets to discuss the ECK Satsang discourses) or Discussion group (of the ECKANKAR books). Satsang and Discussion classes are not to indoctrinate or for group exercises, but rather for exchanging viewpoints and insights on the ECK material being studied. Many areas have ECKANKAR newsletters to present information on activities and the ECK viewpoint to the public. The ECK Centers also present regular Introductory Talks which are publicly announced and free of charge. Many areas take that a step further and hold regional ECKANKAR seminars through which various ECKists present the ECK way of life and viewpoints on a variety of subjects through talks, panel discussions, music, poetry and sometimes art displays to reflect the culture of ECK. At times Sri Darwin Gross will attend these regional seminars, as his busy schedule allows, to meet with the newcomer and ECKist alike. He travels all over the world to present the message of ECK and to meet with the ECK chelas, many of whom have not seen him in the physical for many years, yet who maintain that strong inner link and awareness of his presence and spiritual guidance.

Where chelas have less access to the Living ECK Master in the physical, more attention is placed on the inner linkup. The Master is present in the spiritual body, and the ECK chelas are very strongly aware of that. In 1979, Sri Darwin had to cancel his appearance at the European Seminar in Oslo, Norway. At first, there was a little disappointment by people who had traveled far to get to Norway to meet with the Living ECK Master, but the spiritual presence of Sri Darwin and the other Vairagi ECK Masters with him lifted the vibrations so high, that many of the seminar participants later said it was one of the best European Seminars they had ever attended.

Major ECKANKAR international seminars held at this time, often with some 5,000 in attendance, include the European Seminar, usually held in late summer; the ECKANKAR International Youth Conference, held on the weekend of Easter; the ECKANKAR Creative Arts Festival, held near June 10 (Children's Day); and the World Wide of ECK, the major event of the year, held the weekend

222

closest to October 22. Sri Darwin personally attends these major events. They are times of great joy for the ECKists and the newcomer alike, for those in attendance share the succor of the Light and the Sound of ECK that the Living ECK Master brings into the worlds, from his words and music, and his very presence.

Speaking of his travels to various parts of the world, Sri Darwin commented: "It's like triple time, it never ceases whether I'm awake or the physical body is lying down trying to get some rest, an hour or three hours. It's very interesting, on a trip to Japan, I had quite a group to talk to in Kyoto; that visit there we were speaking or talking through an interpreter for about 2½ hours, and I could barely move. I was on my feet all this time and the extra current flowing. After an hour had gone by, I tried to shut it off somewhat, but the offshoot was the physical damage to the body was swollen feet and some of the nerves which carry the electricity in the body, the nerve-endings on the bottom of the feet were very, very sore, sore to touch, let alone to walk on.

"The current comes down from above through the top chakra, the top of the head, the crown chakra and goes on out through your hands and, of course, your feet and other centers. I was very much taken up by the interest of the Japanese people that attended this meeting and this causing some problems physically, I tried to go too far. Anything past a half-hour to 45 minutes becomes a physical problem for me. I can go beyond myself a good half-hour and work from out and beyond time, space and matter in the Soul body when I'm giving a talk and this is where the knowledge and the material comes from, the seven Golden Wisdom Temples, as well as the Soul plane. This is felt by the person whether they realize it or not, sometimes as much as a week, a day or a couple of hours later, maybe several months. That person that has attended that seminar or that gathering, information filters through to them and some realize it, others do not until later.

"When I was over in India, I didn't go out hiking. I was washed out from Hong Kong and New Delhi; I was working all this time. The bottom of my feet actually burnt, they swelled up. I could barely walk when I was in Hong Kong from the current going through me. People there begging, many who had given up their path, whether it was the Buddhist way, Christian way—they were ready for a more universal teaching. They were sincere, I must help them. So I'm working during the day, talking to ECKists or in the evening and hours around the clock, anytime I go into a new area. But that can happen even if I'm in California. It's not just unique with them over there.

"A physical vehicle is needed and many times I'll manifest the body. If I don't travel physically, I'll manifest a body in certain countries and appear there, just so there is a vehicle. Like when an ECKist travels, I get asked the question: 'What can I do, I'm going to such-and-such a country?' I say, 'Nothing, just be yourself and visit. Don't try to change anything, don't try to change their ways. Take a book in and leave it there, with someone who is interested. If you can get it into the country, that's the greatest thing you can do.' The rest of their visit is just that—a visit.

"Being a vehicle for God allows the Spirit to work through you. We as individual human beings don't know what is needed in that country or what is needed in the way of guiding someone or helping them. I might have that ability to look, but I don't spend all my time to seek out this person, they find me. It works out as Spirit wants it to, not as I wish it to be."

When Sri Darwin travels to non-English speaking countries to speak at a Seminar or to a group of chelas or other individuals, he uses an interpreter to translate his words into the respective languages. In consultations with individuals, an interpreter will be present if the individual wishes, but many times it turns out that the awareness of the individual is so expanded that an interpreter is not necessary. One such case was when Sri Darwin spoke with a young lady on his visit to East Berlin. In the beginning, the interpreter translated both Sri Darwin's and the young lady's words, since she had studied Russian in school, and very little English. However, pretty soon it was no longer necessary to translate the Master's words, for she understood perfectly what he was saying. She began answering in halting English, and it was not long before the interpreter remained silent because she was speaking almost fluent English.

For the first time since the 13th century, Sri Darwin Gross is a Living ECK Master who presents the message of ECK not only through the spoken and written word, and his own example, but through song, through music, using the sound as a direct vehicle of communication. Occasionally at a seminar, and especially at the ECKANKAR Creative Arts Festival, Sri Darwin will sing a few of his songs or play the vibraphone. The healing and soothing effect of the harmonies and overtones produced are uplifting to an extent not describable in words, but can only be experienced by the individual. Remembering the origin of one lovely melody, Sri Darwin notes: "I wrote a song. It wasn't my song, I'm just a vehicle for it. This song came out of the dream state—a song that should be sung by a choir without any note of any instrument. A beautiful experience. I was coming back from taking a certain group of individuals to a Wisdom Temple, a Golden Wisdom Temple in one of the higher planes, and coming back through and into this universe, there is a beautiful blue sky and fluffy white clouds. I look about and there's nothing there but myself and Spirit. The name of that song—just out of the blue came this burst of beautiful voices, started very high, high soprano, along with some harmony to it — 'Where Spirit Leads Me.' It was just quite an illuminating experience for me. The choir—these weren't angels — these were voices in a choir beyond and above. The angels derive from the causal plane, of course, and have wings, in a sense, as some of the pictures show of various artists down through history, but they don't go beyond those planes. They may come down—they might lower their vibratory rate. God never will, nor those Masters that have gone beyond, such as Jesus or Mohammed, lower their vibratory rate and return to the ash can of this universe, planet Earth.

"There are some up and coming composers who will be reaching into these pure positive God Worlds, who are ECKists, and who have, perhaps, come into this lifetime and who are working from that point spiritually and will compose great music, who may not have stepped on the path yet. Ultimately they'll learn about it and put the two together. We'll see a trend or a change in some of the worldly music to a better sound which is more uplifting, harmonious."

Regardless of how one may first hear about ECKANKAR, whether through a book, radio or television show, introductory talk, pamphlet, word of mouth, seminar, etc., it offers the individual something nothing else can. Sri Darwin once commented on his first impression of the people in ECK: "I attended the Third World Wide Seminar and I was very curious as to what kind of people were in ECKANKAR. I had been studying ECK for some time. I found that there were doctors, merchants, woodsmen, the average person off the street as well as children. They were enjoying themselves. They seem to radiate something that I hadn't ever seen before in other groups, or just in life, period, other than in the heavenly worlds. And this was very uplifting, and their music and the art seemed to have a much greater vibration to it. I didn't get a chance to talk with Paul Twitchell at that time. I met him later at a seminar and from there I was taken very swiftly actually up to the Soul plane, and from there I had to proceed on my own to the God-conscious state."

The goal of all ECKists anywhere in the world is the same: Self- and God-Realization. But the benefits and effects of ECKANKAR as a way of life may differ greatly

226

from country to country, or from culture to culture. In many parts of Africa or South America the presence of the Living ECK Master offers the chelas protection from the practice of black magic still widely used in those areas, despite efforts by the Christian churches to stamp out ancient tribal practices. Especially in Africa, people are joining ECKANKAR by the dozens, for their immediate proof of the validity of the ECK teachings is the complete protection they at once receive. As many of these countries are frequently at war or under military dictatorship, the individual lives at a much greater peril to his life. But to the ECKist in Africa, Asia, South America or in communist countries, this only makes the protection more apparent.

It is written in the works of ECK that when the chela (spiritual student) is ready, the Master appears. In this regard, one ECKist wrote to Sri Darwin about a friend of hers:

Dear Darwin,

I am writing for your assistance in interpreting an unusual experience being reported to me by a friend at work.

I joined ECKANKAR late last year. My friend is clairvoyant and a registered medium. We often discuss ECKANKAR. However, she is following another path.

Several times she has reported seeing you here at work. Today she said, 'Hi, Darwin' and the person looking like you replied, 'Hi there,'— then went into the rest room, saying 'Bye now.'

My friend is excited, and also somewhat frightened, because she does not know what you are trying to teach her. (She is 100% certain that she is seeing you.)

We both want to do what is right.

Respectfully,
F.

227

Sri Darwin answered this young lady with a personal reply:

Dear F.
I want to thank you for your continued reports. I certainly enjoy hearing from each initiate.

Your concern about your clairvoyant friend at work and the meaning of my appearing to that individual—do not be alarmed for I am sure you recall that in the writings that when the individual is ready the Master will appear.

Please keep in mind that when your friend understands what Eckankar really means and can do for the individual that the choice will be hers as to stepping onto the path of Eckankar for there is no need to rush and it does take some of the individual's time to drop the present path.

I want you to know that the Master is always with you and because I love you spiritually I am as close as your heartbeat and your breath. My only desire is your spiritual growth to God-Realization.

My love always surrounds you.
Affectionately,
Darwin Gross

The spiritual love and protection given by the Living ECK Master to the chelas is beyond the ken of the average man. When Sri Darwin says to the ECK chelas "My love always surrounds you," the impact of his communication sometimes comes through subtly and quietly, other times loud and clear with sudden and unmistakable certainty. Attesting to this divine protection a chela wrote: "One day I was driving home and in a hurry. I was going much too fast and approaching a hill when I noticed someone next to me out of the corner of my eye—then I heard Darwin say, 'Slow down to 30'—then he disappeared. I did, and it saved my life; coming over the hill was a car full of kids going faster than I was, only they were passing another car and we would have hit head on if I did not slow down. I have just had so much guidance and direction in all areas of my life that it would take forever to write about all of them."

The natural expansion of consciousness and growth in awareness that comes with the study of ECKANKAR will often pleasantly surprise and amaze the individual. This housewife and mother wrote: "I IMMEDIATELY noticed a change—it was very momentous to me and difficult to describe. A lot of hang-ups I had, began to drop away ... especially anything to do with fear and guilt. I was no longer afraid of flying and high places. I think all of us carry a certain amount of fear and guilt instilled in us by religion—that left. I became a much better parent because I no longer worried and fretted about my children's experiences. I learned about karma and realized they had their own karmic patterns to work out—they had to learn from their own experiences, not mine. I could give them guidance sometimes but I had to be willing to let them make mistakes, better to do it while at home than later. If allowed to make their own choices then kids learn to make wise choices later in life—anyway, I knew they were also guided and protected by the Living ECK Master."

ECKists all over the world belong to all races and backgrounds. Generally, the students of ECKANKAR very rapidly transcend the racial consciousness and see all men as Soul, regardless of their color, age, sex or position in life. For some, however, there is the difficulty in the beginning of accepting a Living ECK Master who is a white man in the physical. The white man in recent times has dominated positions in many areas of the globe, and is not always looked upon too kindly by the yellow, black or red man. There was one young man in Malaysia who had been guided for many years by Shamus-i-Tabriz, a Persian Adept of the Vairagi Order of ECK Masters. This young man was ultimately told by Shamus-i-Tabriz to seek out the present Living ECK Master, a man by the name of Darwin Gross. The Malaysian was shocked to find that Darwin Gross was a white man. He nevertheless decided to become a member of ECKANKAR and study the ECK discourses. This he did for five years without ever seeing the Living ECK Master in the physical. Then a group of ECKists from the United States visited the small number of Malaysian ECK chelas who by that time had become members of ECKANKAR. When the Americans entered the meeting room, they found this young man crouched in a corner, unwilling to even meet these white people. But as the meeting went on, the young man realized that the "white people" were first and foremost ECKists, just like he was, and he gained confidence to come forward and meet them. A little later, Sri Darwin visited the Far East and by that time the Malaysian was able to meet the Living ECK Master, who had guided him so long on the inner, without any reservations as to his race.

Even the fear of what man calls death falls by the wayside as the ECKist begins to understand his true identity as Soul and the continuity of life in the inner planes. One Mahdis, a Fifth Initiate in ECKANKAR who is authorized to perform weddings and funerals in an official capacity, remembered an occasion when she was asked by a fellow ECKist to perform a funeral service for her five-year-old son who had just translated. She did so, reading from *The Anitya* and from *Stranger By The River,* both by Paul Twitchell. "I discussed the son with the mother about a year later," she recalled. "I asked her if she had seen him. She said, 'Oh, yes. I see him quite often and I am able to hug and kiss him and enjoy being with him. It is funny, the last time I saw him he kind of squirmed and said, "Oh, Mom ... I do have other things to do." ' I know that it is a very traumatic experience for most parents to lose (or

THINK they are losing) a child that age, so it was wonderful to see the way she was able to adjust to his being on the inner planes instead of in the physical. There is some kind of old saying that the proof of the pudding is in eating the pie. ECKANKAR works!!! It changes our lives and does what it says it will do—for a very large percentage of the people that get into it. We are given the tools and if we use them the way we are told, it works in our lives."

Even those individuals who have searched from path to path in this lifetime, only to meet limitations and disappointments again and again know when they have reached that point and are ready to take that next step. A concerned parent explains: "My son's questions about life and his inner experiences instigated my search for truth. I perused many spiritual and religious paths including the Mormon faith, Science of Mind, Edgar Cayce, Lobsang Rampa, yoga, and Transcendental Meditation, but always I felt there was something missing. One day when I was alone in my house, I screamed out as loud as I could, 'God, I know there is one path that you want us to find, so why don't you show it to me.' A few days later I came across an article in *Fate Magazine* on ECKANKAR, the Ancient Science of Soul Travel. I sent for several books and after reading Paul Twitchell's account of the heavenly worlds in *The Tiger's Fang,* I realized that there were more answers than I had questions for. I realized that my seeking had ended."

"The ECKist," says Sri Darwin, "is a very active person and he finds as he progresses spiritually that if he isn't active, something's wrong. If he isn't doing something in order to not only be a vehicle for the good of all, but if he sits home and thinks 'I'll let George do it,' pretty soon there's something wrong inside. He feels it, he senses it. He's unhappy with himself and the moment he goes out and becomes a 'seed carrier'—a vehicle for Spirit to work through, the essence of God—his whole perspective and attitude changes. So once he gets a little of that experience, presenting the message of ECK in some manner, not necessarily talking, it could be writing letters, articles, putting up a poster. I still today enjoy doing that myself.

"We as individuals in this world are at the place in life where we should be. You cannot run a grocery store or department store without some sort of guidelines for each department and the personnel to run it—there's the janitor, the clerk, the cashier, the manager, that sort of thing. In this physical realm we're speaking of order only, this is very necessary. In order to get things done as we think of progress, whether it's science or what-have-you. When it comes down to getting the message of ECK out, there has to be certain rules and regulations set up to go by, whether it's presenting the teachings, holding a class, there has to be some sort of structure, just look at this galaxy!"

The outer structure of ECKANKAR as a spiritual teaching is made up of the Mahdis, appointed by the Living ECK Master, to oversee activities in certain areas. Then responsibilities are delegated to Area Representatives, the Arahatas and the Chelas. Satsang classes provide the spiritual vortex for the Master to work through. The Living ECK Master, as well as other ECK Masters are present in each ECK meeting, in their Soul body and seen by some. Membership in ECKANKAR has grown twenty-fold since Sri Darwin accepted the Rod of ECK Power. There are many Satsangs and numerous discussion classes additionally around the globe.

The need for organization and physical structure in the physical world led to ECKANKAR becoming a California non-profit corporation when the move was made from the Las Vegas office to larger quarters in Menlo Park for more efficient service to the membership. The ECKANKAR Board of Trustees oversees and makes recommendations concerning the physical aspects of ECKANKAR, alert to the most efficient and effective ways to make the message of ECK available to the world with the resources at hand. Sri Darwin, as President of ECKANKAR, gives guidance to the Board in their decisions as well as interacts with various co-workers in the ECKANKAR International Office and in the field.

At the February 1979 ECKANKAR Board of Trustees meeting Sri Darwin indicated: "The next Living ECK Master shouldn't have to help run or work in the ECKANKAR Office with the physical aspects of ECKANKAR. He should concentrate on his spiritual functions without the physical work of the office. If I step aside as Living ECK Master, I may help on administration if I have my health and am still around. There's no way I can predict what the next Master will do. This might happen in three years or more, but I know I will still be around for some time to help with this great message of ECK.

"It's always hard for the new man. It was hard for me and it will be hard for the next one. There are a lot of spiritual situations to resolve. There's a lot of things to do. One way or another, I'll be here to help."

One of Sri Darwin's major projects and concerns has been to strengthen the true "organization" of ECKANKAR—the chelas, the spiritual students, in their areas and their interaction and coordination with the spiritual network of communication he has established among the Mahdis, Area Representatives, Arahatas and Chelas themselves. He has done this through his many travels throughout the worlds, with the special training programs he has established for Area Representatives and Arahatas, special training video cassettes for the leadership in ECKANKAR, and by putting special attention on the Satsangs and simple, direct and honest presentation of the Message of ECK.

"Now when Paul put together *The Book of Spiritual Instructions for the ECK-Satsang Classes*," explained Sri Darwin, "this is for all of our classes, not just the Satsang. It's used for all of the classes as guidelines, it was necessary. There are Satsang classes on the various levels or dimensions of heaven in the Golden Wisdom Temples and there are guidelines there as well.

"You don't have to memorize these rules, it comes naturally. If a person has the desire to hold a class or to be a vehicle for the ECK, he'll seek out the information he needs providing they have the foundation in Spirit. For instance, when I was covering the countryside before stepping into this area of responsibility, even before I had received my Fifth initiation, I was doing the works of a Mahdis, but I wasn't going around telling people about it. So I was giving, not only of coin, but of myself, without looking for anything in return, and this is one of these spiritual laws that when one gives without looking ahead or looking with attachment, with strings, then it is that which is given truly from the heart. Then you are being a vehicle for God, you are assisting someone for the good of the whole and in doing so you meet various obstacles and tests.

"A person has to decide for himself as no one else can do your thinking or make your decisions. If it's a talk he wants to give, know the subject. Stick with the simplicity of the message. If it's a brand-new group we're trying to reach, talk about the ECK books and weave it into history and keep it simple, lead them to the books and let that person make up his own mind.

"I recently put out a guideline for speakers, that they could talk for 45 minutes if they wanted. I'd heard some complaints from some that a half-hour wasn't enough, so I said, 'Okay, let's go back to what it used to be, which was 45 minutes, maximum.' Who wants to sit and listen to me or anyone else for more than that? It's human nature that, if we say, if something is put forth in print, they take it as gospel. One, I was taught not to believe everything I read or that I hear. An experience, and it's the only way you can gain wisdom—that's something that cannot be given to us —it must be earned. If a person wants to talk ten minutes, then talk ten minutes. You have to use some common sense, in all things, whether it pertains to the physical life, or the spiritual life."

To those individuals new to ECKANKAR, who are taking a look at the teachings, Sri Darwin says: "I would recommend to those that they seek out an Area Rep or a Mahdis in their area, a Higher Initiate, and chat with that person. A lot of people, in their spiritual life, they like to keep their relationship secretive, in a sense. It's a very personal relationship, that relationship between themselves, their spiritual relationship I'm talking about—God. It's like a love affair with a young lady, and if you're in a small town and you have eyes for this young lady or vice versa, they don't want the whole town to know about it. They have something very special, and when the time is right, and these two lovers that I'm talking about, reach the point where they have agreed to make a life together, they are full of joy, and they don't mind letting the whole world know about it. They might even write songs about it, or poetry. The same thing exists with the love affair between the individual and this personal relationship between them and Spirit, the vehicle of God ITSELF.

"The uninitiated will be alone and they will be lonely. They don't have the spiritual guidance that the ECKists have. The ECK Masters could show themselves if they wanted to, but they don't want to. As individuals of the Vairagi, as well as a group, co-workers, we don't want to attract millions of people all at once. Man calls that phenomena, that which he doesn't understand. There is no phenomena nor are there coincidences in ECK. There's always a reason, a purpose for everything that takes place, even the learned man doesn't understand it whether he's a physicist, a doctor, a psychic investigator—I don't profess to know everything, but when I need a piece of information I know how to get it and this is the difference—I don't misuse that. To say I'm better than the next person, it's just a matter of having certain tools available to me that no one else has and this is true of up and coming Initiates on this path of ECK.

"In my training for Mastership, I found that I had to learn how to give openly without any strings and I knew that, I thought, when I was a child, but I gave beyond what I thought I could actually, both in service and in material goods that I had. I gave to the Living ECK Master of the time, including the property I had, for I was alone and my responsibilities were only to God, myself and my country. It was quite a lesson; I didn't really have to, but I was being tested, evidently, at the time. A lot of people want to give in ECK and my recommendation to them has always been not to go beyond their means and overstep their bounds of responsibility. If they have a family or other responsibilities, they're caring for their mother or some member of their family, the main key is not to jeopardize it.

"There are those that are very close to you that you don't mind giving to, but to help perpetuate something that is of a negative nature... It's fine for a person to be successful but when you get into that area of greed which many of the businessmen aren't aware of and some of the people aren't aware of the greed of the various religious orders. A religion has no business being in politics nor have they any business in medicine. What are they doing with the money that they are going to be making from their hospitals and other physical interests? The accumulation of some of these dollars aren't being utilized properly for the benefit of the whole, as they had said they would do, and you'll see some changes in the next three to fifteen years, changes in —we've already seen drastic cuts in individuals dropping out of churches, and ECKANKAR has nothing to do with that, because we don't stand on the street corner and preach our word to the world. We hold open public meetings, some free, some may have a charge to help pay for the facility.

"For the person to understand the difference between ECK and ECKANKAR, there are two aspects to that, should this be understood, then you'd see quite a change take place in this world, especially in this country. And for the better. When one is evolving spiritually, it's always for the better but as long as a person is looking to an ascended master, one who has gone on and cannot help him here in this physical world and guide him through the lower worlds, they are going to stay in their state of consciousness for the rest of this life and the next lifetime until they realize and start to broaden their viewpoint a little bit. And the only way they're going to broaden that viewpoint is to get that desire within themselves to do that.

"To what degree would you devote yourself to spreading the message of ECK? When one steps on the Path of ECK and learns of this great message it has to offer the individual, you must understand that whatever you take into your consciousness is going to be the determining factor in your life. You alone determine to what degree you will attain the ECKshar consciousness. If you wish to devote an hour, half-hour to an hour to this great truth every day, it will benefit you that much more. Such as doing your spiritual exercise once a day is all that is necessary or some do it twice, once in the morning and once in the evening. However, should you decide that during some part of every hour of every day you allow the ECK to circulate into your consciousness you will have much more of the spiritual fruitage in your life.

"Your consciousness when imbedded with truth becomes a law of harmony not only to you but to those who come in contact with you. You cannot be the light of the world and keep the light hidden under a bushel basket. If you are the light of the world, the world beholds that light and benefits by it. But you cannot be the light except in proportion as truth is consciously imbedded in your consciousness.

"The ECKists find that as they unfold spiritually and gain greater knowledge of the heavenly worlds and accepting more initiations that they cannot sit still, that they must always be doing something in this world in the form of spreading the message of ECK. This too is the law of Spirit, of the ECK. As one gives to it, it will demand more of you.

"This world is a world of getting, achieving, accomplishing, struggling, striving; it is a world of two powers as well as the lower heavenly worlds. To some extent however, you have already left the world if you've come to realize that life need not be lived by power, by might or by struggle, but that life can be lived in a state of adorn and that you are on this Path of ECK to experience that beauty in the greatest possible measure. Should you have any other goal than to know God and to seek the realization of the kingdom of God and his righteousness, you are setting up a barrier between yourself and the MAHANTA in reaching your goal."

"In my travels and at the seminars," Sri Darwin explains, "I am frequently asked how the ECKists can help me as the Living ECK Master. My answer has been, to individuals, just be yourself. There's one thing that not only will help the Living ECK Master but help you as an individual as well, that is to drop the stimulants such as Coke, Pepsi, coffee, wine, etc. If one is to be a channel for Spirit and the Vairagi ECK Masters as well as the Living ECK Master, one can be of great assistance by not having these negatives in one's aura. Keep in mind that of these items, they tend to make one nervous or short in temper, as well as make one react in negative ways and you wonder why you are reacting to situations as you are. However, more than that, if you are being a vehicle for Spirit and the Living ECK Master, under any influence of these items or some type of stimulant, those who are Higher Initiates and working with the Living ECK Master will pass this on to those under them in a negative way for the Kal and be a burden to the Living ECK Master with his great spiritual load.

"This is why certain religions down through history have stressed that in their teachings, that these things are a negative for somewhere in the line of their teachings this was known. Yet one must keep a balance and remember that one can not be so pure as the driven-snow. This must always be kept in mind. There are those that will tell them-

238

selves that it won't matter, who will know? But I tell you that that person who is working as a spiritual assistant with the MAHANTA, the Living ECK Master, are only fooling themselves if they think they can get away with this sort of thing. For not only does Spirit and God know, but the Living ECK Master as well."

CHAPTER 11

The Sacred Teachings of ECK

The aim and purpose of ECKANKAR has always been to take Soul by Its own path back to Its divine source. The successful devotee is he who, by practice and use of the spiritual exercises of ECK, lifts himself as Soul to Its real abode with the help of the Living ECK Master. This frees Soul from all bonds, both internal and external, gross, subtle and causal. It separates the mind from the physical worlds and gives Soul freedom to move in any direction, either upward into the heavenly worlds or downwards into the psychic worlds. The perfect devotees or true lovers of the SUGMAD are only those who reach the final stage of the journey to the heavenly source of all things. Those who talk of the MAHANTA, the perfect Guru, or read his teachings to others without practicing them, are only intellectually educated people.

        —*The Shariyat-Ki-Sugmad,* Book Two

Every student of the teachings of ECKANKAR at one point comes into the realization that these teachings have always existed. Although the terminology and the way it is presented has changed over the ages, its essential message has always been the same. There are references to ECKANKAR in man's writings as far back as the Naacal Scriptures, reputed to be over 30,000 years old, and the symbol EK is found in the ancient Egyptian and Sanskrit scrolls. All through history there have been ECK Masters who, under the guise of mystery schools or religious teachings, have brought the message of ECK to a select few, Masters like Pythagoras in Greece, Zoroaster in Persia, Quetzalcoatl in Central America, Gopal Das from Egypt, and Shamus-i-Tabriz, a 13th century Persian poet, to name just a few.

To quote Sri Darwin: "In a book printed by the University of Chicago in 1953, *Philosophers Speak of God*, this author points out up in the front of the book 'ECK, EK' and this didn't come from Paul Twitchell; it didn't come from somebody who wrote about ECKANKAR in the fifteenth century, which was Guru Nanak because he got his instructions from Fubbi Quantz and Gopal Das and Rebazar Tarzs. And he went out and started the Sikh Order with what he called 'The Jap Ji' and he uses ECK and ECKANKAR in his works, for he did not dream of his work going beyond his own life span."

In the "Introduction" to *Philosophers Speak of God,* the authors Charles Hartshorne and William L. Reese, in a philosophical and intellectual treatise, speak of the ECK and various offshoots of IT. They define ECK as "The Supreme Consciousness." At one point they state that "it is to be observed that knowledge is deficient unless it fully and literally contains its objects. ECK is the paradox of a knowledge whose objects change, though the knowledge-of-these-objects does not change, and which is wholly necessary, though the objects are not."*

Sri Darwin states further that "Plato spoke of the ecstatic regions. He was right on and knew it, and he was given instructions and he was teaching the word, when he spoke of the ecstatic, meaning that ECK was constantly flowing, and man has expressed it, 'I've got a hold of Spirit and boy, I'm going to give it to someone else!' It's an awakening.

*Charles Hartshorne and William L. Reese, *Philosophers Speak of God* (Chicago: The University of Chicago Press, 1953), p. 18.

"The ECK has been brought forth, the ECK or the EK, in different forms, different writings and languages down through history and the oldest records on earth, the Naacal Records mention this; over in Nepal, India, EK means *come home,* or Number One; the EK also appears in the Greek language as well as the Russian and Polynesian languages. The Naacal Records are tablets that date from a period of 30,000 years long gone. There are some of these records housed in the Katsupari Monastery. Jesus spent some time in the physical body at the Katsupari Monastary. John traced Jesus' steps from the Jerusalem area after Jesus left Earth, from Damascus up into Kashmir and to Tibet. These records are in different places. Over in Srinigar, there are some descendants of Jesus' family and he's supposed to be buried there, as well as Mark and Moses. There's a book available, *Jesus Died in Kashmir** which is fact. The crucifixion did not kill Jesus, but it was a good story.

"The closest path to ECKANKAR has been the Sufi teachings, but they don't have any Living ECK Master nor the succor, per se, that the teachings of ECK has, and it is older than man, yet it's fairly young and fit for modern man.

"There are other religious groups in the east teaching the light and sound of God or attempting to, but they don't have the Rod of Power or that succor to give to their followers."

The path of Soul back to Its original home in the pure positive God Worlds has always been available to those with eyes to see and ears to hear. In the course of time, however, there have been many individuals with a certain knowledge of the ECK teachings who formed their own paths or religions, splitting off from the original path. Not being the Living ECK Master, these teachers were and are capable of leading their followers to a certain point, the

---

*A. Faber-Kaiser, *Jesus Died in Kashmir* (London: ABACUS edition/Sphere Books Ltd., 1978)

lower levels of heaven, only. Sri Darwin, the MAHANTA, the Living ECK Master, describes these as steps on the God Worlds chart:

"It's true that there are some eastern terms in ECKANKAR, but there's also terms from other sections of the world. A few words that come to mind like Anami, Agam, Alaya, as well as Ashanti, a tribal name in Ghana and Sewa from Africa, come from the worlds of God as stated in the teachings of ECKANKAR which engulf all teachings. It recognizes all teachings. They are looked upon as if one is able to develop this 360 degree viewpoint—will find, ultimately, that each of them, not only the religious, but philosophical thoughts as well, are a step. Think of a stairway or a ladder, perhaps the best way I can describe it, and at some point on this ladder, the ECK teachings will have a spiritual awakening for the individual's state of consciousness. Some individuals will have nothing to do with some of these steps in ECK, because they know that ECKANKAR has something that goes beyond their path in a way of thought or in a way of philosophy.

"One, all life originates from one source. The consciousness of the world today is such that more people are receptive to that, so, some men ask, 'Why, then, do we have so many different religions, and fields of thought?' There have been great thinkers down through history, and some of these thinkers have been guided by the ECK Vairagi Masters, even though in their day, they may have been on a certain path or in a certain faith. Some have changed their faith in the course of time, as well, and gone from a religion to no religion, as man thinks of a religious teaching, because they learned to lean upon Spirit and go to the temple within; thus they had met a spiritual guide that guided them, and they are very much aware of that. I can think of musicians, politicians, even laborers—the man on the street. This is nothing unique to me.

"There are other flavors in the teachings of

244

ECKANKAR, I mean from Egypt, or Greece, or Europe, as well, in terminology. The east was a melting pot for most religious teachings at one time, meaning that part of the world, whether it was from Israel to India, and from Tibet to Egypt, it makes no difference where. Europe has its tie-in, in its day, different philosophies, different teachings have derived from so many sectors of this world. The teaching of ECK, in ECKANKAR, recognizes each of these steps. I nor the teachings put them down, even though I have my own personal viewpoints about certain steps—how man is held back, perhaps, in his way of thought, and allowing him to grow, consciously to develop this 360-degree viewpoint."

The teachings of ECK constitute the whole—that total awareness of God expressed in the term of a "360 degree viewpoint." Thus, it can be said that, without exception, all religions, philosophies, cults and doctrines are offshoots of ECKANKAR. They represent "a slice of the pie," as Darwin put it. The Living ECK Master and what he teaches is truly representative of the ECK, the pure life essence emanating from the SUGMAD (God), and this has been so since the beginning of time.

In the *ECKANKAR Dictionary,* by Sri Paul Twitchell, a compilation of the definitions of ECK terms, one can find the following explanation of the ECK, as well as the Ancient Creed of ECK:

ECK   The Audible Life Current; all that is life; the eternal truth and eternal paradox within all; encompasses all the teachings of religions and philosophies; stream of life force; the science of Total Awareness that grows out of the experiences of Soul Travel; the realization of God-consciousness; the thread that binds together all beings in all planes, all universes, throughout all time and beyond all time into eternity; life force;

self consciousness; Holy Spirit; the source of all; the creator of all things; the great forming force; is everywhere; the essence of the SUGMAD, the holy spirit and the science of God-Realization.

ECK CREEDS (Ancient) (1) Perfection has no limitation nor is it temporary or changeable, while pleasure and suffering are the conditions of material existence. (2) All life flows from the SUGMAD, downward to the worlds below, and through them, and nothing can exist without this cosmic current known as ECK, which can be heard as sound and seen as light. Therefore it is necessary for man to always be aware of the sounds of the ECK and see the nuri (light body) of the SUGMAD in order to live within the highest spiritual realms.

EK Modern form of "Ecstasies" or "ek-marg," used to describe both the result and the techniques of "exteriorization." Known to the pagan Greeks, and to the Romans (as "superstitio"), the practice consisted in reaching, through concentration, a mystic state in which the subject believed his spirit to have left his body. Buddhism fostered similar techniques through meditation. This was researched by Paul Twitchell.

In the modern western world, the practice was revived in the mid-twentieth century by the American savant Paul Twitchell, who set forth a number of methods for "leaving the body," with the object of achieving total awareness of the divine ground of Divine Being.

The ECK Current has a centrifugal and centripetal flow. In Its centrifugal flow, It emanates from the SUGMAD and creates all the levels of existence, starting with the Agam Lok, the Nameless World and abode of the SUGMAD, down through the various levels of God-consciousness to the Soul Plane. These regions are called the pure positive God Worlds, because here there is no time, space, energy and matter, and the ECK force is undivided and free of maya, or illusion. Then, the ECK is split into the dual aspects of positive and negative, creative and destructive, forming the realm of polarity which consists of the etheric, mental, causal, astral and physical planes.

"HU is the word, the sacred word of ECK, of God; it has been long before man has been on this planet or even in this universe," states Sri Darwin. "HU is that sound that issues out of God and is as exacting as mathematics; reduce it to the simplest denominator, and that is H-U. It is the Voice of God; It knows all things, sees all things through Its vehicles, all life. The vehicles of Spirit as It issues out from IT and comes down out of the Soul Plane down to the Etheric plane and divides. There are two main currents—the positive and negative—but there are lesser currents off of those, streams, whatever you want to call it, of atoms. These atoms are unmanifested Souls in that sense, yet being the vehicle of God. If you listen for it, you can hear the sound of HU in everything. It's all right here."

Souls are created in the higher spiritual worlds, and transported or taken to the lower worlds of duality by the downward flow of the ECK, placed on that level of the lower world to learn and gain experience in order to become conscious co-workers with the SUGMAD. In the dual worlds, they struggle against the negative force which tries to hold them back and tie them to the negative reality which is relativity or illusion. Darwin explains:

"Normally, over a period of eons, as we think of it as

247

time, for instance, the normal process for all of man when he leaves this physical plane of existence—in what we call death—he drops the physical body and will go to the astral plane, unless he has unfolded himself spiritually to the causal or mental worlds. From the astral plane, the entities that reside there, or the individuals, they feel they have reached immortality because the life span is equivalent on Earth standards about a thousand years, and you'll find many of the past inventors or great men that we think of that have even helped form this country that might be residing there. If the lessons are learned there, the spiritual lessons, we're talking about, they'll go on to the next plane of existence. It's a continuing thing. If the individual doesn't learn their lessons there, they'll come back to the physical realm and, I might add, they don't come back in a lesser state. Once you're a human being, you remain in that state, should you come back into the physical. This is mentioned in the following biblical references:

Hebrews . . . . . . Chapter 9, Verse 27
Malachi . . . . . . Chapter 4, Verses 5, 6
Ezekiel . . . . Chapter 16, Verses 48 thru 55
Ezekiel . . . . Chaptèr 37, Verses 1 thru 14
Ecclesiastes . . . Chapter 1, Verses 9 thru 11
Ecclesiastes . . . Chapter 3, Verses 15 thru 21
Matthew . . . . . . Chapter 11, Verses 12 thru 15
Matthew . . . . . . Chapter 17, Verses 10 thru 13
1 Peter . . . . Chapter 3, Verses 19, 20
1 Peter . . . . Chapter 4, Verse 6

"Ever since I was a child I had certain experiences, and I wanted to be shown where I am going, what I am going to do, and how to get there, during this lifetime, as some of the great teachers had. There is much written about different levels of heaven, and as a child I'd been experiencing up to four levels of heaven. I would go beyond the physical body, not only dream state but in the awake state, and travel beyond myself. As a child three, four and five years old, coming back into the physical body, I tried to reject it. I didn't want anything to do with it, because of what I experienced in the astral world or in the mental world. It's a freedom and it's beauty, but yet at this early age I learned that there's work that the entities do there, just like on this plane of existence of Earth. There are laws and rules more strict.

"There isn't enough gold, silver or gems that could be traded for the value one gains by learning how to cope with the different levels of heaven. For instance, what is referred to as the 'lower worlds'—they're very negative! These are the first levels of heaven or the 'rooms' in God's heavens as spoken of in man's scriptures. These are the planes of heaven up to the etheric, each with its own deity. They are under the control of the negative deity or what is called Kal Niranjan, known as the devil or Satan in the scriptures. Yet that entity reports to the Supreme Being or the SUGMAD or God, and takes its direction from God as well, for his dark force is unable to withstand the pure white Light of God.

"Some people have not seen these inner worlds, for it isn't necessary that they see them. They may have experienced them in a previous lifetime and won't be shown; perhaps, these lower planes of consciousness may not be necessary for their spiritual unfoldment."

Darwin points out some of the pitfalls, or tests the individual may go through on his journey back to the pure positive God Worlds, just as Job did.

"There are so many pitfalls, one can use *The Tiger's Fang* by Paul Twitchell as a guide, a road map through the lower worlds. I've said many times at talks I have given around the world that when someone appears and claims to be a Silent One, the Living ECK Master, or says they are an agent of God or the MAHANTA, just call on 'Darji' or Rebazar Tarzs or Paulji or call on SUGMAD. They'll find out right quick whether that person is for real. There are a lot of hoaxes or pitfalls in going through the lower worlds, and one of the best things for anyone or the initiate on this path who is aware of that and encounters an entity in the astral or causal or mental world, is to let go, don't push, say, 'OK, you're a Master, so what? Show me the God World planes, take me.'

"An entity off the astral plane can't go beyond that plane. It it's someone trying to poke fun at the person from the astral or mental plane, they can't go any farther than that because they have no business being here on Earth. They love to poke fun; the Kal will use subjects like that and give them certain powers on that plane of existence and allow that person to appear to him with great mystical powers, great spiritual powers, but only on that plane of existence. And these are some of the tests we are faced with, everyone —I've been faced with it, Paul was faced with it, Rebazar Tarzs was faced with it, Fubbi Quantz had to go through it. We all do, even the great saints had to go through these tests.

"One can always ask for clarification of an entity's identity. And keep a history of your dreams, write them down in the morning while they're fresh. I keep a pad and pencil by my bedside for things I bring back from the Wisdom Temples or a song, things I should do at the office, do out here in the physical world, that sort of thing. You'll find that there's a story or a picture that is being fulfilled and a portion of a dream you didn't understand last month or last week will fall in place."

The centripetal flow of the Creative Life Current, converging like circles on a pond from the outermost bounds of creation back to the center, the source of the flow, is the positive force or the vehicle soul uses to get back to Its original home in the true heavens. The spiritual exercises of ECK enable It to make contact with the Light and the Sound, the visible and audible aspects of the ECK, which raises Its consciousness upward through the various planes of existence.

Since this great cycle of the ECK Current has existed since the beginning of creation, the method of traveling back to God on the return flow has also always existed. And there has at all times been a Living ECK Master, a representative of the SUGMAD, present on all planes to lead souls on this path of ECK. These ECK Masters form an uninterrupted succession, and their order is known as the Ancient Order of the ECK Vairagi Masters. There are other spiritual guides, but they themselves are working under either the Vairagi Adepts or under the dark force. Sri Darwin comments:

"A spiritual guide can be working under the guidance of an ECK master, but you'll find that the majority of the spiritual guides are ECK Masters, working from one of the Golden Wisdom Temples. There are a few individuals that do assist, that are in training, whether it's to follow me or the next Living ECK Master, there is always someone ready to take over that responsibility.

"This line of ECK Masters, the Vairagi ECK Masters of ECKANKAR, has never been broken and never will, because the hierarchy, the structure of it existed before man existed on this planet, long before. Some of the past Living ECK Masters are working silently, others in the Golden Wisdom Temples on the various planes of existence, starting with the Soul plane and beyond that, on down to this physical level.

"The whole goal of their work is to bring this awareness to those ready for It and of being available—some people are guided by these ECK Masters and have been with them in previous lifetimes. There's a good share that have no spiritual guide and have not been aware or met any of the ECK Masters, whether it's in this lifetime or the past. I've not stopped to take inventory of how many ECK Masters are in the lower planes, from the etheric down to the physical, versus the God worlds."

These Temples of Golden Wisdom are located on each plane on up to the Soul plane, and in each temple is kept a section of the Shariyat-Ki-Sugmad, to be studied individually in the Soul body by the chelas who are brought there by the Living ECK Master. The Inter Master knows what section of the Shariyat-Ki-Sugmad the student is ready for, and he is individually taken there in the dream state or his contemplation. The importance of individual study is stressed by Sri Darwin, the Living ECK Master, because of the difference in understanding and spiritual unfoldment:

"Every man, woman, plant or animal is at a different state in his spiritual unfoldment. Take an example, in my youth, being taken to my mother's church. They collectively were attempting to unfold spiritually—collectively. And it cannot be done, because of the difference of understanding. Myself, personally, I think that the old scriptures were fine, even though man was unable to follow the rules that were set down. The basic scriptures of the old book were good. The New Testament has been rewritten so many times, was handed down and written down by somebody else, second and third parties, and in some cases, a fourth party down the line. The old scriptures and most of those stories are mostly based on dreams, and interpretations of dreams. So, again, it is not concrete evidence as so many people look to the 'good book,' as it is called, as being the last word. It isn't. It's a good book and makes a good story and just as any other book, it should be read, read again, perhaps, and learn from it, but not use it in a sense that it is the last word. The last word has not been written anywhere here, in this physical world. You'll find that it is in one of the seven Golden Wisdom Temples. And, even then, when you read it from the tablets and the books in the seven Golden Wisdom Temples, one has to, after they have gained that knowledge, go beyond that, starting again from the temple within and being adventuresome and bold.

"For the spiritual traveler who knows how to go in the states of consciousness into these worlds, whether subjectively or objectively, when the individual reaches the Soul plane and is taught by the ECK Master, the Living ECK

252

Master of the time, on a one-to-one basis, he turns loose of him. Then he can go on his own. He's through with those Wisdom Temples, where the tablets exist, and writing. There are other Wisdom Temples, but that knowledge, spiritual knowledge I'm speaking of, is gained by his own initiative by becoming adept at living life—he religiously keeps that love affair going between him and God."

SUGMAD (God), through ITS primal creative energy, the ECK, works only through the consciousness of the individual. IT, of ITSELF, does not descend into the lower realms of the physical, astral, causal and mental states of consciousness, only in ITS lesser forms as the dual forces. Therefore, we find that man exists on all levels simultaneously: just as he has a physical body and physical senses, he has an astral body, which is the emotional body, existing on the astral plane; a causal body, which contains all past and future experiences, instincts, memories, and is part of the subconsciousness; a mental body, which is the mind or intellectual faculty which has at least four levels; an etheric body which is that unconscious part of the mental body that is intuition, and whose function is to transmit impulses from Soul to the mind and vice versa. Lastly, there is the Soul body, which is the vehicle for Soul, or the true consciousness of the individual, the divine spark. All lower bodies are mechanical and lifeless, unless activated and sustained by Soul, who uses them as instruments on the lower vibratory levels.

The ECK flows through Soul, or the consciousness, and gives impulses to the mind which creates thought. Thought gives rise to images, and, coupled with emotion, manifests the image as an object on the physical plane. This is the process of creation and shows how each individual is the creator of his own life and environment. Each person manifests the Divine Spirit individually in his life, and this is why ECKANKAR is an individual path. His attitude is what shapes his creative processes, and when his attention is directed to the Living ECK Master and the higher spiritual worlds, his attitude being that of working for the good of the whole, his life becomes infused with the Divine Essence and he is raised into the realization of his true self and God.

ECKANKAR, therefore, is not a religious path to be observed only at certain times or on Sundays, but it becomes a way of life of each moment. Sri Darwin Gross, in a booklet called *ECKANKAR, A Way of Life,* examines what this means in the life of the ECKist:

"In ECKANKAR we place the emphasis on the Soul body as the vehicle we prefer for experience. Soul can't be aberrated in the manner the other bodies can. It is indestructible. The mind can be developed, but it is limited. Once an individual grasps the movement of Soul—it is swifter that the speed of light.

"Why is ECKANKAR a way of life? Why is it a path that I follow along with many thousands of modern citizens of this planet Earth? The ECKist follows the manmade laws. He is not out to change the social structure or to become politically influential. The ECKist is far more interested in experiencing God during this lifetime. His experience is that success which will make him more effective in every aspect of life. The goal of the followers in ECKANKAR is spiritual liberation within this lifetime, the realization of self and God, and the preservation of the individual self throughout eternity. The essential nature of ECKANKAR is freedom from all things—the complete independence of Soul. Soul is the central reality of the individual. Soul, being a happy entity, will not be controlled by anything other than the Spirit. Thus we must devote ourselves to the practical work of our daily lives and try to realize the guidance of ECK (Spirit) in every affair. This depends on our maintaining a non-attached attitude. The moment we start creating special points, ideas, and distinctions, we exile ourselves from the state of God consciousness, and miss the infinite freedom of reality. ECKANKAR is the science of certainty. The ECKist will not accept these things on faith—he proves them for himself. In this way he becomes spiritually mature and eventually a master in his own right.

"The ECKist follows the beat of his own drum. He acquires and lives by the highest attributes: total freedom, total awareness and total responsibility. He is unfettered by the guilt and fear that have been imposed upon the race of man for centuries, yet his goal is not social change or reform. He acts within the laws of man while placing his attention upon the worlds of God. At the same time he lives a responsible, involved existence, paying his own way, serving a useful function in society, and fulfilling his commitments to himself, his family and employer.

"In the above ECKists are busy translating their inner unfoldment into everyday life terms all around the world."

Soul is indestructible and immortal and evolves in the lower worlds through a long series of incarnations, manifesting and taking on the shapes of the various life forms. It, Soul, evolves from the lower life forms to the higher through the accumulation of experiences, which are brought about by cause and effect. This law of cause and effect, action and reaction, which brings back to the originator the effect of the causes he has created, is called the law of karma in Eastern terminology. It is a purely mechanical mode of learning and evolution that governs all worlds from the physical to the etheric.

Speaking about past lives and accumulated experiences, Darwin said:

"We as individuals have an accumulation from previous existences whether in this universe or another universe, such as a young lady or young man who takes to music or art, creativeness very naturally, and may not have the talents but have the desire and opens himself to Spirit, through the spiritual exercises in ECK, and this unfolds for them very naturally. The accumulation of one's life in the past has some bearing on it but in ECKANKAR one doesn't need to go back and find out whether they were a musician or such. It doesn't pertain to the here and now.

"We are taught that we may have traits from our father and mother and this isn't necessarily true. The individual brings these traits with him; it's a record that is retained in the causal body as well as the Soul body, and the father and mother are just vehicles for us to be germinated and brought forth to this outer life."

Once the individual comes into ECK, he has the opportunity to transcend the mechanical method of unfoldment and expand his consciousness under the spiritual guidance of the Living ECK Master. No longer does he depend on cause and effect to bring him enlightenment through trial and error, but now the MAHANTA has conscious control over each step in his unfoldment. The individual no longer suffers from the feeling of guilt and fear about so-called sins committed in the past, but is aware that each event in one's life is a step in one's spiritual growth. He is now able to drop whatever actions and habits that are holding him back, and advance at his greatest capacity towards the two main goals of ECKANKAR: Self-Realization and God-Realization.

The attainment of these goals may happen in an instant, yet the student needs a thorough spiritual foundation to be able to have these experiences and stay balanced. Sri Darwin speaks about sin, and Self- and God-Realization:

"There is no sin. Emerson, Jesus and Buddha spoke of it very nicely: it's compensation, for we earn what we sow. We reap that which we sow. This is very exacting, especially for those who unfold themselves spiritually to a point.

"The first step is Self-Realization, whether the person comes to this path with Self-Realization or develops it— that is the first step into the heavenly worlds. Without that, if a person attempts to go beyond that—because some do attempt to get into the heavenly worlds into certain areas of knowledge that doesn't exist in books, that you can't get from books—he is pushing against that door. That door that I'm speaking of is that temple within. He might know how to open it slightly, and have a look at what is out there, or maybe he is being tested and hasn't prepared himself with a foundation, spiritually, he starts to have some difficulties — of the Dark Night of Soul. Some people go through that without any hassle. The majority of us, individually, do have a difficult time with various aspects of it.

"Now, to the individual that takes the time to develop himself spiritually and builds that foundation of Self-Realization with the spiritual blocks, and then takes the next step when he is ready, and has the guidance of the Living ECK Master of the time, he'll have a lesser problem. Now, some of the tools are in those Five Passions of the Mind, to develop — not to rid oneself completely, but get ahold of, be aware of some of those negative aspects of one of the divisions of those five passions, such as anger, lust, greed, attachment and vanity.

"The 360-degree viewpoint is consciousness. You could think of it as an attitude, developing this in unfolding spiritually and to progress while we're here in this physical realm, to progress spiritually. We must have and be open to other viewpoints and understand other viewpoints.

"At the Soul plane, the first step is the Self-Realized state. Then, is what the Christians call the Christ-consciousness — theirs takes place in the astral or mental realm. The closest state in ECKANKAR is the ECKshar consciousness which takes place on the Soul plane. There's a great difference—semantics and terminology get in the way and tend to cause arguments, but there are similarities. To the occultist and metaphysicist, they think of it as cosmic consciousness. It's similar to the Christ-consciousness. The Christ-consciousness and cosmic consciousness deals with the dual worlds. I'm not saying that the ECKshar consciousness is greater, for it just *is*. It's not for me to say that, but it emanates from the Soul plane. From that point of illumination or spiritual unfoldment, the individual then has the spiritual guidance when he needs it. He can call on the Living ECK Master or the ECK Master he was initiated under—whether it is one of the other ECK Masters, in his time, such as Paul Twitchell, as he is still helping to guide individuals through these lower worlds. They're off and running if they choose to, into the invisible worlds, the endless worlds, and ultimately, the God-conscious state, while they're here in the flesh.

"It is something greater than recognition of SUGMAD. He becomes aware of the SUGMAD and realizes the SUGMAD at the ECKshar consciousness. As high as one can travel and unfold to a state of consciousness from this physical level, while being here, is that Hukikat Lok, the God-conscious state. Beyond that, one drops the physical body. We don't look to the past or the future, because there is no beginning or ending. It's all right here, in this moment, and looking to the past—moment, days, or years—we always are creating frustration and trouble and arguments bringing it up. It's gone, and it's over with. To the future, in this world in making our way, we can set goals, but then let go of it. Let the Spirit guide us, and the Inner Master — for spiritual growth, and our outer, material growth."

Spiritual foundation is achieved through the daily practice of the spiritual exercises of ECK. They strengthen the link-up between the individual and the ECK, and open him gradually for the guidance from the Living ECK Master. The creative process working through the mind, emotions and desires needs to be directed towards the true spiritual benefit of oneself and others. The necessary effort in this regard is pointed out by Darwin:

"One must be careful with what one insists on and wishes for others as well as one's self, especially someone who's unfolding spiritually, and blending into the Sound Current and the Light, those pillars of God that sustain life. And if we wish for something it's going to happen, and it might not be what we want. So we must think out our thoughts very carefully in what we want to happen to us and what we want in life. And above all, not to be wishing something for someone else, because that other person may not be able to accept it and it might be very harmful for that person. A person may not want accelerated spiritual unfoldment when he gets it because someone wishes it for him.

"That is why it is stressed in the teachings of ECK to take your time and go slow, and take a look at each step and know that you want to take it. It's not like some of the evangelists out there say that you can have your piece of pie in the sky right now. You want to go at it a little step at a time. But you have to earn it, and work and pay for it. That is one of the big misconceptions in the religious world that all we have to do is ask God and it will be given. That's not true—up to a certain point there are things that are, but beyond that to gain further spiritual knowledge and enlightenment of God and the heavenly worlds now, not waiting till death but now in this lifetime, we have to earn it. I had to."

Controlling the mind and thought is not so much an effort of concentrating the will and forcing one's self, but more of letting go mentally of inner turmoil and being active under the guidance of the Inner Master. According to Darwin:

"The Inner Master will always listen, and will always be there with that person. The uninitiated, those that aren't on the path of ECKANKAR, get into a troubled area and have a negative sort of circumstance come up. They should be aware that if they pray and use the power of prayer, the more that they pray, the worse the situation will get. The more that person might meditate or talk to God or whatever their faith or belief is, the worse it gets for them, the more pressure Spirit puts upon, or more of the karma, because the negative forces of the Kal or the Devil, whatever one thinks of the dark force—the more pressure it will put on, in trying to get this resolved from that individual's point of view, because the negative force doesn't want to lose that

Soul. That Soul is destined to go into the heavenly worlds and the best thing is you've got to let go. Don't pray, don't seek out anything in the way of further spiritual enlightenment. That is, turn it over to Spirit, turn it over to the Inner Master, and let go of it and know that it's going to be handled, and use that middle of the road commonsense approach. The person that is struggling is pushing on the inner door.

"The more one prays or does any spiritual exercise, the more this force of ECK comes in, and is showered upon us, and the worse things get. Don't try to take personal problems to the temple within. Don't try to take it to God. Or to Spirit. It'll just get worse. It's up to us, as individuals, to work out our problems here. God could care less about it. Spirit doesn't want to know about it—IT already knows. These are spiritual tests, and it's the attitude one might have during that moment of time. It's that simple. So the problems themselves are tests that Spirit is issuing out to us. And it's how we handle these problems that determines our spiritual growth."

There are four constructive modes of action and five destructive modes of action of the mind. The four constructive ones are: to take notice of form, beauty, color, rhythm, harmony and perspective. Second, to receive and register impressions through the senses of smell, taste, hearing and feeling. These impressions are passed on to the third faculty, that of thought or the intellect. This faculty passes its judgements on to the fourth part, which executes the orders.

The five negative activities are called the five passions of the mind and include: Anger, Greed, Lust, Attachment and Vanity. All negative traits and motivations of man can be classified under one or more of these five. Fear, for instance, comes under attachment, because being afraid only means having fear of losing something one is attached to. With the spiritual exercises of ECK one can raise oneself into a position of being able to handle these mind passions

260

so as not to let them interfere with one's well-being and spiritual unfoldment. There are hundreds of spiritual exercises given throughout the literature of ECKANKAR, for the individual to try out and take as a framework to create his own exercises. Darwin frequently speaks about a spiritual exercise developed by Sri Paul Twitchell called The Easy Way:

"You look very gently to the right or left without straining, with your eyes closed. Place the image of whoever you look to as a spiritual giant, be it Jesus, Buddha, Paul Twitchell, Rebazar Tarzs or myself. After a few long soft breaths to slow the heart down, repeat the word HU (HUUUUUUUU) or you can use the word AUM (Ah-oom), an ancient Oriental word that has been used down through the centuries, a verse that is uplifting from any scripture that you yourself choose. You can even use the word 'God' if you choose to. Repeat your word HU no more than ten to twelve times.

"Repeat the verse or word or sing it, either silently or orally, at least a half dozen times. Then sit quietly and just listen and look for the Light or listen for the Sound. The first thing that should happen will be a very small dot of light and it's subtle, could be blue or ultraviolet. For some it has been gold or white. This will depend upon your spiritual unfoldment. After sitting and gazing into the spiritual eye for a period of time, of three to five minutes, repeat the word or the verse that you had used for another half a dozen to a dozen times.

"Once again, sit very quietly and looking very softly, do not strain, to the right or left and keep your attention there throughout this whole exercise. But one does not have to strain; it should be gentle and easy. Do this two to three times and you'll find that if you do this once a day, whether it's in the morning, afternoon or evening, whenever you can find the time, and do it on a regular basis, that things in your daily life will straighten out. In time, spiritual insights will start to flow in.

261

"Have no fear for you are not going to be leaving your body or no one will be taking you out of your body. The first thing that takes place for most people will be a wave of light which is usually blue. Should you go beyond yourself, a spiritual guide will be with you. However, you may or may not see him.

"This spiritual exercise will help in expanding your consciousness. You may not notice it immediately and you may not see or hear anything the first few times or two to three months. It may, for some, take six months before they experience the Light or Sound of God. Others it might take two to six days. It takes patience, and, above all, persistence, for unfolding spiritually, and gaining the secrets of God takes time. There is no need to hurry. I have found that most people in the western world find it difficult, initially, to sit still longer than 3 - 5 minutes in their first try at the spiritual exercises. Don't be disturbed by that. Just do the spiritual exercise if you choose a time, try to use that same time each day, even if it is three minutes. You'll find, as you perform this spiritual exercise, that the time will ultimately draw out to one-half hour and that is all that is necessary to carry you through a 24-hour period. Not only are you helping yourself spiritually to the knowledge of God, but you'll find that you'll be assisting yourself in the physical realm as well. There are many ways in which there's not enough paper or words to tell you. You'll meet the right people, find the right work, heal yourself or someone else, as well as learn to prophesy for yourself.

"The only suggestion that I can add to this spiritual exercise is that it should be done once a day, regularly. Even if you pray daily, and do this exercise, you'll find great strides in your spiritual unfoldment. Use the word 'Jesus' if you wish or 'Allah' or 'Jehovah,' etc. However, keep in mind these spiritual teachers that walked this earth do not carry the vibrations they did of their day.

"During the quiet period in-between repeating a verse or singing the word HU or Aum, or chanting a word, even if

262

it's A-men, that quiet period is a period of time when you should contemplate on that which you do not understand, either about yourself, this world which you live in, or God. Now when you contemplate about God, remember that there are two pillars which are Light and Sound. Do not try to contemplate on both the Light and Sound at the same time. I suggest you choose the Light first, for light is knowledge and there's a vast amount of knowledge available just for the taking, through this simple, easy spiritual exercise.

"It is through this spiritual exercise that you'll begin to expand your consciousness and viewpoint. One must be patient, for as you prepare yourself, through this spiritual exercise, the answers will be given as you can accept them. Do not be surprised whether it be through a newspaper, an animal, some other person, or in the dream state; however, it could also take place during the spiritual exercise and during that quiet time in between the singing of your word.

"These spiritual exercises will start one out on the path to God. If he doesn't have a spiritual guide, one will be assigned. There are spiritual lessons to be learned, so one doesn't want to be afraid of either going out, objectively, or subjectively within himself. There will always be someone there to assist him. If they become afraid, they could call on the present Living ECK Master, Darji. If they're allowed to go out, there will be someone standing by to assist that individual. No one else can take over your body. Not in this type of spiritual exercise, whatsoever. An ECK Master won't enter that temple unless asked. They'll help guide, only. They won't go in unless invited, and even then, it's made sure that one's sincere in their spiritual growth. If one is looking for phenomena from the psychic worlds, which are lesser steps on this path, or takes a look at it, he'll be disappointed, because what is learned is beyond the psychic realms and the tools that are gained allows one to do miracles and be a vehicle for miracles to be performed, and a person sees and knows this, but doesn't talk about it. He's not asking for a miracle to happen in his life. He is doing it."

The ECK teachings help the individual rise above fear, instead of using fear to conform them to the spiritual path. Sri Darwin and all of the Vairagi ECK Masters are gentle, who give each person total physical and spiritual freedom. Sri Darwin has said:

"Now, one day, these lower planes will be cleansed, all the Souls will be taken up into the pure positive God Worlds and the lower worlds destroyed and reconstructed again. This is going to happen, but I'm not going to use a fear factor to people that read this book and say, 'Hey, you've got to get right with God.' I would be doing them an injustice if I said that because they would have that fear within themselves. There's enough of that done by the evangelist and preachers and priests. And other religions. This world is good for approximately forty thousand years.

"To try to sway the person to find God, and you can't find God, in this physical realm or while locked up in the body. It has been stressed by all the great teachers, and the saints included, that one must separate Soul from the body. Through the spiritual practices in ECKANKAR, one does this at his own volition, and there's nothing to be afraid of. He can't harm himself. There's change that takes place, moment by moment, and one needs to prepare for change.

"The individual needs to know the difference between ECK and ECKANKAR. They are two different functions, and I'm speaking of all individuals, not just the ECKists. The movement of ECKANKAR doesn't have or play a part in a sense of trying to change society. Many other types of groups do. It's not an occult group, so therefore it's not concerned about changing the way man lives in his world. The individual himself is his biggest problem. We all are taught things in our childhood that are of a negative nature. Many times he grows up into an adult with these fears, also with these no-no's or don't's. This is ingrained in his magnetic sheath, mental, astral as well as causal bodies, and unless he is aware of it and knows how to rid himself of these traits, they'll linger up to when he translates or leaves this Earth plane."

When a chela has learned to be in control of the five passions of the mind, knows how the laws of the universe work, listens to the guidance from the Living ECK Master, and lives ECK as a way of life, then the result is a life of the highest ethics known to man. Every ECKist knows that greater ethics come from greater spiritual unfoldment, not vice versa. There are no rules or commandments in ECKANKAR, only understanding. Sri Darwin explains:

"The Living ECK Master is standing by that door all the time with the individual and this happens, persons do unfold and get to the point when he thinks the wrong thing and he immediately knows it. That knowingness is so exacting that he can have some fun, but they know how far to go, whether it's in the office or out in the field or out in the street.

"Anything that happens to us, stems from within ourselves. There are five passions of the mind; these are items that are not being taught in the religious spectrum of this world. The uninitiated don't know of this. One doesn't work on all five passions at one time, take just one category at a time—anger, greed, lust, vanity or attachment, and work on it until he has a handle on it, then go on to the next item. The individual on the path of ECK gains a much better insight not only into himself and has a better understanding of himself, but he gets through that area of self-realization by getting a handle and getting complete control of anger, complete control of lust, etc. He becomes aware.

"The five passions are negative traits that are embedded in us, some to greater degree, some to a lesser degree. They are the tools of the negative force, called Kal Niranjan in ECKANKAR, in which he binds the individual to the lower worlds by the use of these, such as anger, greed, vanity, lust and attachment.

265

"Each one is like a claw, a string to the effect and in some instances there are little holes in the aura. Until one has patched up those holes, where there isn't some negative current flowing down through that string into the aura, into that particular body it's associated with, it will continue to bother that person. The easiest way to get around this is the spiritual exercise technique called *The Easy Way*, using the word HU or the word one gets in his initiation.

"Sometimes a person might get a word and he feels it might be negative and won't use it and it really isn't a negative word. The individual isn't used to cleaning out some of the negativeness in his aura and feels it might be negative because he's started to rid himself of some of the negative traits that have clung to him through the negative dark force, some actions from the past as well as from this lifetime. And the only way to get control of that is to get above it and be able to rise above it in a state of consciousness and clean up one's aura, which no one else can do for you. This is done by the spiritual exercises of ECK, practicing them once a day, from twenty minutes to one-half hour. If the passion continues to persist and doesn't clear up, I wouldn't worry about it or fret over it. Let the Inner Master know about it either in writing, whether you mail it or not, or let him know via the inner channels, and for those who have the inner connection — they will know how to use it.

"And suddenly you realize that little claw of Kal is gone. It's a form of spiritual healing."

In his talks and writings, the Living ECK Master will subtly state insights into the effects and results of human actions in relation to their spiritual unfoldment. He will not give his followers outright orders or forbid them to do anything. It is up to the individual to take for himself what he accepts as truth and wants to practice. The message of ECK is, therefore, for those who have eyes to see and ears to hear. If they are open and willing to look beyond the concepts previously formed, then there is a wealth of knowledge to be gained from the words of the Living ECK Master, covering many aspects of life:

"In the spiritual field and especially in this teaching of ECKANKAR, there is no competition, whatsoever, whether it is between this Satsang class or that one over there, in another city or within the same city, or between us as individuals. That competition belongs in the business world, and not in a spiritual teaching. It is really not necessary for man's survival, physically, materially, or spiritually. It's like getting into an old track, like a stuck record, going back into history, whether it's in this present era of time or the early Roman and Grecian era or prior to that, there was the same problem. Civilizations got too materialistic, too competitive.

"Our sports, for instance. It was great when the price tag wasn't put on a player. There should be some sort of way to assist those who have talent, musically, creatively, in some manner — whether it's football, basketball, with an instrument, or vocally, or with dancing or acting. To eliminate that competitiveness, because that competitiveness invites greed, so many aspects of greed — of trying to influence certain parties or judges who judge them by a little payola under the table. And there's a lot of that. Competition is very definitely of the Kal force, very much so. It's that way.

"There should not be any competition in ECKANKAR. There's nothing wrong with being competitive to succeed in the world. The ECKist can be competitive, but he puts it in its place, as a function in the lower worlds.

"A person can have a greater piece of that pie of understanding of the whole circumference, or just a very little slice. It's up to the human state of consciousness. Now, the consciousness we are dealing with is a link between the human, the astral, causal, mental, and the Soul. We don't have anything to do with these lower bodies, in developing spiritually, in ECKANKAR. We develop the Soul body to its full extent, but in turn, that has a link, a communication link, down to the human state of consciousness, and when one is working, for an employer as an employee, he must go by the rules, regulations laid down by that person, and has to be careful. He can voice his opinion up to a point, but when he starts to go beyond that, he is liable to upset his supervisor or his employer and lose his job. Now, that's his own decision. It's a spiritual freedom that is gained, not a physical freedom. It's a total spiritual freedom.

"This viewpoint is spoken of in *Stranger By The River*, as well as throughout the rest of the writings as *The Shariyat-Ki-Sugmad*, as well.

It's referred to as The Way of the Eternal in that set of books. The Everlasting Gospel, it's referred to. There are three attributes that come with one's unfolding spiritually. I don't try to recall everything or memorize everything, I don't have time for it, but these attributes are: Spiritual freedom, wisdom which comes through the experience gained in unfolding spiritually, and charity, which is love. That charity that Paul spoke of is not charity in giving your things away. It's of love, unattached love, divine love, not a physical love. A physical love has its purpose only in this respect, for reproduction. Keep in mind that there are various levels of consciousness, and these levels of consciousness have their function.

"In the plant life, reproduction there is for flowers or timber, and those trees have a function of helping keep the air clean, to a great degree. In the human life, to perpetuate life, we must have individuals be aware and be careful not to misuse that. Some do. I'm not saying that one must abstain from enjoying their partner. That is not what I'm saying, but Paul stressed it, very subtly, in the writings. It appeared and a lot of people overlooked it because they want to. We must be very discriminate.

"Being a channel—there's a number of ways developing that. The creative techniques is the best way. But once you learn how to use one of these creative techniques, or I'll say, 'The Easy Way,' that spiritual exercise in ECK, the contemplative exercise, to be a vehicle for God, and allow ITS essence, that vehicle, Spirit, to work through us, we don't want to direct It towards any person or any group or nation. It knows more of what is needed—whether it's next door or on the other side of the world or some other part of the universe—than we, in the human state of consciousness. I don't know what's good for my neighbor, nor for my loved ones. And, this is an area that—like it's the parents' responsibility to give their children guidance in the home, not only love, but spiritual guidance and understanding. They get that foundation and the tools to work with at a very early age, that you don't go out there and take your neighbor's hoe or something that belongs to your neighbor, because the neighbor is going to learn of it, he is going to miss it and when he sees it in your yard, he's going to call you a thief or a liar or call the police. For every action there is an equal and opposite reaction, and this is a law in the physical sciences, and this is true in the spiritual worlds. As one unfolds spiritually, this becomes more evident.

"As long as you live anywhere in the lower worlds, the higher you go on the spiritual ladder, the more exacting these laws become. This is the reason it has been written in the teachings of ECKANKAR that the ECKist develops responsibility as he unfolds spiritually. Not only is he going to be looked upon as someone with high morals, but ethics greater than man knows. And if he isn't getting beyond the mental world, doesn't know the meaning of ethics, he has not gone and developed spiritually beyond those mental worlds."

CHAPTER 12

The Radiant Body of the MAHANTA

First there is the absolute primordial, the eternal MAHANTA, called the clear voice of God, which dwells in the heart of the Ocean of Love and Mercy. There is no way to compare this with anything in Christianity, Hinduism or Buddhism.

Second is the body of glory; the ECK, the Cosmic Spirit, the Sound Current that which is in all life, giving existence to all things.

Third is the body of manifestation, the transformation, the historical MAHANTA. This is the Living ECK Master in every age, who is the Eternal One, the bodily manifestation of the SUGMAD.

—*The Shariyat-Ki-Sugmad,* Book One

The story of Sri Darwin, the 972nd Living ECK Master, would be incomplete without a statement about that wondrous Being, that total awareness, the MAHANTA, which uses the vehicle (Soul) of Darwin, spiritually known as Dap Ren, on all planes of God's universe, in all galaxies, planets and constellations within space and time and beyond. The writings of ECKANKAR, authored by Sri Paul Twitchell and Sri Darwin Gross, present vast material on the subject of the MAHANTA, and these books will be widely throughout this chapter in order to familiarize the interested reader with the works of ECK.

The SUGMAD is the Creator and Source of all existence. Without IT, there would be no consciousness and nothing to be conscious of. ITS essence, the ECK, stepped down in ITS vibratory rate from plane to plane, penetrates and sustains all life. In ITS pure form, however, IT uses the MAHANTA state to flow to each individual living being. Therefore, it can be stated that the MAHANTA is the Source of Divine Essence for each Soul. The difference this makes in the beingness of each person is explained by Sri Darwin in his book *Your Right to Know.* Using a scientific approach and wonderfully simple words, he makes this spiritual interaction with the MAHANTA understandable to every man:

A polarization of the atoms takes place when the sun is out, and it produces warmth. The same thing is true when the Living ECK Master of the time is amongst chelas. Whether in the physical or radiant body, there is polarization of the atom structure and they feel that warmth and love. In the shade, the unmanifested atoms are not polarized, but when the sun is present in view they are. There is a particular energy, the work force, that takes place. The light photon and the properties of the light are actually what activate the polarization.

If the ECKist recognizes this, and places his attention on the Living ECK Master at the time of need or stress or any time, that polarization will take place. Then he could be in a dark spot and be warm, or in trouble and know that he is being guided through it, or going through a rough area whether it is physical or spiritual.

Above space, time, energy and matter, Soul is one. Each individual Soul is not separate from the MAHANTA, except in the state of limitations It has placed upon Itself. Expanding the awareness through the spiritual exercises of ECK, It becomes more and more conscious of being a part of that infinite Divine Essence —like a spark in the body of an immeasurably vast ocean. This body is often referred to as the Body of the MAHANTA.

Without the true Godman, nothing could exist. All the worlds exist in Him. The macrocosm of the universe is He. Therefore, man as the microcosm is only the little world in movement whose divine self can travel at will throughout the body of the MAHANTA's world, or the universal self of God.

—Dialogues with the Master

This statement by the great ECK Master Rebazar Tarzs, who dictated *Dialogues with the Master* to Paul Twitchell, emphasizes the fact that all life exists in the MAHANTA, yet man has the opportunity to become conscious of this and gain a greater freedom and ability for himself. The MAHANTA, the Living ECK Master has achieved total awareness of His spiritual body and can become conscious of any one or more parts at will, just as the human being is conscious of his physical body and can selectively put his attention on his feet or the tip of his right index finger or any other part. He is with each and every single part of His body at all times.

For that individual who takes on the task of being the vehicle for the MAHANTA consciousness, the responsibility is awesome. Sri Darwin describes it the following way:

"The Radiant Form of the Living ECK Master, when he accepts the Rod of ECK Power, he's accepting responsibility beyond the scope and concept of the human mind can grasp. It's Life itself. The Light one sees is the Body of the MAHANTA, the vehicle, being a channel for the SUGMAD, but yet part of IT, and the atom structure. I'll retain my identity and individuality. I know what I'm going to do when I leave this physical plane of existence. This is what Sri Paul Twitchell had chosen, the kind of work he's doing and the ECK Masters we work with and for the Living ECK Master, the next one in line.

"I try not to have people put me up on a pedestal, I'm

273

just as human as the next person. Some of the spiritual knowledge I've gained and is utilized in the radiant form, in the Soul body, there is a difference. I'm very thankful that I can be of some assistance to all, not just for one person or a small group of individuals. The Initiate of ECK that's initiated into that lifestream of ECK can unfold to do the same kind of work. There are millions of people that are performing miracles and don't dare talk about it, so if I can bring about an understanding to that person or persons longing to understand God and Spirit—there's quite a difference. Spirit is that life-giving force that is the vehicle of God."

The MAHANTA consciousness, therefore, uses a human agent, an individual person, to embody Itself in the flesh so It may be contacted and perceived by those in the physical senses. The manifestation of the MAHANTA is known as the historical MAHANTA, and it is the physical vehicle that changes. The eternal MAHANTA is always the same, changeless and unlimited God-consciousness, but as the Living ECK Master, there is an unbroken succession. Hence, Sri Darwin is the 972nd Living ECK Master, since that time when ECK Masters first appeared on this Earth planet, his predecessor, Sri Paul Twitchell, being 971st, and so on. In *The Spiritual Notebook* there is a complete history of the past Living ECK Masters who figured prominently in the history of humankind. For always have the ECK Masters been present with the human race to guide their spiritual progress.

"The ECK Masters have been with every chela since the beginning of time upon this Earth and with other planets and the beings on those worlds," Darwin states. "The Living ECK Master has assumed another embodiment with each life spent in these worlds. It has always been the ECK which has brought about the existence of the Living ECK Master upon this planet and other worlds. It has only changed forms and handed down Its power from one departing Master to his successor.

"The Living ECK Master then takes up his duties in this world, to serve humanity and gather up as many souls as possible to return them to the heavenly worlds. He is only interested in the spiritual welfare of man, whom he hopes will have the understanding of ECK and ECKANKAR during this lifetime.

"The Living ECK Master serves as a wayshower and spiritual guide. His only mission is to gather up Souls who are ready and return them to the heavenly worlds. He is only interested in the spiritual welfare of man. The Living ECK Master is the exemplar of the Light and Sound of God. His primary function is to bring light and love into the world so that all persons may benefit from those wondrous aspects of the SUGMAD (God). Those who step on the path of ECK are given spiritual assistance and begin the realization of the higher self and of God, should they take some initiative."

The role of the MAHANTA, the Living ECK Master, as the teacher and wayshower of humankind is laid down in many of the ECK works, such as in *The Shariyat-Ki Sugmad,* Book Two, brought forth from the Temple of Golden Wisdom by Sri Paul Twitchell:

The ECKist has a visible place in the life of the world as well as of the Satsangs. The history of the world would be totally without the influence of the ECK Masters and those who have followed ECK over the centuries from the beginning of time in the physical universe. It was the ECK Masters who civilized the human race, who kept not only learning and even literacy alive, but taught the primitives farming and, during the latter ages after the golden era, the raising of cattle. Those who have done the most for the human race in its intellectual and spiritual aspects, as well as its materialistic life, have been the ECK Masters of the Ancient Order of the Vairagi. But anything other than giving the

275

human race an uplift of spiritual value, has never been the aim of the ECK Masters. Rather all that, other than the spiritual air, has been the consequence, almost the by-product, of their search for helping man to reach perfection through the spiritual exercises of ECK.

Although the MAHANTA consciousness always stays the same, It chooses to reveal Itself to mankind in great evolutionary cycles or periods. At the beginning of each cycle there is a tremendous change and upsurge in the spiritual understanding of man. During each period the Living ECK Master has the choice of working up into that MAHANTAship. If he does not, the Living ECK Master who did remains the MAHANTA until another individual reaches up into that state.

In one of his books Paul writes that there will be eleven more such MAHANTAships, or leaps in the revelation of the Divine Consciousness. The periods may last from several hundred to thousands of years, and each is characterized by its own color or rate of frequency. This appears somewhat in the maroon colored robes many of the previous Living ECK Masters of the past cycle wear. "In October 1965 quite a change took place, not only on this planet but throughout the universe and all universes, when the Rod of Power of the ECK Mastership was passed from Rebazar Tarzs to Peddar Zaskq (Paul Twitchell)," Sri Darwin writes in his book, *Your Right to Know.*

A new cycle of the MAHANTA consciousness had started with Peddar Zaskq, to be carried on by his successor, Dap Ren. More information on this point was given by Sri Darwin in an interview:

"There was a great step taken when Paul Twitchell received the Rod of ECK Power and these steps and segments range greatly from the lower vibratory rates, like red on up to blue, but the blue existed even then. There was always the variations of color and there is an ECK Master that is in charge of that part of the spectrum, pertaining to that vi-

276

bratory rate, whether it is black, red, blue, green, yellow or white, and on up to ultraviolet. The greatest light that emanates out of God is yellow and goes into the pure white light; the pure white light is directly from the SUGMAD to the vehicle.

"The blue light is knowledge coming off the mental and subconscious levels, light being knowledge, the color is going to reach different stages of that individual's capabilities of absorbing information, which are at different levels of frequencies."

Few people outside the teachings of ECKANKAR realize the universal work the MAHANTA, the Living ECK Master does. He is not only present whenever someone Soul travels, whether consciously or unconsciously, but steps in whenever anyone is open to spiritual guidance from the Godman.

"The person who turns their life over to God, not to some past savior, saint or holy man who doesn't exist in the physical body, but has come to the end of the world of their religious practices or beliefs, and says, 'OK, God, I give up, I'm in your hands,' this is where I step in, even though they are not aware there is a Living ECK Master. I've appeared to them through their dreams or their prayers or meditation. Many times I'll give assistance and they'll think it came from God. I'm just a vehicle for it."

This statement by Sri Darwin, the Living ECK Master, is one of the most important aspects of ECKANKAR. There is no personal relationship involved between Darwin and the seeker of God, but only that of Spirit ITSELF. It is not the ECK Master's responsibility to manipulate the individual towards God-Realization, but to assist him in his own efforts. The Inter Master acts as a spiritual guide and counselor, always leaving the final decision up to the individual. Sri Darwin explains:

"One American out of ten suffers mental illnesses at one time or another, mostly because he or she believes they go through life alone. The ECKist should always be aware

277

that the presence of the MAHANTA is with him as a living, working partner. What is often not understood by the individual, despite religious, metaphysical or occult teachings is that man in the lower worlds has been given freedom of choice. Man is free to refuse to cooperate with God. When man refuses, he is free to make his own decisions and take the consequences.

"Those who disdain the spiritual teachings will have difficulty grasping the change of consciousness and the impact it has on their lives. The uninitiated have a difficult time. They need the guidance of the Living ECK Master and the Inner Master who in ECKANKAR is known as the MAHANTA. The individual can develop himself up to a point, but without that spiritual guide he may have difficulties, doubt, confusion, preoccupation with physical problems and responsibilities. All contribute to the spiritual retardation that composes the worry belt.

"ECKists know that there are no coincidences in daily life. Everything happens exactingly through Spirit. If one is placed in a negative situation, they rise above it to a higher state of consciousness. They know that the outcome will be positive and for some specific reason, for the good of the whole.

"This by no means relieves the individual of the responsibility for dealing with his everyday problems. In this physical realm we cannot just sit aside and say, 'I'll leave it up to the ECK; It'll find me a job.' It won't happen that way. One makes an application for a job and then forgets it, leaves it to Spirit. Then continues making applications. And the right job with the right people that one can get along with for the right wage will come to pass.

"The individual asks how to change his life, how to become more spiritual. One doesn't. He needn't change his living habits to become a spiritual person. As he becomes a more spiritual person, Spirit may change his life and the details of living, how he lives, his attitude about his life, his habits, his awareness, his thoughts and actions. As he grows in spirit, his actions will be his own regardless of what others say or think; yet he will not call attention to himself or make others uncomfortable with strange dress, hairdos or lifestyles. He will live the middle path, employing common sense and discretion."

The sense of freedom the student experiences on the path of ECKANKAR is essential for his own unfoldment. If he is to become a Master in his own right, the director of his own life and destiny, then it is not by living by the dictates and rules of dogma and spiritual authorities. What he does with his life and his spiritual progress is his own responsibility, and for each individual the necessary steps will be different. When approached, the MAHANTA, the Living ECK Master will offer advice for the person to ponder and contemplate, nothing more. His answer will most often be indirect, referring to the spiritual principle involved, so that the questioner may rise above his immediate emotional entanglement, and gain an understanding of lasting value. An example may be Darwin's response about marriage and partnership:

"Neither I nor any ECK Master will interfere with the personal relationships between an individual and his spouse. In marriage or commonlaw, when two people become emotionally attached, they should let go and they can experience truly being together. Honesty is vital, as is open communication, and peaceful resolution of the inevitable problems of any close relationship in the physical world. By understanding divine love with detachment, one allows his mate complete spiritual freedom.

"Divorce, like marriage, is a personal decision. If an individual and his spouse agree to go their separate ways peacefully, in respect and divine love, without hatred or bitterness, there is no adverse karma.

"There is some confusion between marriage and the concept of Soul mate. Soul mate is really a misnomer; it is the completion of Soul, neither male nor female, on Its journey to God. This occurs only on the Soul plane of existence and is unrelated to intercourse, human love or marriage. The human form of love is for reproduction only. Family life is very important to ECKANKAR. It is the parent's responsibility to give their children the best spiritual guidance that they are aware of. ECK tries to hold families together rather than separate them. Some individuals attempt to use Spirit as a cop-out to dissolve their misunderstandings."

It is for the same reason, the freedom of choice to accept or not accept, that the MAHANTA, the Living ECK Master does not perform miracles in public. Since he is the ECK, the highest creative force in all universes of the SUGMAD, all spiritual and physical laws, including the laws of nature, must obey him. He could change the face of the Earth, the structure of society, or any other situation within the blink of an eye, yet to do so in order to convince man of the path of ECK would be a violation of the spiritual law of freedom. The Truth must be presented to the individual in the subtle way that is for his spiritual benefit.

"It is unfortunate in these times that people instead of believing in the works of ECK, run after the teachings of the orthodox and the false, even without any visible evidence in their favor. The Kal has so cleverly designed this world that people easily believe what suits their purpose, but they will not seem to believe the MAHANTA, the Living ECK Master, who tries to present truth to all in the best possible manner, but demand miracles of him. This shows they are the victim of the Kal, because they believe what his followers say without evidence, while they demand miracles of the MAHANTA," writes Sri Darwin in *Your Right to Know.*

The Kal force is the power of the intellect within the individual. Usually, the intellectual person will demand proof for the physical senses in the form of a miracle from the MAHANTA, for it is the intellect that relies on physical facts and mental deductions to arrive at its conclusions.

Physical facts and mental deductions, however, prove nothing at all in the spiritual realm, and, therefore, the intellect will never be satisfied and always demand more miracles and answers from the MAHANTA. That the experience of Truth does not lie in the realm of the intellect was discovered by this chela who wrote Darwin about his changed attitude:

Dear Sri Darwin:

All my life, I've considered myself an intellectual. So much so, that I've spent endless hours arguing and writing as an anti-intellectual. A friend introduced me to ECKANKAR because of some things I told him about my views of Soul. For two years, I read everything I could get my hands on—but my only reaction was to criticize the literary style, the simplistic assumptions, the syntax and grammar, the organization and the claim of strange experiences.

Then one night I decided to try a spiritual exercise, the "easy way" you called it in one of your tapes. The mental worlds were on my mind as usual. I focused my mind's eye on your image. You seemed to be laughing and showing me a huge temple. From my reading, I assumed it was the Golden Wisdom Temple overseen by Sato Kuraji, the ECK Master of the intellect. Nothing was said, but suddenly everything seemed to fall in place for me. True, the intellect is an important part of me, a beautiful thing, a great instrument; but in my case, the intellect has nothing to do with my spiritual progress. I realized my studies in ECK are important. I have to start over, to experience Spirit rather than study it; but what joy, what a blessing, what a feeling of adventure . . . that now I can begin unburdened with intellectualizing everything.

Thank you Darwin.

Love in ECK,
A.

Paul Twitchell once stated: "A true miracle is a changed consciousness." The aim of the MAHANTA, the Living ECK Master is therefore to raise the individual in his state of consciousness, working with him on the inner as well as the outer, so that he may experience contact with the Divine Spirit himself. On countless and infinite levels, this is true for the whole of humanity and all life. The MAHANTA works quietly and mostly without recognition to raise the consciousness of all Souls who contact Him. In *The Far Country,* by Paul Twitchell, Rebazar Tarzs tells us:

"The SUGMAD has ITS way of leading men to the light. There are two methods used by the Supreme One: First, is the method of the whole world, led by natural law, personal experience and experimentation—trial and discard. The second is finding the MAHANTA who will help you and give you his benefit by taking you with him on trips into the Far Country until you're able to travel alone."

To receive this spiritual guidance and upliftment from the MAHANTA, the person who is of a particular religion or a certain cultural background need not disassociate himself and burn all bridges behind him. Sri Darwin Gross writes in *Your Right to Know:*

"The Universal Body of the MAHANTA is made up of people of all races, religions and moral fiber. These various people are not obligated to rescind all connections with their traditional values and change to a new set of so-called ECK values, because the only thing recognized as being of any value in ECK is Soul, in the total expansion of consciousness of Soul."

In fact, one of the principles of the MAHANTA consciousness is that It acts as a stimulant to any kind of spiritual endeavor. To quote Sri Darwin:

"One of my responsibilities, and the Shariyat bears this out, is to stimulate the religions and this has been happen-

282

ing. Paul started it and I carried it on even further, an upsurge that's been seen the last 3 - 4 years."

Preserving the freedom of worship is a primary object of the MAHANTA, the Living ECK Master, and the Adepts of the Order of the Vairagi, because it guarantees the right of the individual to choose his own steps to God, rather than being pressed into a uniform pattern of approach to the Deity. One of the reasons behind the discovering of America, and the later founding of the United States, was that this new country allowed the individual freedom of religion that the churches of the old world tried to restrict. Darwin stresses the importance of religious freedom:

"You are not asked to believe everything you read or hear about ECKANKAR. However, It's been pointed out in the books how Columbus was guided to this part of the world by two ECK Masters, Fubbi Quantz and Rebazar Tarzs. Moreover one learns in the teachings of ECK that when Washington knelt to pray and asked God for help, it was Fubbi Quantz who showed him how to form the colonies. And it is not by chance that our Constitution was established the way it was. This great country of ours is to show the world that all people of different colors and backgrounds can not only work and live together but be happy and free to move about without being followed and spied upon as I experienced behind the Iron Curtain of various countries. Would you want that to happen in America? In America, to not allow a person to worship as he chooses, whether it be a stone, a live master or an ascended master, would be the downfall of this great nation."

Earth has been named the "ashcan of the universe" by the ECK Spiritual Travelers, because of the unusually strong negative forces that cause conflict among the nations and groups, and darken the spiritual light in the world. Sri Darwin continues:

"You find the big world powers use a lot of psychic means against each other, like Russia, France, and other countries, use clairvoyance and other psychic means to get classified drawings and information and specifications out of the U.S.A. on the SST. America had that plane in its hangars before any one of those countries started building it, and America knew it was going to be a fluke, but there is quite a hassle that most of the masses aren't quite aware of. A lot of our secret documents have been obtained through psychic means.

"The world is still good for another 400,000 to 500,000 years, depending on whether or not man wakes up and does not destroy himself with his own nuclear devices. It's quite possible. Not all of the race would be wiped out, but there would be a very funny place to live. Cities depleted of people due to the neutron bomb or something like that. There are other ways of doing away with individual human life very subtly, and man's got to be very careful of that. If it gets in the hands of the wrong persons, there goes a complete nation, not just a city.

"We're here for spiritual progress but it's a warring universe and always has been a warring universe, and the peace that Jesus spoke of and all the other teachers on Earth, was not for this nation or any other nation. It's individual peace and understanding that one comes into between him and God. Anywhere in the dual worlds, the worlds of duality from the etheric plane to the physical, one can never find peace.

"Maybe we're depleting some of the fossil fuels; however, one can use other ways to heat the rooms and warm up, and you can carry that warmth with you all the time. All the money being used on nuclear missiles can be used in other ways, but how do you tell the nations of this world that, how do you bring about an understanding about it? It's a lack of spiritual understanding.

"Getting into the space program, we have power sources that we use in outer space that also could be utilized as in an automobile, and that power plant or portion of it is at least good for 25 years or so. The car would last longer; perhaps, it would not break down as often. A lot of people fear that there will be many people out of work, if we had electric cars, and that's nonsense. There's other ways that individuals can be productive. It's politics and greed mostly. But our space program surely is important. Our next war will probably be fought in space, not on Earth. Not necessarily among ourselves, it might be with another race from another world or planet or galaxy. We have ECKists and some individuals teaching on these planets, as well as here on Earth, and it's just as difficult to get the message out there and in the lower worlds, as it is here. There are states of consciousness that exist there on other planets just like here, and there are people that do know how to travel and break down that barrier, you might say, without the use of a vehicle, just with the utilization of Soul."

There is quite a bit of traffic between the various planets and worlds, be it with machines or in Soul, with several way stations located on Earth. In an interview with the *ECK Mata Journal,* a yearly publication by ECKANKAR, Sri Darwin commented on visitors from outer space:

"The visitors in the physical vehicles are from different planets and different galaxies or universes that exist. As I mentioned earlier, the Earth has been mined in various places by some of these visitors in space vehicles. As the various countries on Earth are exploring the outer space, they too are being watched very closely, for not all of the people that reside on Earth were born and raised here. Many have reincarnated from another planet or a level of heaven such as the astral, causal or mental worlds where they have not learned their spiritual lessons. In addition, some have been planted here for various galaxies and universes. The visitors are very intelligent and are no different than you or I in appearance. There are different colors as on Earth, black, brown, white, yellow, red, as well as green.

"There are various vehicles from different planets, different galaxies and universes. The source of power varies greatly; the majority though today that are seen in the skies of this world, utilize the magnetic forces and that known as

ECK or Spirit which flows through all life. That is what causes the glow."

At another time, Darwin spoke about space vehicles and how they affect the magnetic and atmospheric shields around Earth:

"When a vehicle is shot out into space it not always punctures the Van Allen Belt, because of the angle when it's shot out, but it's true, when it punctures the Van Allen Belt, you can look at the newspapers of past history of every shot, there is something very negative that happened on Earth. This is caused by negative currents from the astral worlds. Some of the vehicles that come in from outer space come in through the North or South Pole, that doesn't puncture the Belt and they know that. They know if they come through the Van Allen Belt something negative is going to happen, and they'll be responsible for it. It will be traced right back to them. The ECK Travelers don't use machines, they use their Soul body. Agam Des is the prime way station for an individual that is traveling in their Soul body or a vehicle coming from another planet or galaxy. They have used the way stations for centuries. Not all visitors are spiritual travelers. They think of it as a train depot or bus depot or an airport. It allows that person to come in there and change their rate of vibration. This is so much lower than from where they came from, they must adjust to this environment. Agam Des is a spiritual city that's above the Himalayan range. They come there and rest, change their vibratory rate to adjust to the lower vibratory level here on Earth. Then they'll come down into the physical world."

When asked how this Earth planet compared in progress and development to other parts of the galaxy and universe, Darwin replied:

"Paul coined Earth 'the ashcan of the universe' and it really is. We've been watched for many generations and there have been times during the history of this planet, where it has had its space ships. You look at our moon as it orbits around the Earth and there were colonies up on the moon at one time and other planets as well. There was a ruling group of individuals who pretty much bombed it out; those pock marks aren't all craters by volcanic action, they're by huge bombs. A good part of Mars was bombarded the same way, masses of people just diminished, obliterated.

"There are greater civilizations on other planets, greater in this respect that they've utilized a greater form of energy in warming their buildings or moving about in their vehicles. They have just as difficult a task in some of these worlds or planets of spreading the message of ECK as we do here, and that is utilization of the Soul body. You don't really need that physical vehicle to visit someplace whether it be another planet or the other side of the world.

"The fear factor that the religions are using on the masses is very negative. People looking for Jesus to come back as they have, for centuries. The Moslems are looking for Mohammed to make his trip back here, and they won't be coming. They're going to be very disappointed, and I do feel sorrow for the people because they cannot see beyond that aspect, wrapped up into, emotionally, yet they are at that state of consciousness. Until that person takes the initiative, on their own, to take a look at various other aspects —go to that temple within, and try to develop that 360 degree viewpoint and learn how to ultimately go beyond himself, this is what Jesus taught, and taught by Pythagoras, etc. All the ECK Masters have taught it. There's no need to be afraid of the end of the world. We need to be afraid, more so, of ourselves, and our neighbor who is a threatening factor. I am not an advocate of arms, but as long as other countries have arms, we have to protect ourselves. In the early days man had to be strong, in the sense of bows and arrows and spears; he had to develop his armies to protect himself from invaders, and that, in a sense, is still true today, because, as a whole, in this world man is still afraid. Still has fear within himself—fear of animals, fear of his

287

fellowman, and fear of his fellow beings in the universe that might come from another world or another planet. You can't rid all the people of all the countries of that fear factor, overnight. Some people want to use that factor, they lean upon that fear factor, they wouldn't want to change themselves. It'll probably take many years — I hardly doubt in the span of this 400,000 years, that'll change very much, even though this is the ashcan of the universe. There are other worlds and societies where life exists as we know of life, and they, too, have machines and ways of doing away with their troubled people. They fight battles and it's a warring universe and will always be, until it is destroyed by God and reconstructed. Now, those Souls that are taken up during that period of time will be placed back on some part of the physical world, or a world within the universe, and continue their spiritual growth."

All the planets and worlds are not isolated from another, but they are connected through the bonds of karma, of causes and effects, just as the various nations on the globe are linked together by the karmic ties that have been built up over the ages. Each individual constantly influences the entire universe, in however great or small degree, by this constant chain of causes and effects he is creating. For a conscious co-worker with the universal creative force of the ECK, a clear channel, this provides an unlimited field of operating for the good of the whole. As Darwin points out:

"We have individual karma, groups, small groups, cities, nations. As a whole the Earth might be related to the rest of the galaxies and the galaxies to the rest of the universe and that universe to other universes. It just goes on and on. With a good number of clear channels that are working as co-workers for God, too much destruction that could come about can be prevented by the number, say, Rebazar Tarzs would like to have 50,000 good, clear channels, individuals who are co-workers with God that will allow Spirit to work through them openly without that individual's will trying to direct it in any direction, towards any purpose. Then we'll see some great changes come about and that's what we're working for right now to prevent some of the holocaust that could happen with nuclear destruction."

The MAHANTA, the Living ECK Master and his followers throughout the worlds and planes of creation do not strive to change their respective society towards a goal they think would suit themselves or humanity, but work in accordance with Spirit flowing through them for the good of the whole as seen by this omniscient essence of God. Each chela of ECK has his place in the great network of the body of the MAHANTA, and none is greater than the other in the eyes of the Spiritual Traveler.

In conclusion, these words from *The Shariyat-Ki-Sugmad* may serve to emphasize the responsibility and function of each ECKist as a channel for the MAHANTA:

If the doctrine of the body of the MAHANTA as the spirit in and of the ECK is taken seriously, and due significance given to the variety of tasks within the body of the MAHANTA, then the ECKist's life can be seen as one of those tasks, complementing others and complemented by them. For every chela there are spiritual exercises and other activities, but the relationship of these two sides of life in ECK will vary from individual to individual. There will be many within the body, who, if they are doing the tasks to which they are spiritually called, will have little time for the conscious offering of the spiritual contemplation and worship of the SUGMAD. Because this is so, such active lives are not a second best but just as valid as a vocation within the whole body of the MAHANTA.

289

Suggested introductory books published by IWP
on ECKANKAR, the most ancient spiritual
teaching in all the universes ...

THE FLUTE OF GOD (Psychology of Spirit)
THE TIGER'S FANG
(An understanding of levels of heaven)
THE SPIRITUAL NOTEBOOK
(History of the ECK Masters of the Vairagi)
STRANGER BY THE RIVER
(If you enjoyed *The Prophet* by Gibran, you will love
STRANGER BY THE RIVER, the greatest piece of
literature to come along in the 20th century)
IN MY SOUL, I AM FREE
(Biography of the Living ECK Master Sri Paul Twitchell
by Brad Steiger)
YOUR RIGHT TO KNOW
(Compilation of articles on contemporary subjects)
GEMS OF SOUL
(Excerpts from the works of Sri Darwin Gross)

Books on ECKANKAR can be found or ordered
at your local book store.

In many areas around the world, discussion classes on the introductory books of
ECKANKAR are being held, which the public is welcome to attend. ECKANKAR
Centers will be listed in the local telephone book. For more information on
ECKANKAR and/or ECKANKAR activities, please write to:

ECKANKAR
P.O. Box 3100
Menlo Park, CA 94025 U.S.A.

For a free book catalog, write:

PUBLISHING
P.O. Box 2449
Menlo Park, CA 94025 U.S.A.

BOOK ORDER COUPON

Mail to:

 **PUBLISHING**
P.O. Box 2449
Menlo Park, CA 94025 U.S.A.

☐ Please send me a complete IWP catalogue.

I enclose $ _____ for the book(s) checked below.

Foreign countries: Please remit Int'l M.O. or check payable in U.S. funds.

☐ **The Flute of God** $2.95 $ _____
☐ **The Tiger's Fang** $2.50 papbk, $8.95 hb $ _____
☐ **The Spiritual Notebook** $2.50 $ _____
☐ **Stranger by the River** $5.95 $ _____
☐ **In My Soul, I Am Free** $2.50 $ _____
☐ **Your Right to Know** $1.95, papbk, $8.95 hb $ _____
☐ **Gems of Soul** $4.95 $ _____

Total $ _____

Add 10% shipping $ _____
75¢ minimum

6% sales tax $ _____
(California only)

TOTAL ENCLOSED $ _____

Name _____

Street _____

City _____ State _____

Zip _____

(detach here)

Photo Album

**Flights of swans on a lake where Darwin
grew up and ice-skated in the winter.**

The Great Northern Line through Denhoff

—Photos by Alan Hammond

From Darwin's window, the view of the pond

The house Darwin was born in—now a shambles

Darwin's Grandfather Schmidt on his mother's side

Grandpa Gross— Darwin never wanted to be held by the preacher in black and always fussed when held by him.

**Darwin's Grandmother Gross
and Aunt Susie**

The Grosses and the Schmidts

Darwin and friends skinny-dipping!

A second grader

A cowboy star at heart

Jacky, Ron and Darwin

Darwin, Jacky and Ron—A winter on the farm

Dapper Darwin

**Walter Froeber and Darwin
on a Sunday afternoon**

**Darwin on the
steps at home**

The effect of looking at
pretty girls instead of keeping
his attention on pole vaulting

Imagination is a great thing

Darwin organizing the neighborhood to pick cherries

The beach at Moto, Japan

Airborne buddies in Jamachi, Japan

A mountain shrine near the meeting place with Sato Kuraji

In front of a temple in Japan

At ease!

A soft
flight
through
the air

—by Ripley

AIRBORNE

THE SHOULDER PATCH OF THE 11TH AIRBORNE DIVISION

ALTHOUGH "TOKYO ROSE" REPORTED THAT THE DIVISION WAS WIPED OUT –IT WAS THE FIRST TO SET FOOT ON JAPAN – AND ACTED AS A GUARD OF HONOR FOR GENERAL MAC ARTHUR.

The patches Darwin wore

ANGELS

HELL FROM ABOVE

Dad, Ron and Darwin

A family affair

On the way to work, trumpet in hand

The Subtle Tones—

—Lee, Bonnie and Darwin

Paul, Darwin and friends at Portland Semina

Link Ordinance
at Sunnyvale, then
a Division of GPT
(now Singer-Link)

Darwin and son Tim at Medford, Oregon

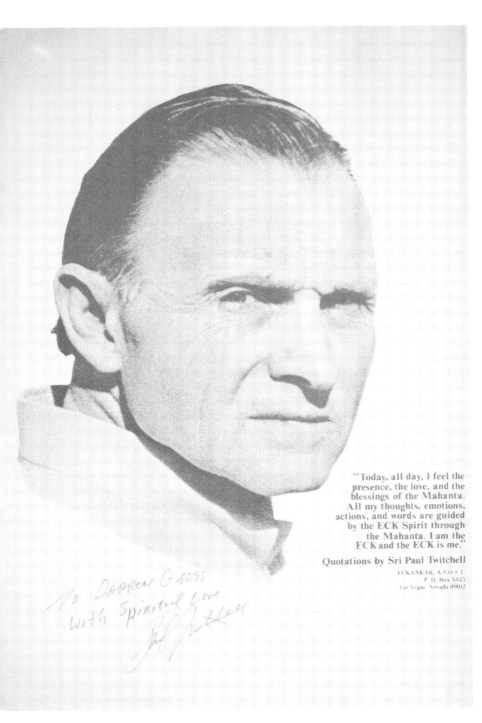

"Today, all day, I feel the presence, the love, and the blessings of the Mahanta. All my thoughts, emotions, actions, and words are guided by the ECK Spirit through the Mahanta. I am the ECK and the ECK is me."

Quotations by Sri Paul Twitchell

ECKANKAR, A.S.O.S.T.
P. O. Box 5325
Las Vegas, Nevada 89102

**The poster Sri Paul Twitchell gave to Darwin
upon receiving the Ninth Initiation, March 1971.**

The Office of ECKANKAR at Menlo Park

—Photos by Kerby Smith

Television: On the Beulah Hodges Show, Austin, TX 1974

MEDIA INTERVIEWS

Radio: Questions from Barry Farber, New York City, Jan. 1975

Phil Donahue interviews Darwin—Chicago, IL 1973

Darwin with Tom Snyder and bear, New York City 1974

Darwin with Sherry Witcher interviewed by Russ
Coughlan, KGO, San Francisco in 1972. Initially to
be a half-hour program, it ran four hours due to

interest in ECKANKAR from call-in audience. Mr.
Coughlan is now Vice-President of ABC Television
in New York.

The Joe Franklin Show, New York City, 1978

—Photo by Joseph Kennedy

Darwin at seminars   —*Photos by Kerby Smith*

**The Subtle
Sounds with
Darwin at
the vibes**

At the ECKANKAH

International Youth Conference, Sacramento, California 1978

**Love that can only be
experienced!**

**At the World Wide of ECK Seminar,
Baltimore, Maryland 1979**

—Photo by Tom Brennan

Sri Darwin and Interpreter Elena Favale
with ECKists from Africa, Baltimore 1979

—Photo by Tom Brennan

**The love that surrounds
the Living ECK Master**

—*Photo by Sarah Epps*

Darwin, Ti Ling and Big Thunder

Darwin at the Vibes—Hilton Hotel, Las Vegas, Nevada 1976